100
Ways
to Build Self-Esteem

and Teach Values

Other Books by Diana Loomans

The Laughing Classroom
(co-author, Karen Kolberg)

For Children

The Lovables in the Kingdom of Self-Esteem
The Lovables
(a board book for young children)

Positively Mother Goose
(co-authors, Karen Kolberg and Julia Loomans)

100 Ways

to Build Self-Esteem and Teach Values

Diana Loomans with Julia Loomans

H J Kramer

New World Library

An H J Kramer Book
published in a joint venture with
New World Library

Editorial office: Administrative office:
H J Kramer Inc.   New World Library
P. O. Box 1082   14 Pamaron Way
Tiburon, California 94920   Novato, California 94949

Editor: Nancy Grimley Carleton
Editorial assistant: Claudette Charbonneau
Cover design: Mary Ann Casler
Text design and typography: Tona Pearce Myers

Library of Congress Cataloging-in-Publication Data
Loomans, Diana
100 ways to build self-esteem and teach values / Diana Loomans
with Julia Loomans.
p.   cm.
Originally published: Full esteem ahead. Tiburon, Calif.: H. J. Kramer, © 1994.
Includes bibliographical references.
ISBN 1-932073-01-9 (alk. paper)
1. Self-esteem in children. 2. Self-esteem.   3. Parent and child.
I. Loomans, Julia.   II. Title.
BF723.S3L65   2003
158'.1—dc21   2002043279

ISBN: 1-932073-01-9
Printed in Canada on acid-free, partially recycled paper
Distributed to the trade by Publishers Group West

10   9   8   7   6   5   4   3

To the Caretakers of the Children,
who do the most honorable and challenging work
on the face of the Earth
in raising other human beings.
May you live with compassion
and teach with great love.

And to the Keepers of Joy,
the children, who live life fully,
with arms open.
May your song live on forever.

— Diana and Julia

Contents

Chapter One: Esteem Each Day

Chapter Two: Esteem Each Night

Chapter Three: "Esteeming" with Pride: Positive Self-Management

Chapter Four: Learning Esteem

Chapter Five: Playful Esteem

Chapter Six: "Letting Off Esteem": Creative Conflict Resolution

Chapter Seven: Esteem Extras

Chapter Eight: Esteem Holidays

Chapter Nine: Global Esteem

Chapter Ten: Spiritual Esteem

Resource Guide

Foreword

Consider yourself blessed. You are about to read the best book on parenting and self-esteem that I know — a book that will transform the quality of your and your children's lives. In addition to helping you build high self-esteem, *100 Ways to Build Self-Esteem and Teach Values* offers an encyclopedia of informational insights and practical ideas for creating more love and less fear, more joy and less pain, and more achievement and less failure in people of all ages. Every page of this remarkable resource is filled with a love of children, a passion for life, and a deep wisdom gained from many years of conscious parenting.

The profound wisdom contained in these pages will bring laughter to your heart, tears to your eyes, and new dimensions to your thinking. Esteem team Diana and Julia Loomans share more than mere prescriptions for building self-esteem and self-confidence. They illustrate each idea with heartwarming stories, inspiring poetry, powerful techniques, and informative charts that apply to hundreds of real-life situations.

What will teach you and touch you the most, however, is the sharing of their own journey together as mother and daughter. Their candid self-disclosure will make you feel as if you are sitting in the kitchen with wise friends and neighbors discussing the lessons of love we are all asked to learn in the classroom of our family relationships.

Be aware that there is more information in this book than you could possibly integrate in one sitting. I suggest that you read this book slowly — a little at a time — and begin to utilize the hundreds of practical suggestions it so richly presents. Return to it each day for new ways to create the quality of life you and your children have always yearned for, so deeply deserve, and now will be able to experience every day for the rest of your lives.

— Jack Canfield
Co-author, *Chicken Soup for the Soul*
President, Self-Esteem Seminars

Acknowledgments

100 Ways to Build Self-Esteem and Teach Values was influenced by the love and wisdom of many great souls from the past and present. We would like to extend our thanks to the following people who contributed their unique gifts: Hal and Linda Kramer, our visionary publishers, who supported this project in every way possible from the beginning. We are most grateful for their dedication and love. Our editor, Nancy Grimley Carleton, whose flexibility, caring, and skill brought the book to a new level of excellence. Uma Ergil, Mick Laugs, and Jan Phillips from H J Kramer, who continue to share great ideas, warmth, and support. Thank you for being a caring staff of fine human beings.

Thanks also to Diana's inner mentor circle of literary masters, who have shared their wisdom and eloquence on many occasions, including William Shakespeare, Lao-tzu, Kahlil Gibran, Walt Whitman, William Blake, Ralph Waldo Emerson, Robert Louis Stevenson, William Wordsworth, Anne Morrow Lindbergh, and D. H. Lawrence.

Thanks to Alexander Everett and Thomas Willhite, for their dynamic workshops that provided a framework twenty years ago for much of what would follow. Lou Loomans, for fathering Julia over the years, and for the gifts that he continues to bring to her life. Don Dinkmeyer and Gary McKay, for the wonderful gift of the STEP program when Julia was still an infant. Charles Dreikurs, for his innovative ideas in the field of childrearing that reinforced much of what we were already doing. Polly Berrien Berends, for the spiritual wisdom she has provided on parenting over the years. Nathaniel Branden, for his insightful work and important contribution to the self-esteem movement and our work. Jack Canfield, one of Diana's earliest mentors and a pioneer in the field of self-esteem. It is an honor to have his words grace the book's foreword.

Thanks to Burt Wood, a "pragmatic mystic," who saw the big picture and put Diana on the platform twelve years ago. Beverly Galyean, inspiring teacher and mentor who encouraged Diana on her path and envisioned this book in print long before we did. Dan Millman, for inspiration about living the life of a peaceful warrior. John Bradshaw, for helping us to become more understanding with ourselves and for the wonderful inner child weekend in San Diego. Joseph Campbell, for his powerful work on mythology from around the world. Our many wonderful friends and relatives in Wisconsin, who have shared their love over the years. To the ACOA groups in the Midwest, which shed light on some dark areas and provided a safe place to begin to come out of denial. To the CODA group in San Diego, for the many moments of truthfulness and candor, and for modeling what it means to be a healthy family. Virginia Satir, for her loving spirit and devotion to self-esteem for all. Wayne Dyer, who has inspired us to reach into more of our potential on many occasions. Clarissa Pinkola Estés, our wild woman mentor who has helped us to awaken the creative spirit within again and again. Jack Kornfield, for his dedication to mindfulness and his words of wisdom on the retreat at Mt. Madonna that renewed us as we finished the book. Marshall Rosenberg, for the gift of his heartfelt teachings in compassionate communication. We share more openly and love more fully because of the skills he has passed along to us.

Thanks to Thomas Berry, Matthew Fox, and Brian Swimme, three powerful teachers and Earth stewards who opened our eyes to the wonders of creation. Deepak Chopra, for enriching our lives with his wonderful ideas. James Redfield, for his transformational ideas and the energizing ritual in Anaheim that came at just the right time. Micki Erwin, for the gift of Sedona and the wonderful healing rituals. Jim and

Marie Fitzpatrick, for encouraging us to develop our creativity and for offering their love and support over the years. Colleen Donohue, for her courage, honesty, and ongoing support, and for being a true friend and wonderful aunt. Tom and Mike Fitzpatrick, for all of the times we've laughed, cried, and learned together, through the good times and the hard times.

Thanks to Sky Schultz, for his playful spirit and keen insights over the years, and for writing a wonderful introduction for the book. Michael Taibi, for his love, enthusiasm, and great ideas for the book, and for offering a listening ear and a word of encouragement through each phase of the book. Kelly Bryson, for editing the "Empathy Each Day" section and for the wonderful empathy coaching. Emily Smogard from Hazelden Publishing, for her enthusiasm and important feedback about the title of the book. Scott Kalechstein, for being a true giraffe friend and for offering his wisdom and encouragement throughout the writing of the book. Debra Tadman, for her deep commitment to the well-being of children and her invaluable feedback on the book. Charmaine and Jack Diehl, who have given their friendship and love over the years and have supported our work from the very beginning. Helice Bridges, for the many blue-ribbon acknowledgments, her insightful contributions to the book, and her vivacity for life. Jean Gabardi, for her commitment to excellence and her enthusiastic support over the years. Meiji Stewart, for his valuable feedback on the book and his wise insights regarding self-esteem and recovery. B Z Betsy, for her cheerful and efficient administrative help over the months. Mark Rosenberg, for the invaluable bodywork during the endless weeks of computer work.

For the caring friends who offered valuable contributions to the book, including Bonnie Burn, Jan Seligman Newman, David Lane, Sally Barbau, Jessica Christian, Celeste Cowell, Denise Paccione, and Omar Wilder. Friends at the Book Forum, the Writers Guild, and the Authors Networking Group in San Diego, who willingly share their vast knowledge with fellow authors, along with a rich appreciation for the power of the written word. Dan Burrus, for his ability to envision a positive future and his valuable contributions to the section "Glimpses of the Future." Friends and colleagues from the National Speakers Association, many of whom paved the way with their great ideas and wonderful books. The hundreds of parents who have attended Diana's workshops over the years, and the thousands of teachers who have attended her college classes and workshops. Their willingness to explore new concepts and share their insights is the basis for many of the ideas within these pages. Finally, we wish to thank parents, teachers, and mentors from all corners of the Earth, for the countless acts of kindness and the innumerable services that they perform on behalf of the children. May they live to see the acorns grow into giant oaks.

— Diana and Julia Loomans

Introduction

100 Ways to Build Self-Esteem and Teach Values is one of those rare, groundbreaking books that can truly make a difference in the self-esteem of the adults and children who have the good fortune to read it. It wasn't written by a team of medical researchers or clinical psychologists, but instead by a parent-child team, Diana and Julia Loomans, who have lived the teachings in the book firsthand, through the ups and downs of everyday life. Diana has a remarkable ability to take the profound and make it playful and practical, as she has done in her previous best-selling works, such as *The Lovables in the Kingdom of Self-Esteem*. Her daughter, Julia, has a striking ability to speak openly and share from the heart. Together, they encourage you to craft an authentic relationship and build more self-esteem by exploring the heights and the depths together, as they have done.

As a friend and clinical psychologist of twenty years, I can say with admiration and deep affection that Diana and Julia are the most authentic parent-child team I have ever met. To me, they are everyday heroes, not because they are perfect, but because they have the courage to be imperfect and to continue to find new ways to relate to each other. I have spent many inspiring hours over the years in the company of these two pioneers of play, marveling over their ability to use creativity and humor to transform the mindless grind of everyday life into mindful games and to express their love and affection for each other in unique and innovative ways. Being around the Loomans's household is always an adventure, since one never knows when a "love note" might turn up on a mirror, in a drawer, or on the bottom side of a plate. I remember finding a love note in my pocket from Julia after one of my visits that said, "I'm glad that you haven't become too 'a-dull-tified,' you big overgrown kid!" They have become masters of the "put-up," rather than the put-down with each other! I have found humor on many occasions as I watched Diana stop herself midsentence and reframe her words: "Julia, stop that...I mean, Julia, can you please be quiet?"

But I have also admired how Diana and Julia have moved through some of the painful times and difficulties that inevitably surface in close relationships over the years. Diana had grave doubts that she would be a good parent when Julia was conceived. She was still carrying a number of her own childhood wounds and wondered if she was ready for the awesome challenge of raising a human being. After Julia was born, Diana decided that she would learn from her young daughter whenever possible, and be honest with her about the struggles in her life as well as the dreams and successes. It was this honesty and willingness to be vulnerable that Diana now realizes set the foundation for a relationship that continues to grow and unfold.

Diana does not claim to be a model parent, and she is realistic about some of the disadvantages that Julia grew up with in her presence, as well as the advantages. Diana was a seeker of wisdom and a highly creative person by nature, with a passion for stepping out of the ordinary and trying new things. This gave her a natural ability to come up with new ideas and express herself as a parent in playful and unconventional ways. But she also had a tendency to be driven, controlling, and somewhat compulsive. Over the years, Julia has watched her mother struggle through workaholism, bottled-up anger, and codependency. I will never forget a discussion I had with the two of them while Diana was in the depths of recovering from some of these lifelong patterns. Diana was expressing her concern that Julia might be adversely affected as she watched her mom learn to become more "emotionally literate," which, by her definition, meant feeling all of her feelings and learning to express her needs in healthy ways. Julia piped in with, "If you're wondering if you've messed me up, Mom, don't worry — you have! But I think you're really courageous for admitting it." All three of us broke into a fit of laughter, and I had a feeling of tremendous relief that a child of ten could speak with such candor to her mother.

Diana also made a commitment to continue to co-parent with her once husband, now friend, Lou, after their divorce. Co-parenting from two separate households has not been easy, and Diana and Lou have struggled at times to find creative ways to raise Julia in different homes. Although it was a challenging passage for them to cross, their similar values and deep desire to stay in connection with their child have been a shared link that has motivated them to keep the lines of communication open.

When Julia was very young, Diana became personally and professionally involved in the self-esteem movement, to renovate her own self-esteem and to raise Julia with greater self-esteem. She considers it to be one of the most important decisions she ever made. Julia was taught to say affirmations as she learned to talk, and Diana often posted positive phrases on the refrigerator for all to see, such as "I am lovable," or "I have a genius mind!" She realized the impact that this was having one day when she became frustrated while searching for her missing keys. Four-year-old Julia said, "Mom, I know that you can find them if you'll just relax and let your genius mind take over."

In my opinion, self-esteem is the most important contribution that an adult can make to a child's life. It is the bedrock on which most other personality traits rest and will do more to determine a child's future than any other single factor. But in order to teach self-esteem to a child, an adult must first have it within. For many adults today, this is no easy task. Many of us have watched our significant adult role models struggle through their lives with careers that brought drudgery and with relationships that were less than fulfilling. In my work as a family therapist over the past twenty years, I have witnessed the severe damage that ill-chosen words, physical beatings, or even gestures of disapproval can have on a person's sense of self years after the fact. The laborious process that must take place in most cases to restore self-esteem after physical or emotional trauma occurs is time-consuming and difficult. In my work in various prisons and hospitals, I have witnessed the subtle but all-pervasive effects that result from low self-esteem. Almost all of the prison inmates whom I have counseled were told that they would never amount to anything in life, and they suffered without exception from low self-esteem.

It is possible to go through life with low self-esteem, and, indeed, there are many people who do, but it's like trying to ride a bicycle with flat tires. Fortunately, we live in an age that is beginning to recognize the importance of building self-esteem in our children. *100 Ways to Build Self-Esteem and Teach Values* is a book that is full of wonderful ideas for parents and teachers who would like to build more self-esteem in themselves and the children in their lives. The real beauty of the book is that it offers very specific suggestions that have been tested over time by a parent-child team who have "walked their talk." The book has been divided into ten sections so that you can hone in on a specific area of need. For those seeking an array of good ideas on building self-esteem, simply read the book from cover to cover. Virginia Satir once said, "Children are like seedlings — they grow best when they are in a nurturing environment." *100 Ways to Build Self-Esteem and Teach Values* offers a cornucopia of practical and playful ideas to help you to live, love, and learn together, and to create a nurturing environment where children and adults can flourish.

— Sky Schultz, Ph.D.

chapter

1

Esteem Each Day

Self-esteem is like good nutrition — the more our children have it, the healthier and stronger they become. Chapter 1 offers ideas that will show you how to create a safe and loving environment, and help your child's self-esteem grow each day. One-minute love connections, esteem themes, a life celebrations book, and love notes will provide daily doses of self-esteem. Using reframing, empathy, everyday etiquette, and the gift of acknowledgment will plant the seeds of respect and harmony in the house.

The following list, "Ten Caring Ways to Connect with Children Each Day," offers practical steps that will help adults create an atmosphere where children can thrive. Use it as a guide as you help children to develop more esteem each day.

Ten Caring Ways to Connect
with Children Each Day

1. **Compassion:** Honor all of your feelings, and listen with empathy to each other.

2. **Clear Communication:** Express your emotions simply, and speak from the heart together.

3. **Creativity:** Try new things, be playful, and invite the unexpected.

4. **Consistency:** Do what you say, and say what you mean each day.

5. **Challenge:** Approach problems with positive expectancy, and learn from the challenges.

6. **Cheerfulness:** Embrace the day with lightheartedness, and learn to enjoy life.

7. **Confidence:** Trust and believe in your own talents and in the abilities of others.

8. **Calmness:** Breathe and live from a calm center within yourself each day.

9. **Clear Agreements:** Create clear agreements and rules that everyone understands and feels good about.

10. **Commitment:** Be committed to being true to yourself and honest with others each day.

Cross My Heart and Hope to Fly!
by Julia Loomans

When I was little, my mom and I used to have a lot of fun turning old ideas around and changing the meaning into something we enjoyed more. This was our way of turning old realities upside down. When we heard someone say, "I'm going to kill two birds with one stone," we changed it to "I'm going to feed two birds with one seed!" "What's the matter — cat got your tongue?" was transformed into "Are you dwelling deep in the silence?" That one always made us laugh! "Don't put off for tomorrow what you can do today" turned into "Celebrate tomorrow what you will choose to do today!" "Be careful" became "Be full of care" and "Never give up!" was changed to "Ever look up."

"An apple a day keeps the doctor away" became "A laugh a day brings health my way": I guess we decided that laughter was even more important than eating the apple. "Good night, sleep tight, don't let the bedbugs bite" was changed to "Good night, sleep tight, a big hug and a kiss good night." I liked the thought of hugs a whole lot better than the thought of gruesome bugs under the bed! "Good God, it's morning" became "Good morning, God," which was easier to wake up to than a groan. We started calling "sunrise and sunset" "the morning tilt and the evening tilt," since it reminded us that we were the ones moving around the sun and not the reverse.

One night, when I was about eight years old, I wanted to tell my mom a secret wish of mine, but I wanted her to promise not to tell a soul. "Promise?" I asked her a couple of times. "Promise," she said, with her hand over her heart. "Cross your heart and hope to die?" I pleaded. "No," she said with a grin. "How about: 'Cross my heart and hope to...'" Before she could finish, I blurted out the final word: "Fly! Cross my heart and hope to fly — yes! That's it," I told her. "That's my secret wish — to fly!"

My mom was surprised and said that it was "like finding two diamonds in the haystack." Not only did she guess my wish, but we changed an old phrase, too. Then she asked me to make her a promise. "Promise to follow your dreams," she said. "Promise?" she asked. "Cross my heart and hope to fly!" I replied.

1

Creating a Happy Home

Share ideas with your child on what a happy home is like, and act on some of those ideas more often.

In teaching parenting workshops, I have found that one of the most eye-opening activities has always been the Happy Home Interview. Parents go home and ask their children two simple questions: "What is a happy home like?" and "What makes our home feel good?" Consistently, parents come back amazed by the honesty and simplicity of the answers they receive from their children. The answers are usually about small, everyday things.

Children are messengers from a world we once deeply knew, but we have long since forgotten.

— Alice Miller

Almost never have children mentioned exotic trips, pools, large houses, or expensive clothes or toys. Instead, feeling good, encouragement, kindness, play, and connection with mom or dad are at the top of the list. Take the time to ask your child these two important questions. The answers may surprise you. Here are twenty-four ideas for creating a happy home, submitted by the children of parents from previous classes.

Twenty-Four Ideas about Creating a Happy Home

1. **Hug More:** "When I come home, my mom and dad hug me a lot. That's when my house feels happiest!" (Nora, age eight)

2. **Create Special Moments:** "My home is happy when my mom lights candles while we eat dinner." (Harvey, age ten)

3. **Cook Together:** "I like it when we cook something yummy together — like cookies or bread — and the house smells delicious!" (Robert, age nine)

4. **Celebrate Art:** "My house has a big refrigerator with kids' artwork and magnets all over it, and even some that fall off!" (Tobias, age five)

Sing of love and leisure, for naught else is worth having.

— T. S. Eliot

5. **Express Affection:** "I like it when Dad throws me up in the air and messes up my hair!" (Rebecca, age four)

6. **Relax and Enjoy One Another:** "We have lots of puppy piles — all of us lie all over each other on the couch and laugh a lot." (Katrina, age eight)

7. **Share Special Time before Bed:** "I like it when my mommy brushes my hair for a long time and sings songs to me before bed." (Beth, age four)

8. **Play Games Together:** "A home is happy when everybody has fun playing checkers or Monopoly and eats popcorn, too." (Jason, age thirteen)

9. **Keep Good and Nutritious Food in the House:** "My house feels good when there's lots of really good food to eat." (Merrill, age seven)

10. **Play Together:** "There's cool toys that moms and dads like to play with, too!" (Alexi, age ten)

11. **Enjoy a Pet:** "A happy house has creatures in it — a bird, gerbil, hamster, turtle, guinea pig, rat, fish, lizard, snake, dog, cat, or monkey. I've had all of them in my house, and, boy, does it smell! But in my house, it's okay." (Jerod, age ten)

12. **Dance and Play Music Together:** "In my house, when it's happy, there is music playing and we all dance together. My dad teaches us the cha-cha-cha!" (Amber, age eleven)

13. **Appreciate One Another:** "My mom sits and looks at me and smiles sometimes when my house is happy." (Kalenda, age four)

14. **Listen to One Another:** "Everybody listens to each other instead of yelling or screaming." (Samuel, age fourteen)

15. **Remember the Extras:** "A nice house has wind chimes hanging, and you can hear birds singing outside the window." (Tara, age five)

16. **Pamper One Another:** "Happy houses have big bubble baths for kids that they can stay in until all the bubbles are gone." (Lauren, age seven)

17. **Communicate Openly:** "When people like each other in their house, they sit around for a while after dinner and talk about all kinds of stuff." (Amy, age thirteen)

18. **Show Interest in One Another:** "In a house that is happy, people ask you how your day was, and they really mean it!" (Lisa, age fifteen)

19. **Share and Read Stories Together:** "Happy people read books together and tell stories by the fire about neat things." (Morley, age twelve)

20. **Wrestle Together:** "Families that get along like to wrestle and giggle together!" (Bo, age eleven)

21. **Keep Plants or Flowers in the House:** "I like it when we have flowers on the table and the whole house smells good." (Jonah, age six)

22. **Have Family and Friends Visit Often:** "Our house is fun when everybody has friends over and there's lots of laughing going on!" (Abe, age sixteen)

23. **Acknowledge One Another:** "Everyone compliments each other and does special things for each other." (Shanti, age fourteen)

24. **Create a Friendly and Safe Environment:** "When I'm gone, I can't wait to get home because I just like being there!" (Carlos, age twelve)

Fortunate are the people whose roots are deep.

— Agnes Meyer

Consider "interviewing" your child on what he or she thinks makes a home happy. Ask for at least ten ideas, and then surprise your child with them, one by one.

7

I have a simple philosophy. Fill what's empty. Empty what's full, and scratch where it itches.

— Alice Roosevelt
  Longworth

I asked Julia when she was ten years old to write down some ideas about what made her home feel good. Ironically, one of her answers was, "When my mom is doing some of the neat stuff that she tells other parents to do with their kids. That's when my home is happy!" Out of the mouths of babes come words of wisdom!

2

One-Minute Love Connections

Create meaningful moments with your child a few times a day with one-minute connections that build self-esteem and offer reassurance in the midst of a busy schedule.

As a busy parent, I have found that one-minute connections have become a vital part of my relationship with my child. The one-minute love connection is a time to pause, be in the moment, and connect with your child from the heart.

Although short in duration, one-minute love connections have a threefold purpose — to build confidence, to offer acknowledgment, and to reassure your child that you are connected even when the day is busy. Here are a few ideas you might want to adopt into your one-minute connections.

The best inheritance a parent can give to his or her children is a few minutes of time each day.

— O. A. Battista

Nine Ways to Make One-Minute Love Connections

1. **The Extra Long Look:** Take a deep breath, and look at your child for a full minute with a smile or a look of appreciation on your face. Every child has a need to be seen and appreciated each day.
2. **The Big Snuggle:** You'll be surprised how good your child will feel if you take a ten-second hug and extend it to a full minute. That extra fifty seconds will give your child the kinesthetic reassurance that "I am lovable!"
3. **Love Phrases:** Stop all activity and thought, look

directly into your child's eyes, and say, "I love you more each day," or "You're wonderful!" Even if some of your phrases are repeated often, if spoken from the heart, they will be music to your child's ears.

4. **Creative Gestures:** Since up to 85 percent of all children are visual learners first, don't underestimate the power of gestures. I have gestured "I love you" to Julia in sign language on my way out the door often over the years. This never fails to bring a smile. A friend of ours pinches her own cheek, squints her eyes, and waves good-bye to her now seventeen-year-old son. It's her silent way of saying, "You're adorable," and it still gets a giggle from him.

The cleanest bath a child can have is an esteem bath!

— Rubber Duckie

5. **The Tender Touch:** A father of three children has a habit of cupping his hand on the cheeks of his children or holding their hands while stooping down to hold eye contact with them when he gives them a compliment. These children are very connected with their father.

6. **Silly Connections:** Julia and I have a few imaginary characters we like to act out. One of our favorites is Baby Boop. I walk funny, talk funny, and say something in garble to Julia, such as "You sure rar a ruvable rirl!" A father-son team has a "get a grip" handshake that involves hilarious hand movements, claps, a hip gesture, and a quick twirl, followed by a final high-five gesture.

7. **Esteem Builders:** I often use one-minute connections with Julia to give her affirmations. A big hug, along with saying, "I love your playfulness," or "Your brilliance is amazing," is like a short esteem bath for her.

8. **The Empathic Connection:** When there isn't time for a longer connection and your child is in need, giving one minute of empathy can be soothing and healing. For example, saying, "It sounds like you

will need longer than you thought for your home-work. I can see that you are feeling frustrated about that," can be reassuring.

9. **Friendly Messages:** When you can't be there for an in-person connection, a friendly note or phone message after school or in the evening can be a great substitute.

Creating a few one-minute love connections with your child will only take several minutes, but the seeds planted will reap a rich harvest in your relationship.

3

Empathy Each Day

Practice the art of listening with empathy and communicating with compassion, and let children know that their feelings and needs are important.

A four-year-old boy was having a tantrum on a crowded elevator as his embarrassed mother reprimanded him by saying, "Stop that ridiculous whining and act like a big boy. You're disturbing everybody!" This just caused him to bellow out his shrill cry even louder, as the adults on the elevator fidgeted and rolled their eyes, waiting impatiently to reach their floors. The child began to sway from side to side and screamed out, "No, no . . . get me out of here, Mommy . . . now!" The tension mounted as his frustrated mother reached out to give her crying child a swat on the behind. At that very moment, an elderly gentleman crouched down and looked into the boy's eyes. "You don't like this elevator; it doesn't give you much room to move, does it?" he said to the boy with empathy.

The boy stopped abruptly and put his hands over his face. Peeking through his fingers, he said coyly, "No, and my bear doesn't like it either." He held up his worn-out teddy bear for the man to examine. "The bear doesn't like the elevator either?" the man asked attentively. "No . . . people get hurt on elevators," was his reply. His mother smiled at the man and said, "He's been watching a lot of television," and went on to explain that he had recently witnessed a violent scene in a movie that took place in an elevator. As they reached their

When it comes to kindness, any size will do.

— Emma Carin

floor, the gentle old man reached out to touch the young boy's hand. "Movies can be frightening sometimes," he said, shaking the small hand. The little boy let out a sigh and said, "Yeah, they sure can!" After the elevator doors closed, he waved to the man and held up his bear. As the doors closed, the man turned to me and said, "The boy was frightened, that's all. He just needed someone to know that." He walked off the elevator, and I realized that I'd missed my floor.

Instead, I'd just witnessed an example of the healing power of empathy. All too often, parents have been taught to reprimand their children or to offer sympathy rather than empathy in a moment of need. Although sympathy appears to be supportive, it actually encourages children to feel like victims rather than providing comfort or connection. I went to a party at a friend's house recently and found her six-year-old daughter Janice lying on the floor near the front door, wailing, "But I really wanted to go to my friend Alison's today. She's waiting for me. I don't wanna stay home with the company!" Her mother's sympathetic response was, "Poor baby, she has to stay home all by herself!" She was trying to comfort her child with a dose of sympathy, but her daughter continued to cry even louder. If Janice were being raised in another nonempathic home, she might have been reprimanded rather than receiving sympathy — an equally ineffective response. Here are a few possible scenarios.

One of the most valuable things we can do to heal one another is listen to each other's stories.

— Rebecca Falls

Six Common Nonempathic Responses to Children

1. **Shaming:** "Stop that ridiculous fussing! Do you want our company to think that you are a baby?" (Result: The child is judged and labeled and may feel anger or shame.)

2. **Discounting:** "There's nothing to be sad about. You're blowing this way out of proportion. Dry those tears right now." (Result: The child's feelings are discounted, and the child is likely to feel

frustrated, angry, or doubt his or her own feelings and reality.)

3. **Distracting:** "Come on, let's go play with the dog until the company arrives." (Result: The child is distracted and may feel frustrated or confused.)

4. **Bargaining:** "If you're polite while the company is here, I'll take you for some ice cream later." (Result: The child is likely to feel confused or frustrated.)

5. **Threatening:** "I'll give you something to really cry about if you don't stop that nonsense!" (Result: The child is threatened with violence, and most likely feels scared or angry.)

6. **Shunning:** "Go to your room and stay there. I don't want to talk to you or see you when you act this way." (Result: The child is isolated and may feel lonely, scared, or sad.)

To resolve conflict, you need to create a safe space. A safe space is one in which you feel free to share your vulnerabilities, knowing you won't be judged, attacked or reacted to.

— Danaan Parry

All of the above responses have something in common: Janice's feelings are not being heard, and she may absorb the unspoken message, "My feelings are not important or not acceptable." What Janice most needed in the above situation was simply to be heard and acknowledged without judgment.

According to international peacemaker Dr. Marshall Rosenberg, the founder of the Center for Nonviolent Communication (see "Resource Guide"), communicating with compassion is one of the most important skills we can teach our children. He has created a simple and effective model to follow for communicating with compassion. Here are the four steps, in response to Janice's feelings, as an example.

Four Simple Steps to Compassionate Listening

1. Acknowledge the situation contributing to the feelings: When you hear me say that you can't go to your friend's house...

2. Check in with the feelings: do you feel sad...
3. Acknowledge what the desire is: because you would have liked to play with your friend Alison?
4. Check in with the current need: And would you now like to know when you will get to see her again?

Putting it all together, the statement goes like this: "When you hear me say that you can't go to your friend's house, do you feel sad because you would have liked to play with your friend Alison? And would you now like to know when you will get to see her again?" This simple approach to communication emphasizes compassion and connection, while minimizing the likelihood of creating defensiveness in children. Of course, giving empathy is only half of the formula. Expressing yourself using the empathy model is just as important as listening to your child with empathy. Here is how the model works in reverse, using Janice's feelings as an example.

Communication is to relationships what breath is to life.

— Virginia Satir

Four Simple Steps to Compassionate Communication

1. State the observation: When I hear you say that I can't go to my friend's house...
2. Express the feeling: I feel frustrated and sad...
3. Express the desire: because I wanted to spend the afternoon with my friend.
4. State the current need: And I would like to call her and plan another time to get together.

Putting it all together, it sounds like this: "When I hear you say that I can't go to my friend's house, I feel frustrated and sad because I wanted to spend the afternoon with my friend. And I would like to call her and plan another time to get together." Note that there will be times when "translating" your child's message will be necessary, especially when there is labeling or name-calling. Learn to listen to the feelings and needs in the statement made, regardless of how it is expressed. As Dr. Rosenberg says, "Labeling or name-calling is a tragic expression of an unmet need."

The four steps to compassionate listening can be stated one at a time in response to your child, or all together, depending on the situation and what you are comfortable with.

Here are a few more examples of listening with empathy.

Examples of Listening with Empathy

1. "I don't want to go to the dentist's office again! I hate the sound of the drill!" Empathic response: "When you're at the dentist's, do you feel scared because you would like to know you won't get hurt? And would you now like to find out more about how the drill works?"

2. I can't do the work, and I'll never be able to do it!" Empathic response: "When you go to your class, do you feel frustrated because you would like to understand what is going on in class? And would you now like to get some support and decide what the next step will be?"

3. "I don't want to be Ed's friend anymore. He didn't come over today the way he said he would." Empathic response: "When you wait for Ed and he doesn't arrive, do you feel angry because you would have liked Ed to let you know that he wasn't coming over? And would you now like to find out what kept Ed from coming?"

What I'm for empowers me. What I'm against weakens me.

— Wayne Dyer

The most important thing to remember when expressing yourself with compassion is to share your feelings simply and from the heart. When giving empathy, listen to the feelings and needs that are being expressed and mirror them back until your child feels heard. Listening with empathy lets children know that their feelings and needs are important. Children who are heard with compassion grow up to trust their feelings and to know their own needs. They are able to give empathy to others and communicate in a nonviolent manner. Make it a habit to communicate with empathy, and help your child to practice compassion as a way of life.

Words are windows or they're walls.
They sentence us or set us free.
When I speak and when I hear,
Let compassion flow through me.

— Marshall Rosenberg

The tin soldier melted down into a lump, and when the servant took the ashes out the next day, she found him there in the shape of a little tin heart.

— Hans Christian Andersen, "The Steadfast Tin Soldier"

4

Love Notes

**Leave fun or encouraging notes for loved ones
in different shapes, colors, and sizes
in unexpected places, and "Say it with notes!"**

Julia came home from school in second grade with a long face
and no smile. "What is it?" I asked with bewilderment. "It's
Mark," she said. "His mom writes him nice notes on his
lunch napkin every day. Mine are always plain."

I felt a surge of sadness as some old "inadequate parent"
messages began to play on automatic in my mind. At the
time, I was going through a divorce, running a business
full-time, and traveling fairly often. My worry turned into
guilt over the next few days. In fact, if parental guilt were
electricity, I probably could have lit up the whole city.

It took me a few days to muster up the wisdom to realize that little extras such as this were a wonderful way to
make up for some of the times I couldn't be there to express
my caring in person. I started out with a note on Julia's napkin that said, "Have a great lunch, I love you a bunch!" It was
a hit. I progressed to Post-it notes on mirrors, in coat pockets, under pillows, and, one of our ongoing favorites, on the
refrigerator. Some of the messages were encouraging, such as
"Being in between the trapeze bars can be fun!" or "Just a
little note to tell you that I understand and support you today."
Sometimes I left short quotations for her on the love notes,
such as "Shared sorrow, half sorrow. Shared joy, double joy," or
"Every problem contains the seeds of its own solution."

*There is no difficulty
that enough love will
not conquer.*

— Emmet Fox

18

Some of the notes took a humorous twist, such as "Did you know that you have a few of my favorite problems?" or "I've figured out why we had a tough time last night — we were mountain climbing over molehills again!" And then there was the love note that she enjoyed so much she posted it on her mirror: "Julia, everything I have ever told you might be wrong!"

Julia picked up the habit as well. I started finding love notes in my glove compartment, suitcase, and jacket pockets, which was always a delightful surprise. She enjoyed starting themes, which would travel back and forth, sometimes for weeks. During the "vegetable phase," she started with a note that said, "Avocado tell you I love you!" I wrote back, "Mustard bean a beautiful baby, cause baby look at you now!" She responded with, "Lettuce be kind to each other this week," and, after an endless round of nutritionally sound tidbits, I finally held up the white flag with, "Let's celerybrate the end of this corny trend!"

Recently, I was traveling on a bus en route from the airport to a downtown hotel, preparing to give a speech to a large group. I was exhausted after a long delay with planes, I had a cold, and the airline couldn't find my luggage, which meant that I would be giving my speech in blue jeans. When I got to the hotel, I reached in my pocket to discover a small note. It read as follows, "Mom, all of this will be funny in ten years, so why not laugh now?" How did she know how much I needed to hear that, I wondered, feeling my mood shifting for the better. A few hours later, I opened my keynote speech in my sweatshirt and jeans. My opening sentence was the quote — from my love note. Try your hand at writing love notes. It may become a habit that sticks!

Do you know what you are? You are unique. In all the world, there is no child exactly like you.

— Pablo Casals

5

Everyday Etiquette

**Teach your child the basics in treating
others with dignity and respect by modeling
good manners and polite habits at home.**

In a national survey by a leading university in the Midwest,
one thousand teachers were asked in which areas they per-
ceived that American children most needed improvement. Their top three answers were good listening skills,
self-discipline, and good manners. Good manners, of course,
start at home, with parents or guardians acting as models.
Many parents teach their children to be polite and respectful
to neighbors, strangers, or authority figures in the community,
but they don't practice basic principles of good manners under
their own roof, with the most important people in their lives.

I'll never forget visiting the home of a neighbor and
watching him interact with his young three-year-old son. He
expected his son to display impeccably good manners to me,
but he was very rude to him. In the hour that I was there, he
called his son a "little twerp" in an impatient voice, shamed
him for not completing a task, and demanded that his son
fetch him a glass of water and never said thank you. His
son will probably not grow up to be particularly respectful to
his own family. He will most likely grow up displaying the
same double standards with his children that he received
from his own father, unless he works hard at reversing the
poor mind-set that he has learned.

On the other hand, children who grow up being treated with dignity and respect usually pass the good manners on to others. I know a large family of seven who treat one another with remarkable consideration and caring. After I had dinner with the entire family, it became clear why manners seemed second nature to all of the kids. The father complimented all of them openly at the table, and he was very affectionate with his wife.

In the course of one meal, he acknowledged his children in a positive way, and included a "thank-you for my wonderful family" comment in the prayer at the beginning of the meal. The family members were polite to one another and each one offered the dish of food that was being passed around to the next person before taking some for himself or herself. The result wasn't a stiff, rigid bunch as one might suspect, but instead a lively community of family members who cared about one another and went out of their way to express it.

Everyday etiquette involves teaching children the basics of respecting others and treating them with dignity. In our fast-paced, changing world, basic rules of etiquette are sometimes shunned and considered provincial or dated. And yet, being treated with respect and dignity is a basic human need no matter how much the times are changing. Here are some etiquette principles to model with consistency to your children if you wish them to do the same.

Baloo, the Teacher of the Law, taught him the Wood and Water Laws: how to speak politely to wild bees . . . what to say to Mang the Bat when he disturbed him in the branches at mid-day, and how to warn the watersnakes in the pools before he splashed down among them.

— Rudyard Kipling, The Jungle Book

Six Everyday Etiquette Principles

1. **The Basics, Please:** Starting with the very basics, saying *please* when asking for something and *thank you* after receiving something, encourages cooperation and always improves the atmosphere. When it comes to *please* and *thank you,* the obvious can hardly be overstated. Saying *excuse me* whenever appropriate, or *I'm sorry* (quickly and willingly) when feeling regret for something, brings mutual respect for everyone. There are many adults in the

world who are frustrated over the fact that when they were children, their parents didn't admit that they made mistakes. If you grew up in a similar environment, check to see if the pattern is repeating itself.

2. **Eating Habits and Table Manners:** Good eating habits are life skills that every child needs in order to feel confident in social settings. This includes knowing where to put all utensils in a table setting, putting one's napkin in one's lap, chewing each bite of food slowly and thoroughly (some experts recommend chewing each bite twenty-one times), putting the fork down in between bites, eating enough food rather than too much, having one helping of dessert rather than three, and drinking in a relaxed way, rather than gulping.

3. **Giving and Receiving Appreciation:** Expressing appreciation to others for the many small things that may otherwise go unnoticed is one of the greatest forms of everyday etiquette. This includes giving acknowledgment and being able to receive it graciously by saying thank you rather than minimizing the kind words or contradicting them.

Appreciative words are the most powerful force for good on earth!

— George W. Crane

4. **Communicating Feelings:** Expressing anger or frustration in a respectful way is one of the most challenging and rewarding ways to treat another with dignity. This includes using "I" statements rather than "you" statements (i.e. "I feel frustrated that the dishes aren't done," rather than "You didn't do the dishes you were supposed to do.") Name-calling and swearing are also best left "off-limits," since they usually just increase the conflict.

5. **Community Cooperation:** Taking care of the community space is a significant way that we can show consideration for the needs of others. This includes picking up after oneself, rinsing and stacking dirty dishes, throwing all garbage out,

volunteering to do small tasks, and keeping all community areas neat and clean, as well as taking pride in the yard and neighborhood.

6. **The Extras:** Be aware of the extras that everybody so much appreciates, such as reaching out first to shake hands with a new person (this includes friends), opening the door for another, or pulling back a chair to help someone sit down, knocking on all private doors and bathroom doors before entering, greeting guests with a friendly smile, and knowing how to strike up small talk by conversing with others about their own interests.

Help your child learn basic skills in everyday etiquette by communicating with respect for your child's dignity. When it comes to manners, children do live what they learn.

A considerate child commands more notice than a double rainbow!

— Nancy Baltimore

6

The Gift of Acknowledgment

Make it a habit to give ten words of acknowledgment each day to your child, and watch the closeness grow.

A four-year-old boy anxiously took his mother's hand and led her over to the dartboard. "Mom, let's play darts," he said. "I'll throw the darts, and you stand and watch and say, 'Wonderful!'" An eleven-year-old girl was asked by her affluent Indian parents what she wanted for her birthday. "You can have anything you want," they said. "Anything?" she queried. "Yes, anything" they reassured her. "How about a whole day of everybody telling me what they like about me!" she said enthusiastically.

If you treat an individual . . . as if he were what he ought to be and could be, he will become what he ought to be and could be.

— Goethe

An eight-year-old boy was dying from leukemia when the Make-A-Wish Foundation contacted him and asked him if he had a wish that he would like them to bring to life for him in his final days. "Oh, would you?" he asked. "I'd like my dad to play with me again, like he used to when I was little!"

A prominent medical researcher recently said that more people are suffering from a lack of acknowledgment than from all other mental diseases combined. Most of us are longing for more recognition and affirmation. Children need appreciation from the significant adults in their lives, since they need to connect with them, and parents need acknowledgment from family and friends, since parenting can be a lonely job that too often goes without notice.

A great teacher from India was once asked what families could do to love each other more. His answer was very simple.

He said, "Each and every day, give ten compliments away. This will bring more harmony than can be imagined in the common hours."

If you would like to experience more connection with your child and move "full esteem ahead" together, begin by giving small acknowledgments to your child each day. If it seems difficult at first, you might be experiencing "stroke dehydration" yourself. Begin by acknowledging yourself for all of the things that you take for granted in yourself, such as:

The deepest desire in human nature is the craving to be appreciated.

— William James

- I enjoy your creative spirit.
- Thank you for all of the nice things that you do for yourself and your children each day.
- I respect your courage to be imperfect and show your vulnerability as well as your strength.
- Thanks for exercising and putting a high value on being healthy.
- You are always continuing to grow and improve! I like that!
- You inspire me with your persistence.

When you begin to feel replenished, begin to give your child strokes throughout the day, such as:

- I appreciate it when you work so thoroughly.
- Thanks for being cooperative today when you knew I was busy.
- I enjoy how often I laugh and have fun around you.
- I like your creativity and fantastic imagination.
- I like watching you grow up.
- Your intelligent ideas are really fascinating to listen to.

I count myself in nothing else so happy as in a soul remembering my good friends.

— William Shakespeare

Progress to even deeper levels of appreciation over time, such as:

- I'm so glad that I am your parent.
- I learn so much from you, and I appreciate that.

- Having you in my life is an honor that I don't take for granted.
- I cherish our relationship — both the good times and the struggles.
- I'm really glad that you are my child.
- My love for you grows bigger each day.

Helice Bridges, founder of Difference Makers International in San Diego, noticed that people of all walks of life had a deep need for recognition and acknowledgment. Twelve years ago, she created "The Blue Ribbon Ceremony," acknowledging people by pinning them with blue ribbons that simply say, "Who I Am Makes a Difference!" The blue ribbons now span the globe, with over three million people honored with the blue ribbon ceremony in five languages. "When people receive acknowledgment," says Helice, "they naturally rise to the level of their own greatness. A floodgate opens, and they are able to see the contributions that they have made in their own lives, as well as to the lives of many others. There is no doubt about it. When we see the best in others, we can see the best in ourselves." Make it a habit to see the best in your child each day, and pass along the message that "who I am makes a difference!"

No act of kindness, no matter how small, is ever wasted.

— Aesop

7

Reframe It!

**Help children to change old ways of thinking by
substituting empowering thoughts or words
in place of old, disempowering ones found in slogans,
words, story lines, or song lyrics.**

An optimistic child will probably make as many mistakes as
a pessimistic child, but optimistic children have more fun
making mistakes! Reframing is a fun way to teach children
how to empower themselves with innovative thinking, rather
than feeling powerless to change when faced with thoughts or
words that do not serve them. It's also a way to learn to see
the cup as half full, rather than half empty. Reframing isn't
intended to deny feelings that might require empathy (such
as joy, sadness, or anger) but instead offers a chance to try on
another mental perspective when experiencing prejudiced
thinking, distress, or mental stagnation. Here are some simple
ways to use reframing.

*Everything is possible
for him who believes.*

— Mark 9:23

Examples of Reframing

I. **Everyday Language:** Observe your everyday language and words, and call a "reframing time-out"
in a playful way when you hear yourself or your
child expressing an old, worn-out attitude. Here
are a few examples of using reframing to create a
shift in perspective.

- Mondays are always a drain!
  Reframe: Each Monday brings a new start.
- Hurry up or we'll be late!
  Reframe: I'd like to focus on being on time.
- I hate it when it rains.
  Reframe: The rain gives me a chance to relax and do something indoors.
- All children are little pests.
  Reframe: Children have an amazing ability to ask for what they want.
- I never get anything right.
  Reframe: I must be on quite a learning curve with all of these mistakes lately!
- Let's break a leg!
  Reframe: Let's become turbocharged and move into high gear!
- I can't do it — it's impossible!
  Reframe: I'm up against a wall, but every wall has a door! I am going to find the door.
- What's wrong with you? Are you dense?
  Reframe: I'd like to help you to understand what I am saying.

It's important to keep the tone light and playful rather than shaming when reframing. Otherwise, reframing can become just another way to "should" on yourself or your child. Keep in mind that reframing works best if used to establish new thinking habits after one has received full attention and empathy for any feelings and needs that may be connected to the old thoughts. Otherwise, reframing can become a form of denial, or "icing over the mud pie."

The last of the human freedoms is to choose one's attitudes.

— Viktor Frankl

2. **Wordplay:** Play with clever words that help children to turn old thinking patterns upside down or inside out! The more novel or unusual the word choice, the more it has the capacity to turn on a

mental light bulb or to usher in some humor. Here are a few examples.

- I'm really angry!
  Reframe: I'm feeling particularly peeved!
- I am really exhausted.
  Reframe: I need time for some recharging.
- I am overwhelmed by how much there is to do!
  Reframe: I'm in an inordinately inexorable state at the moment.
- I am not very hopeful about the future.
  Reframe: When it comes to the future, I am waiting to become inspirited with eagerness.
- Are you feeling sad?
  Reframe: Have you become chapfallen and woebegone?

3. **Say What You Want rather than What You Don't Want:** Learn to express what you want rather than putting the emphasis on what you don't want when speaking with a child. Children are highly responsive to the messages they receive. If an adult says, "Don't slam the door," the child listening hears the phrase *slam the door,* with the word *don't* in front of it. The child must figure out that slamming the door is the undesirable thing to do, which is difficult to comprehend, especially for young children. The chances for a successful response from a child increase dramatically when an adult says, "Please close the door gently." Now the child has a visual image to follow. The words spoken are congruent with the request, which makes it much easier to understand. Here are a few more examples.

    - Whatever you do, don't come home later than three today after school.

Whatever you place your attention on grows stronger.

— Harold Bloomfield

Reframe: Please be home by three today after school. I know you can do it!

- Stop teasing your sister right now!

  Reframe: How about finding a way to play together that both of you will enjoy?

- Hurry up! You only have five more minutes to do your work.

  Reframe: By concentrating, you'll have all the time you need in the next five minutes to finish your work.

- I'm not going to help you unless you stop that awful whining!

  Reframe: Relax and use words to tell me what you want. I can help you if you'll talk to me more slowly.

4. **Neat Nicknames:** There is nothing more endearing than the host of nicknames that people come up with for their children, spouses, friends, family, and pets — that is, if they are enjoyed by the receiver. On the other hand, there is nothing worse than an undesirable nickname that sticks despite repeated attempts at removal, like old gum to the bottom of a shoe. One of our neighbors refers to his wife as "Old Yeller." Another family calls an overweight sister "Moo-Moo." These are not exactly terms of endearment. On the bright side, one of our friends calls his daughter "Golden One," to her delight. Another parent refers to her baby son as "Baby Genius." Considering the fact that most of us are using less than 5 percent of our brain potential, all of us could be nicknamed "Genius-in-the-Making!" So go ahead, use some of that brilliant potential and be original about nicknames. Just make sure that they are affirming and will be enjoyed by the bearer.

5. **Reframing the Printed Word:** There are many ways to practice reframing the printed word, since

The greatest discovery of my generation is that human beings can alter their lives by altering their attitudes of mind.

— William James

so many of our news headlines, quotations, slogans, fables, and stories could use an "about face-lift." Begin to watch for doomsday predictions, stereotypes, and tunnel vision in the written word, and use these opportunities to practice reframing with your child. When Julia was a baby, I noticed how many of the old fables, stories, and fairy tales were passing along limiting messages that I didn't wish to instill in my young child's receptive mind. I was particularly disturbed by some of the nursery rhymes that were in one of the traditional books that we had. One night, while I was reading "Rock-a-Bye Baby," Julia heard the lines "When the bough breaks, the cradle will fall, and down will come baby, cradle and all." Her body stiffened in my lap, and she quickly turned to me and said, "Who is going to pick up the baby, Mom?" I hesitated for a moment and said, "We are, right now!" That night, we used liquid White-Out and rewrote the ending of the rhyme, changing it to "Birdies and squirrels will be at play, and you can watch them all through the day." Over time, we reframed many more nursery rhymes, and eventually we wrote the now-popular children's book *Positively Mother Goose*. Here is an example of a before and after rhyme from the book.

Whether you think you can or think you can't — you are right.

— Henry Ford

The Old Woman Who Lived in a Shoe

*There was an old woman
who lived in a shoe.
She had so many children,
She didn't know what to do.
She gave them some broth,
without any bread,
And spanked them all soundly
and sent them to bed.*

The Bold Woman Who Lived in a Shoe

*There was a bold woman
who lived in a shoe.
She had many children,
And knew what to do.
"You are all lovable, with
special gifts," she said.
She hugged them all fondly
and tucked them in bed.*

31

6. **Reframing the Media:** The media offers great practice in the skill of reframing. In fact, this could keep any parent and child busy for years! Up to 95 percent of the news that is reported each day across the world focuses on negative events, injustices, and conflicts. What if the news were reframed to include an equal ratio of uplifting stories and reports? Television shows, commercials, and advertisements bombard viewers of all ages with messages that equate materialism, youth, and good looks with happiness. Violence has become so prevalent on television that the average American child will see approximately eighteen thousand murders and violent acts by the age of eighteen. What if self-esteem, nonviolence, wisdom, and living life with integrity were revered as much as the above themes in the media? Songs on the radio sometimes wail of endless pain, violence, or misery. Many love songs foster relationship addiction with despairing lyrics. To lighten up the somber mood of many of the current woe-is-me song lyrics, Julia and I have often rated the songs on a scale of 1 to 10 based on negative or codependent themes. Anything over a 5 becomes a candidate for reframing. This has brought many laughs as we change some of the sad and sorry lyrics into something more palatable, and there are always plenty to choose from!

When old words die out on the tongue, new melodies spring forth from the heart.

— Rabindranath Tagore

Reframing teaches children to discern between thoughts that hurt and thoughts that heal. The child who becomes skilled in reframing is able to "take the best and change the rest." Reframing reminds children that every moment is a moment of choice — to feel powerless or powerful.

8

The Life Celebrations Book

Create a family book that allows you to celebrate the little things as well as the big things in life. Leave it in a place that is accessible for all to write in as well as read.

Today I celebrate my friendship with Aimee. On our ride home from school, we made up some really funny laughs and took turns imitating one another. We ended up laughing so hard we almost cried! I love her playfulness!

I went for a long ocean walk today. I walked briskly and felt alive and full of energy. I felt so appreciative that I had four healthy limbs to move with, and a strong body to live in. I appreciate my body more and more as time passes. What a wonder it is!

Today I bought flowers for a friend and tucked a card in with them to let her know how much I appreciate her. I placed them on her front doorstep where I knew she would spot them when she returned home. Although my intention was to render to her an unexpected gift, the real surprise was for me! After I dropped the flowers off, my spirits lifted greatly for the remainder of the day. I was reminded that one of the best things I can do when I'm feeling down is to reach out to somebody else.

Today I talked to my sister on the phone. She is a true friend. I asked her if she could help me with a challenge I am going through and her answer was, "Of course. I'll help you in any way I can." I knew that she meant it, and I really felt nurtured when we hung up. We've both come a long way in our relationship. Hooray for us!

Each day comes bearing its gifts. Untie the ribbons.

— Ann Ruth Schabadar

33

He is a wise man who does not grieve for the things which he has not, but rejoices for those which he has.

— Epictetus

These are just a few of our recent excerpts from our life celebrations notebook. Since we noticed a tendency in ourselves to take the good for granted, we decided to create a special book just to take note of all of the gifts in our lives. We keep it on a shelf in the kitchen so that we can easily enter a short excerpt. The idea is to leave it out so that it's accessible to all. Sometimes we read it aloud to each other after a meal or in a quiet moment. We have divided the notebook into four categories.

1. Celebrating the Gifts I Give to Myself
2. Celebrating the Gifts I Give to Others
3. Celebrating the Gifts Others Give to Me
4. Celebrating the Gifts Life Brings to Me

There is so much in our lives that passes by without appreciation — budding flowers, a warm breeze, our health, a child's laugh, freshly baked bread, sunshine, a new day, kindness from others, the embrace of a loved one, and even the many challenges we face that help us to grow. Keeping a celebrations book is an excellent way to learn to smell the flowers along the way and to practice developing the fine art of appreciation. Over time, it will become as treasured as a family photo album.

9

Esteem Theme of the Week

Choose a positive theme for the week, such as courage. Read about courage, discuss it, and practice being courageous in small, everyday ways during the week.

Many adults wonder how to instill the values that will be needed in the world our children are growing up in today. Choosing a theme for each week will foster a wonderful burst of self-exploration in the household. If every week seems too often, then choose a theme every two weeks, or even once a month.

Here are some ideas to help you get started.

High self-worth means being able to respond to people but not be defined by them.

— Virginia Satir

Abundance	Enthusiasm	Optimism
Affluence	Excellence	Persistence
Awareness	Faith	Questions
Awe	Friendship	Rest
Balance	Goal Setting	Self-esteem
Beauty	Healing	Surprise
Brilliance	Humor	Trust
Challenge	Integrity	Unity
Commitment	Intuition	Vision
Compassion	Joy	Wilderness
Courage	Kindness	Wisdom
Dedication	Lifelong learning	Wonder
Detachment	Mentors	Zest

A truly great person goes within for the answers.

— Chinese proverb

If, for example, you choose courage, here are some ways that you can explore your theme for the week.

Eight Ways to Explore Your Esteem Theme

1. **New Definitions:** Post the definition of courage for all to read, or read it aloud. For the more innovative thinkers, create your own definition.

2. **Esteem Theme Readings:** Read excerpts from a biography about someone who modeled courage, such as Mahatma Gandhi or Martin Luther King, Jr.

3. **Special Interest:** Post quotations, proverbs, cartoons, or articles on the subject for all to read and enjoy.

4. **Esteem Theme Storytelling:** Share a story about something you did that was courageous, and have your child do the same.

5. **Community Watch:** Be on the lookout for acts of courage among friends and relatives during the week.

6. **Esteem Learning Lessons:** For the daring, discuss some of the ways that you didn't have courage in the past, and what you learned from those experiences.

7. **Esteem Theme Affirmation:** Create an affirmation for the week about courage, such as "We are becoming more and more courageous in our lives!"

8. **Esteem Expanders:** Simply allow the idea of courage to be in your awareness for a week and see what shows up.

Experiment with your own esteem themes, and aspire to greatness together!

Self-esteem isn't everything, it's just that there's nothing without it.

— Gloria Steinem

10

Silent and Powerful Messages

Become aware of the powerful, unspoken messages that your child receives in your presence, and, if necessary, begin to compassionately rewrite the script.

Much of a child's emotional and spiritual nutrition comes from the unspoken field of messages in the household that the child absorbs like a sponge. The Dalai Lama of Tibet, a renowned Buddhist teacher, has said that the children of the world will thrive not only on the loving words of their parents, but also on the powerful unspoken messages that linger long in their minds.

Parenthood is just the world's most intensive course in love. Yet we are not becoming parents to give or get love. Rather we are to discover love as a fact of life and the truth of being.

— Polly Berrien Berends

A few years ago, I wrote a list of some healthy messages that I wanted to permeate into our household, not only for Julia but also for my own inner child. It was an empowering experience, since I now had some positive goals to strive for. Although I can't say that I am able to project these messages 100 percent of the time, I am getting closer and closer to this goal. The more compassion I feel for myself, the more I'm feeling comfortable with the messages that I aspire to give to myself and my daughter. Here are some examples.

Messages for the Precious Infant

- You are a miraculous gift!
- I am honored to be your parent.
- I'll keep you safe and warm.

- I enjoy taking care of you, nurturing you, and holding you.
- I will be here for you no matter what. All of your needs are important to me.
- I'm so glad that you and I will get to grow and learn together!

Messages for the Happy Toddler

Sow a thought and you reap an act;
Sow an act and you reap a habit;
Sow a habit and you reap a character;
Sow a character and you reap a destiny.

— Samuel Smiles

- I like all of your energy!
- I love your new growth! It's exciting to see you learning to walk and talk.
- I like all of the questions you ask.
- I encourage you to explore your world with curiosity.
- All of your feelings are important to me.
- It's okay that you don't always want to do what I ask, but I will gently persist in teaching you.
- I want you to be you. I like your uniqueness!

Messages for the Lovable Child

- I like being here for you.
- I like your growing independence.
- It's okay for you to have many friends and feel connected to me, too.
- I like your curiosity about life.
- I like your opinions, questions, and thoughts.
- I enjoy helping you to learn to ask for what you need.
- You can trust yourself. You are intelligent and capable.
- I believe in you.

Messages for the Beautiful Teen

- I enjoy watching you mature into an adult.
- I like your keen mind. I am interested in your thoughts and feelings.

- I encourage you to grow up at your own pace.
- It's okay to feel like an adult and a child at the same time.
- I will be here for you to help you to make responsible choices.
- I trust you to respect the family agreements.
- It's okay to make mistakes. We can all learn from mistakes.
- It's okay to feel scared or confused sometimes. You can reach out and ask for help.
- You have the talent to make your dreams come true!

Consider creating your own silent and powerful messages. Write them down, meditate on them, and begin to permeate the household with your own nurturing messages. If you experience difficulty sending out these messages, check in with your own feelings and needs by asking yourself, "What am I feeling?" and "What can I do to get more nurturing or support right now?" Remember that taking care of you is one of the best things you'll ever do for your child. One of the most powerful messages that I frequently tell myself is, "The best way to love my child is to first love myself."

We are what we think. All that we are arises with our thoughts. With our thoughts, we make our world.

— The Buddha

Esteem Each Day Chart

Read over the following chart of old beliefs and new beliefs, and help your child move from low esteem to full esteem each day.

From Low Esteem

To Full Esteem

1. Basically, it comes down to this: Adults must lead. Children must follow.

2. Raising children entails much sacrifice and hard work.

3. It's hard to be in the moment with children when adults have so much to do in a day. There just isn't time.

4. The day-to-day routine can't be changed. Children must adjust to the daily schedule no matter what.

5. Children have an easy life. Parents have all the hard work.

6. Children owe a lot to their parents and elders for all that they have done for them.

1. Children and adults are equal teachers and students for one another. Adults teach life skills to children, and children teach joy and playfulness to adults.

2. Raising children is an honor and a rewarding challenge.

3. There is so much value and joy in small moments. Make it a priority to seize the day. Some things can wait. Your child is only young once!

4. The daily routine serves one purpose — to enhance life. We run the schedule. The schedule doesn't run us!

5. Children are naturally light-hearted and playful. They remind us to relax and let down our guard so that we don't take life too seriously.

6. It is a special honor to influence and nurture a child. It is a natural part of the cycle of life to give back that which we have received.

chapter
2

Esteem Each Night

All of us spend about one-third of our lives in slumber — resting and restoring our bodies, sleeping, and dreaming. How many of us were raised to think of the evening as a sacred time to contemplate the day's events, unwind in a spirit of quietude, and prepare for another night's journey into the mysterious unknown?

Chapter 2 offers ideas on how to help children to reflect and relax as they enter the world of slumber, through the use of songs, bedtime blessings, sleep tapes, learning to remember dreams, and other techniques. Adults will learn how to create more golden moments and to plant a few "self-esteem seeds" in the evening hours, even if the amount of time available is just five minutes. From mini-massages and story-telling games to dreaming big dreams together while still awake, this section will help children and adults to have more "esteem, sweet esteem" as the sun sets.

The following lyrics are from a song called "Angel Watch." We wrote it when Julia was five years old. We were searching for some creative bedtime blessings and we couldn't find many, so we decided to write some. "Angel Watch" became one of our favorites.

Angel Watch

A bedtime blessing song by Diana and Julia Loomans

Angels watch you as you sleep,
Tiny elves dance in your hair.
They sprinkle you with sparklings of love,
Just to show you how much they care.

They know that when you're sleeping tonight,
Your happiest dream will come true.
When you think lots of happy thoughts,
Happiness will happen for you.

Being loved is your birthright,
Love is a part of you.
When you love it helps you find yourself,
So look for love in all that you do.

I'll bet that when you're sleeping tonight
Your dreams of love will come true.
When you think lots of loving thoughts,
Love will happen for you.

As I Watch You Sleep
by Diana Loomans

[This piece was written in my journal when my child was six.] My precious, I have slipped into your room to sit with you as you sleep, and to watch the rise and fall of your breath for a while. Your eyes are peacefully closed, and your soft blonde curls frame your cherubic face. Just moments ago, as I sat with my paperwork in the den, a mounting sadness came over me while I contemplated the day's events. I could no longer focus my attention on my work, and so I have come to speak with you in the silence, as you rest. In the morning, I was impatient with you as you dawdled and dressed slowly, telling you, "Stop being such a slow-poke." I scolded you for misplacing your lunch ticket, and I capped off breakfast with a disapproving look as you spilt food on your shirt. "Again?" I sighed and shook my head. You just smiled sheepishly at me and said, "Bye, Mommy!"

In the afternoon, I made phone calls while you played in your room, singing aloud and gesturing to yourself, with all of your toys lined up in jovial rows on the bed. I motioned irritably for you to be quiet and stop all the racket, and then I proceeded to spend another bustling hour on the phone. "Get your homework done right now," I later rattled off to you like a sergeant, "and stop wasting so much time," "Okay, Mom," you said remorsefully, sitting up straight at your desk with pencil in hand. After that, it was quiet in your room.

In the evening, as I labored at my desk again, you approached me hesitantly. "Will we read a story tonight, Mom?" you asked with a glimmer of hope. "Not tonight" I said abruptly. "Your room is still a mess! How many times will I have to remind you?" You wandered off in a shuffle with your head down and headed for your room. Before long, you were back, peering around the edge of the door. "Now what is it?" I asked in an agitated tone.

You didn't say a word. You just came bounding in the room, threw your arms around my neck, and kissed me on the cheek. "Good night, Mommy. I love you," was all you said, as you squeezed tightly. And then, as swiftly as you had appeared, you were gone.

After that, I sat with my eyes fixed on my desk for a long time, feeling a wave of remorse come over me. At what point did I lose the rhythm of the day, I wondered, and at what cost? You hadn't done anything to evoke my mood. You were just being a child, busy about the task of growing and learning. I got lost today in an adult world of responsibilities and demands and had little energy left to give you. You became my teacher today, with your unrestrained urge to rush in and kiss me good night, even after an arduous day of tiptoeing around my moods.

And now, as I see you lying fast asleep, I yearn for the day to start all over again. Tomorrow, I will treat myself with as much understanding as you have shown me today, so I can be a real mom — offering a warm smile when you awaken, a word of encouragement after school, and an animated story before bed. I will laugh when you laugh, and cry when you cry. I will remind myself that you are a child, not a grown-up, and I will enjoy being your mother. Your resilient spirit has touched me once again today, and so I come to you on this late hour, to thank you, my child, my teacher, and my friend, for the gift of your love.

11

Bedtime Blessings

**Create a tradition of sharing a blessing at bedtime
by reciting a prayer from around the world together,
or by creating your own sacred wishes for
one another and the world.**

Many Christian children recite this bedtime blessing, inviting their guardian angel to be with them as they sleep:

> *Angel of God, my guardian dear,*
> *God's love has put you here.*
> *Ever this night, be at my side,*
> *To light and guard, to rule and guide. Amen.*

This simple Buddhist prayer is recited by millions of children before bed each night:

> *May all the beings in all the worlds be happy.*
> *May all the beings in all the worlds have peace.*

This prayer is a translation of an African blessing that tribal leaders sing out to the rest of the tribe:

> *My body is holy, the earth is sacred,*
> *And the Wise One in the heavens is among us all.*
> *May this night bring blessings and promise to all.*
> *May this night bring peace both above and below.*

This Native American prayer from New Mexico is often recited before slumber:

*Our foster nurse of
Nature is repose.*

*— William
Shakespeare*

> *Weave us clothing of great brightness,*
> *That we may walk where birds sing*
> *And grass grows green,*
> *Oh, our mother the earth,*
> *Oh, our father the sky.*

In many cultures around the world, blessings are shared in the evening before sleep. In Africa, some tribes believe that a blessing before slumber will assure a peaceful sleep. Hindus often say the word *namasté* to their children before sleep, which means, "I salute the divine in you." Christians believe that a prayer before bedtime will help to assure a peaceful passage into the next life.

Here are a few ideas to help you to create some moments of bedtime blessing with your child before bed.

Seven Ways to Share Bedtime Blessings

As a small child, I could not understand why I should pray for human beings only. When my mother had kissed me goodnight, I used to add a silent prayer that I had composed for all living creatures.

— Albert Schweitzer

1. **Customized Prayer:** Create your own personal prayer and say it out loud together.
2. **Body Prayer:** Combine words and movement and move through your prayer together.
3. **Prayers from the Great Books:** Read from one of the great spiritual books from around the world together.
4. **Visual Blessing:** Draw or paint a picture of a positive intention for yourself, your child, or the world in vivid detail. Post it in a place where you'll see it each night.
5. **Singing Prayer:** Put the words from a prayer to music and sing or chant it out loud together. Include musical instruments, such as bells, a drum, or a kalimba.
6. **Special Person Prayer:** Send a special blessing to a loved one or to a person in need, which might include anyone you are struggling with at the time. Imagine what it will be like when you reach an understanding once again.

7. **World Blessing:** Hold a prayer of world peace in
    your heart and include it as your last prayer of the
    night.

Bedtime blessings will help your child to move from a
wakeful state to a quiet state before sleep.

Bless the self, and sleep well.
Bless others, and dream good dreams.
Bless the world, and live forever.

12

Touching Moments

**Before bedtime, give your child the gift of a
light face, foot, or shoulder massage while playing
some relaxing music to help him or her unwind.**

For people of many cultures, including members of the Yucatan tribe, touching is a very important part of child rearing from infancy to adulthood. The Yucatan Indians carry their babies close to their bodies all day long in soft burlap wraps. Body massage is part of their daily ritual, along with food preparation and bathing. Their children are notably cooperative and remarkably well adjusted as they grow up. In our Western culture, some of us have become "stroke deprived," as social scientist Ashley Montagu termed it. Many of us have not had the good fortune of the Yucatan children. But it's never too late to "reach out and touch someone you love."

*Touching is a
universal language
that everybody
understands.*

— Ashley Montagu

We were at a friend's house recently, watching him give his son a foot massage before bed. "He used to have trouble falling asleep," he said, "but now he nods off in the blink of an eye, especially when I put on some violin music while I massage his feet." His son was lying on the couch with his eyes half shut and his feet propped up on a pillow, looking calm and content as he drifted off to sleep.

After that, I decided to start giving Julia mini-massages every so often before bed while playing quiet music. These have become a frequent request over the years. Her favorite is a light face massage, which helps her to remove any excess stress from her body as she relaxes into the gentle movements.

Children of all ages love massage. Start out giving your child a short five-minute massage on the shoulders and neck, and progress to the face, scalp, arms, hands, legs, or feet for a more extended massage. For an extra touch, light a few candles and use a small amount of warm, scented oil. If doing this seems foreign, you may be unfamiliar with the bonding effects that daily touch can bring.

Many of us go about our day-to-day lives without tapping into the powerful resource of touch very often. We forget to appreciate the healing effects that a few hugs, some strokes, and some hand-holding can provide. A twelve-year-old American boy named David didn't take touch for granted. Being touched was his greatest dream, since he was born without an immune system that would shield him against disease and as a result could not be touched. He lived his entire life inside of a sterile plastic bubble, and he thus became known as "the bubble boy."

It was not until the final fifteen days of his life, when death was imminent, that he emerged and, for the first time, experienced the touch of a hand unprotected by a glove. It was his mother's hand, and he called her touch the greatest moment of his life. As he lay dying, he could experience his mother's tender kiss and the sensation of her warm hand as she ran her fingers through his long hair. He spoke of the miracle of touch with tears in his eyes, and he was dumbfounded that anyone could take such a thing for granted. In his final hours, he was able to feel his mother's arms wrapped around him one last time. His last expression was a smile and a wink before he slipped into his final sleep.

Take more time to reach out and touch your child in the here and now. You don't have to be a professional masseuse to give a great massage. Just relax, tune into your child's level of tension, and follow your instincts. Your child will appreciate your loving touch and enjoy the extra attention. And so will you.

As the little prince dropped off to sleep, I took him in my arms and set out walking once more. I felt deeply moved, and stirred. It seemed to me, even, that there was nothing more fragile on all the Earth.

— Antoine de Saint-Exupéry

13

Creative Storytelling

**Bring back the lost art of storytelling by
making up stories from scratch or telling stories
in animated detail from long, long ago.**

In Sufi folklore, the tales of Nasrudin are fables that teach life lessons through the art of storytelling. One of our favorites is the story of Nasrudin at the bathing house. Nasrudin went to a local bathing house dressed in very expensive garments, carrying a gold-lined pouch at his side. He was treated like royalty, and at the end of his visit, he surprised the attendants by giving them just one small copper coin for a tip. The next time he arrived, the workers warned one another about him, and they flipped a coin to see who would have to serve the miser. Although he was cordial and polite, they were short and curt with him, anxious to see him leave as soon as possible. After a leisurely stay, he cordially thanked the attendants and handed them a large golden coin. "This, my friends," he said, "is for the service you gave me last time. I believe that I paid you for today's service last time!"

Storytelling is a lost art that is finding its way back into the hearts and homes of story lovers everywhere. Telling a story at night is a refreshing and creative alternative to television, videos, movies, and arcade games (and by the age of sixteen, most American children have spent up to twenty thousand hours in front of a television). Although new technology has introduced a whirlwind of fancy toys and games, nothing will ever replace the warmth, spontaneity, or human

A story is a mind picture painted by the human voice, and the voice is far more wonderful than the hand.

— Edward Eggleston

connection that storytelling offers. Here are some ideas to help you to bring storytelling back to life in your home.

Six Fun Ways to Enjoy Storytelling

1. **The Cocreation Story:** Start a story from scratch, take turns adding to the story line, and watch as the story takes on a life of its own (we like doing this one in the car, too).

2. **The Magical Mystery Ending Story:** Start with a true story from your past, embellish it with a different ending from the actual ending, and see how you like the new memory.

3. **The Animated Tale:** Act out a fictitious story, complete with wild gestures, improvisation, and different voices for each character. Exaggerate each part, and let yourself get goofy.

4. **Great Stories from around the World:** Explore some of the great myths, parables, and fables from around the world, and act out the story line together (adding props or costumes for added effect).

5. **The Fantastic Future Story:** Tell a story from the future in rich detail, the way you would like to see it come out.

6. **The Wild, Wild Word-for-Word Tale:** For those who would like to earn an M.S. (Master of Silliness) in storytelling, narrate a story, switching back and forth word by word, and create a sensationally silly story in the moment. This is one of our all-time favorite ways to tell a story and always brings much laughter.

Fairy tales, myths, and stories provide understandings which sharpen our sight so that we can pick out and pick up the path left by the wildish nature.

— Clarissa Pinkola Estés

Children used to grow up in homes where parents and relatives told most of the stories. Today, television is telling most of the stories to children. Become a storyteller in your own domain, and share in the cultural, imaginative world of storytelling with your child.

14

Imagine That!

Share some of your dreams and aspirations together — the big ones, the small ones, and even the seemingly impossible ones!

D. H. Lawrence once asked, "How can you have a dream come true unless you have a dream?" The more we hold a vision in our minds, the easier it becomes to believe that it will come to life. It's inspiring to realize that every creative idea and great invention started out as a dream in someone's mind. Einstein had a dream when he was a child that as he was flying on a rocket that began to soar rapidly through space, his watch stopped. Years later, his famous $E = MC^2$ theory brought his dream to life, since it proved that time stands still when we are traveling at the speed of light.

Robert Louis Stevenson used to dream of writing magnificent stories that would become timeless classics. Before he went to sleep, he used to enlist the help of his "mental elves," asking them to come up with some great ideas while he slumbered. Eventually, he became one of the greatest writers of his time.

Use your imagination to dream your dreams in living color together. You'll be amazed by the rich ideas that spring forth from this exercise. You can do this anytime with your child, but it's especially powerful before bedtime, since the mind tends to be especially receptive to new ideas while in a relaxed state. Here are a few ideas to help you get started.

Six Questions to Help You Become a Dreamer by Day

1. What is a dream friend like? Describe your thoughts in detail. How can you become more of a dream friend?
2. What is a dream family like? Give some examples. How can you become more of a dream family member?
3. What if all the nations in the world lived in harmony? What would it be like?
4. If money was no object and there was no such thing as failure, what would you like to do as a profession now or in the future?
5. What is a dream parent (or child) like? How can you be more of a dream parent or child?
6. What if you had already accomplished your biggest goal right now? What would your life be like? What would you do next?

I would truly be blind if I did not have vision.

— Helen Keller

Whenever you practice dreaming by day with your child, you make an investment in the grand bank of dreams coming true.

15

Song of Self

Create a special song for your child, either an original piece or your own lyrics put to an existing tune. Sing or hum it on special occasions, such as birthdays, at bedtime, or in any moment of appreciation.

There are African tribes whose members take part in a wonderful singing ritual for children. As parents prepare to have a baby, they sit under a tree and "listen" for a melody that celebrates the coming child. They hum this song for the child during the entire pregnancy, and throughout the child's life. They consider this to be a melody for the soul.

"I have many flowers," he said. "But the children are the most beautiful flowers of all."

— Oscar Wilde

When Julia was still in the womb, I began to play Pachelbel's popular Canon in D within close range so that she could hear it as she was growing. When I would play it after she was born, her eyes would light up and she would say, "Mom, I know this song! I know it all by heart!" Years later, I began to sing a short verse over and over to accompany the music, "Hallelujah, child of light, Julia. Hallelujah, soul so bright, Julia." This song has become her song of self. She often plays it when she needs comfort or relaxation, and she considers it her favorite classical song.

We know a Japanese family with a daughter named Grace. When she was born, her dad created a song for her to the tune of "Amazing Grace." Her parents sing it to her on her birthday, and whenever they rock her or hold her. She absolutely loves it and glows when her parents sing it. Here are the lyrics:

Amazing Grace, how sweet the sound.
Your name fills us with glee!
Your spirit blessed, your light profound,
A gift to all you see!

A Hindu father of four children created a beautiful song of thanks for each child on his or her first birthday that he chants with his family on special religious days. Each child has been taught from a very early age to hum the melody of his or her own special chant in quiet time, and before prayer time.

You don't need to be a singer or a musician to create a song of self, and your child is never too old to receive this special gift. Just find a good tree, become very still, and listen for the melody.

What the mother sings to the cradle goes all the way down to the coffin.

— Henry Ward Beecher

16

The Paying Attention Game

**Create thought-provoking questions about
your surroundings to help your child to pay
attention to the world in a whole new way.**

*The question to ask is
not merely, Am I
paying attention?
but rather, what am I
paying attention to?*

— Socrates

When Julia was very young, one of her favorite children's stories was a tale about a boy who discovered a small dragon under the bed. The dragon gradually grew from the size of a small kitten to a gigantic dragon who began to outgrow the entire house. The trouble was that nobody paid any attention to it except for the boy. "There's a dragon in the house," he would insist, but nobody seemed to notice. Finally, one day, the dragon had one last growth spurt and got so large that he began to carry the whole house away on his back. The boy's mother screamed, "Oh my, there's a dragon carrying our house away," while his father yelled, "Hey, where did that dragon come from?"

Miraculously, the dragon began to shrink back down before the boy's parents could do anything drastic. Before long, the dragon became the size of a kitten once again, sitting in the mother's lap as she stroked its thorny little head. "I guess we do have a dragon in the house," the boy's mother finally conceded. "But why do you think he had to get so big?" she asked with a puzzled look. "Oh, I don't know, Mom. I think he just wanted to be noticed," was the boy's last line as he winked at the dragon.

All of us move through a world of wonder, mystery,

beauty, and infinite variety each day. But how many of us are really taking it in? We get so caught up in our everyday lives that, like the boy's family, we become oblivious to our surroundings. We forget to smell the flowers or notice the face across the table from us, and sometimes we don't see the dragons that may be growing in our own home.

The Paying Attention Game is a great way to help you broaden the scope of your attention span with your child. Don't be surprised if your child can outdo you in the beginning, since children are masters of the sublime and far more attuned to the world that surrounds them than most adults. Here are some examples of questions you can ask.

Twelve Paying Attention Questions

The quality of presence determines the quality of life.

— Jack Kornfield

1. How many windows are there on the first floor of your house or apartment?
2. Close your eyes, and tell me what I'm wearing on my feet right now.
3. What is the very last thing you see at the end of our street on the right side before you turn?
4. Think of a store that you frequently go to. How many trees or bushes surround it?
5. What color is the ceiling in your classroom or at work?
6. What is your best friend's middle name?
7. What is the very last thing I do before I go to bed?
8. What is missing from this room that was here before you closed your eyes? (Remove something.)
9. Where do you see the first speed limit sign on the street after you leave the neighborhood?
10. Close your eyes, and tell me how many buttons I am wearing today.
11. What song am I humming, and what are the first five words of the song?
12. Think of your third grade teacher. What color were his or her eyes?

Because it's so relaxing, this game works well before bed. After just a few sessions of playing this game together, we noticed a quantum leap in our ability to take in our surroundings and notice subtle details. Try it for yourself and stretch your attention span to a whole new dimension.

17

Super Sleep Tape

Help your child to describe an attainable goal in detail, as if it had already occurred. Put it on tape and play it several nights a week until the dream is reached.

When Julia was five, she was so afraid to take swimming lessons that she wouldn't even get into the pool on the first day of class. I didn't want to coerce her since she was adamant about not returning, but I knew that it was important for her to learn to swim. I decided to appeal to her imagination, so I came up with a story called "Julia the Fish." In the tale, Julia became a fish who loved to swim and dive in the water more than anything else in the whole world! I repeated at least three times, "Julia the fish feels safe, happy, and free whenever she's in the water!"

O! This learning, what a thing it is.

— William Shakespeare

I decided to narrate the ten-minute story on tape, playing ocean music in the background for added effect. Julia listened to the tape as she drifted off to sleep each night for a whole week. After "practicing" swimming like a fish for seven nights, she was not only willing to go back to class, but to get into the water as well. She even told her coach that her name was "Julia the Salmon"!

Julia passed the course with "flying fins," and continued to take many more swimming classes. She now considers swimming to be one of her favorite sports. Since then, we have made tapes to help her overcome a math block, adjust to a new school, develop new habits, and reach goals.

The mind responds best to suggestions made in a relaxed

state of mind. The best times to listen to a sleep learning tape for maximal effectiveness are when taking a nap or relaxing, or any time when the mind is quiet and receptive. Consider developing a tailor-made sleep learning tape for your child for any of the following reasons.

Seven Reasons to Make a Sleep Learning Tape

1. To accelerate learning educational material.
2. To review for an upcoming test.
3. To build your child's self-image.
4. To form a constructive habit.
5. To reach a goal successfully.
6. To rehearse mentally for an upcoming event.
7. To improve memory and concentration.

Seven Steps to Creating a Tape for Your Child

1. **Gather Your Information:** Prepare your educational or inspirational material in a form that is easy to read and understand. Include a positive phrase that can be repeated at least three times in the tape.

2. **Recite Your Information:** Read your material into the tape for five to twenty minutes. It is best to keep the tape fairly short. If your child is old enough, encourage him or her to narrate the tape.

3. **Read with a Relaxed Voice Tone:** Read the script as though you were reading a bedtime story — gently and lovingly.

4. **Pace Your Words:** Read with expression and conviction. Leave pauses between your statements. Take your time.

5. **Use Positive Suggestions:** Intersperse suggestions, such as "You are absorbing this information effortlessly," or "You are listening to this tape with ease."

Golden slumber kiss your eyes, smiles awaken as you rise.

— Thomas Dekker

6. **Review Main Points at the End of the Tape:** Reinforce the statements that you have made for one to two minutes.

7. **Use a High Quality Tape:** The quality of sound is important, especially if your child will be listening to it often. Use a tape of high quality that will last over time.

Most important, as you make a tape for your child, have fun! Using the imagination to visualize a positive end result can be powerful and enjoyable for both you and your child.

18

Concert Reading

Read uplifting stories, poetry, or prose to your child at bedtime, playing music in the background to create a relaxing experience.

A researcher in Bulgaria named Georgi Lozanov discovered that people learned much more effectively if relaxing music was played in the background while information was read aloud. He called this process a "concert reading." The results were dramatic. People understood the material better, remembered it longer, and learned it effortlessly.

The best way to learn is through the powerful force of rhythm.

— Wolfgang Amadeus Mozart

A mother with a great love for literature and philosophy began concert readings with her son when he was six months old, reading from the works of Shakespeare, Einstein, Gibran, Emerson, and many of the great thinkers of the past hundred years while playing Bach or Beethoven in the background. Although her friends thought she was overdoing it, she was convinced that it would establish an early memory of appreciation for music and great ideas, and she enjoyed doing it as well. Her son is now a toddler with an enormous vocabulary and a great love for music.

Five Ways to Give Concert Readings

1. **Literature:** Start out reading a favorite short story with music in the background, and progress to reading some of the classic literary works.

2. **Homework Review:** Use concert readings to provide a great review for homework or an upcoming test.
3. **Memorization:** Use concert readings when memorizing a lot of information in a short period of time.
4. **About Your Child:** Create a poem or story about your child, and read it aloud with one of your child's favorite instrumental songs in the background.
5. **Bedtime Blessings:** Read spiritual prose, prayers, blessings, or parables aloud to your child before bedtime for a special bedtime blessing.

Concert readings provide relaxation for the body and food for the spirit. They will help your child to feel special and loved while learning something new.

Learning is a matter of attitude, not aptitude.

— Georgi Lozanov

19

Remembering Dreams

**Since everyone dreams during sleep,
get into the habit of paying attention to dreams and learn
from the movies of the mind together.**

For centuries, Native American culture has considered dreams to be very important. The Lakota Sioux tribe even created a special token they hoped would make their good dreams come true. They called this token a "dream catcher." They would wind colorful string through a round wooden base and hang their dream catcher above their bed so that their good dreams could be captured in the net of the dream catcher. They left a small hole in the center of the woven string so that the evil in their dreams could escape. They looked for messages in their dreams to teach them how to live in their everyday world with more wisdom, for they believed that the world of dreams was a doorway to the soul.

*Dreams are a
window to the soul.*

— Carl Jung

A few years ago, I had a recurring dream about being on a dock waiting for a boat to arrive. A small boat would come to pick me up, but it was so small, I couldn't even fit in it. I looked out into the distance and saw a large sailing ship beginning to sail away. I knew I'd have to jump into the cold water and swim to the ship if I wanted to get on, but I was terrified. What if I drowned before I got there? What if I didn't try to get there and the ship never came back? At the crux of the dilemma, I would always wake up.

After a while, I realized that the dream represented my fear of moving to a new city. The boat that was too small represented the old city, and the ship represented the new city I wanted to move to. Diving into the water was what I would have to do if I wanted to follow my dream — jump into new waters and take a risk. I realized that the large sailing ship was within a reasonable distance and that if I was in good condition, I could easily swim to it. After that, I made the decision to move. It was one of the best decisions I ever made.

Everyone dreams about three to five dreams each night, but most of us don't remember much in the morning. By putting some attention on the desire to remember your dreams before drifting off, you will begin to remember more within a few days. It usually takes children even less time.

> Dreams come to tell us something about our lives that we are missing.
>
> — James Redfield

I was somewhat skeptical about this process, so I tried saying each evening before bedtime, "We are going to remember a few of our dreams tomorrow when we wake up." Within a few days, we were both beginning to tell stories to one another about our dreams. We began to keep a dream journal, and we both learned a great deal about ourselves.

Here are a few of the reasons for you and your child to begin to pay attention to your dreams.

Four Reasons to Pay Attention to Dreams

1. Dreams are a window to the world within the inner mind. Getting to know our dreams helps us to *get to know ourselves,* including our fantasies, hopes, and desires.
2. We spend *one-third of our lives* sleeping. Wouldn't it be nice to know more about what we were doing with that time?
3. Dreams help us to get in touch with *our deepest desires and fears.* Many of the images in our dreams represent the feelings and needs we are not in touch with by day.

4. Dreams often present *creative solutions to problems,* and we can only take advantage of them if we can remember them.

Become dream catchers together and explore new dimensions of yourselves. The greatest stories ever told are going on each night in the theater of the mind. Don't miss the show!

20

Plan the Day in a Positive Way!

Get into the habit of spending a few moments each night with your child, picturing the next day unfolding in a positive way.

A cheerful principal of a large school had a reputation for being incredibly energetic and upbeat at his school. He was optimistic and friendly, and although he had many responsibilities, he was easygoing and relaxed. When some students asked him how he kept his spirits up, he said, "I always place my order for an enjoyable day the night before!"

Taking a few moments to plan the following day in a positive way with your child is a form of "practical prayer." By visualizing the next day's events going smoothly, you and your child can develop the capacity to achieve excellence.

Here are some ways that you and your child can practice planning the day in a positive way.

He who every morning plans the transactions of the day and follows out that plan, carries a thread that will guide him through the labyrinth of the most busy life.

— Victor Hugo

Five Ways to Plan the Day in a Positive Way

1. Prepare for the following day by putting out clothes, keys, and anything else that will be needed for the next morning.
2. Picture yourself waking up full of energy.
3. Picture thoroughly enjoying the people you are with, the places you go, and the things you do.

When I want to think, I sit. When I want to change, I act.

— Japanese proverb

4. Imagine laughing often, showing up for the day's events, but not taking any of them too seriously.
5. Imagine you are paying attention to your feelings and needs as well as showing compassion for others.

A great teacher once said, "You are where your attention takes you." Positive planning will help you and your child place your attention on making the most of the day.

Esteem Each Night Chart

Read over the following chart of old beliefs and new beliefs, and help your child move from low esteem to full esteem each night.

From Low Esteem	To Full Esteem
1. When children are demanding or resistant at bedtime, they must be forced to go to bed if necessary.	1. Children are more likely to co-operate when there is an atmosphere of safety and love in the evening hours.
2. Evening hours with children are often draining and exhausting.	2. Evening time can become a time to unwind, relax, and have a little fun with your children as well as some time for yourself.
3. There should be a bedtime routine that is set in stone. Children must be punished if they disregard the rules.	3. Schedules are important, but flexibility is more important. Sometimes, gifts and surprises reside in the unexpected. At the same time, creating agreements about bedtime helps everyone to win.
4. There is so much that piles up that's left to do at the end of a day. There's just not enough energy to share any quality time with my children.	4. In the evening, make sure you get some free time whenever possible. Taking care of yourself is one of the best gifts you can give to your children.
5. Parents are too exhausted to even think at night, much less be creative or present for their children. It's too much to ask.	5. Connecting with your children is a priority. Become more creative about finding quality moments at night, even if just for five minutes.

chapter

3

"Esteeming" with Pride: Positive Self-Management

Children who know how to manage themselves have a certain glow about them as they move through everyday tasks with confidence. They have a sense of pride in their work, and they enjoy their accomplishments. They are less fearful of the unknown and often take risks that other children wouldn't dream of trying.

Chapter 3 will help you teach your child to establish good habits that can enhance his or her self-esteem for many years to come. Good nutrition, regular exercise, stress management, studying, and time management will be explored, along with skills that prepare children for a positive future, such as setting goals, project planning, successful money management, and creating clear agreements. Keep in mind that patience, persistence, and a positive approach are three vital ingredients needed to help your child learn to delight in self-management.

The following poem, "What All Children Want Their Parents to Know," was written to remind parents that children need patience and understanding as they learn to manage themselves and find fulfillment in life.

What All Children Want Their Parents to Know

by Diana and Julia Loomans

Teach me to love and care for myself
Through your positive example.
I will learn much more from what you do
Than from anything you could ever say.

Notice me often,
And take joy in my very existence,
So that I grow up to feel special
And know that I am loved.

Listen to me
With an open ear and a loving heart,
So that I learn to understand my feelings
And trust that my needs will be heard.

Play with me often.
Let down your guard and be more carefree.
The memories will last long,
And our connection even longer.

Focus on what I'm doing right,
And tell me when you appreciate me,
So that I learn to feel worthy
And motivated to do even more.

Tell me more about your life,
Your hopes, dreams, and successes,
So that I come to know you as a person
And can call you my friend
As well as my parent.

Silverstar the Unicorn
by Julia Loomans

When I was in second grade, I loved to fantasize. I would pretend that I was a royal queen and that the playground was my vast castle. If school was boring, I liked to pretend that I was flying like a bird through the sky or venturing through a dense jungle with Atreyu from *The Neverending Story*. Because I had such a vivid imagination, I was great at writing stories, creating artwork, and coming up with ideas about what to play on the playground. But I wasn't so great at writing down homework assignments from the blackboard correctly or following complicated instructions in class. My teacher started sending slips home with me that said, "Julia needs to learn to follow instructions better," or "Julia did not complete the correct assignment last night."

I felt embarrassed and frustrated about this situation, but I couldn't seem to pay attention to details that seemed unimportant or boring to me. One night, when I was talking to my mom about it, I blurted out, "I wish I could just ride away on a unicorn and never go to school again!" My mom said, "It sounds like you need a friend — you know, someone to help you to pay attention in school. How about taking a unicorn to school with you each day to help? It could be a secret between you and me and the unicorn."

"That would be great!" I shouted out loud. "I'll name her Silverstar." That night I described Silverstar in detail. "She's white with an iridescent blue glow. She can make herself large or small whenever she wants. She's a really good listener, and she whispers in my ear to remind me to pay attention if I'm drifting off."

I liked the idea of taking Silverstar to school with me. The next day, I imagined that she was by my side walking with me to school. When I got to my classroom, Silverstar shrank down so small she could hide in my hair. I pretended that she was nudging and whispering, "Julia, listen carefully with me," whenever I needed to pay attention. It was so much fun! Now I had a magical buddy to help me to follow instructions, and it was my secret.

Taking Silverstar to school with me was working pretty well, so my mom and I made a unicorn chart. I drew a bright picture of Silverstar, and we wrote three sentences underneath the drawing:

1. It's easy for me to write down my homework assignments.
2. Following directions is becoming easy for me!
3. I listen carefully when I'm in school.

Each sentence had twenty squares next to it, one for each school day of the month. With Silverstar's help, I was hoping to put a star in all of the boxes. By the end of the month, my chart was full of stars. My teacher sent home a note that said, "Big improvement! Julia is doing much better." I knew who to thank — the unicorn! Silverstar was becoming a star on the playground, too. All of the kids wanted to play unicorn games when they heard me describe my invisible friend.

When my unicorn chart was finished on the last day of the month, I had forty-nine stars out of sixty. I got a surprise package in the mail that day from my Aunt Colleen in Dallas. It was a Christmas present that had arrived a few weeks early. I decided to open it since waiting until Christmas seemed overwhelming. I carefully unwrapped the shiny silver paper and opened the cardboard box, and there was the most beautiful stuffed toy I'd ever seen — a white fluffy unicorn! "I'll bet it's Silverstar's way of saying congratulations," I said. The funniest part was that my aunt didn't even know about my secret unicorn. But who knows? Maybe Silverstar could travel even farther than I thought!

21

Teaching Children a Wellness Lifestyle

Help your child to establish a lifestyle of wellness by making friends with three things — good nutrition, exercise, and stress management.

A close friend of ours who is a busy forty-six-year-old husband and father with three children checked into a hospital in Los Angeles, complaining of dizziness, migraine headaches, and severe chest pain. He feared that he was dying, and his family was equally concerned for his well-being. After numerous tests, he came out with a clean bill of health. "Don't get overzealous," his doctor told him. "Although you aren't dying, you're far from well. Your symptoms are warning signs for you. If you want to be in optimum health, you will have to make some major changes." The hospital referred him to a wellness counselor, and she recommended that he make a few significant lifestyle changes. He was at least fifty pounds overweight, largely due to his habit of eating like a bird all day and gorging like a lion at night. The deprivation of food all day gave him a ravenous appetite in the evening, especially for food that was high in fat and loaded with sugar. He was immediately put on a plan of three square meals (low fat and low sugar), with two light snacks of fruit and vegetables. Within a few weeks, he was feeling better and beginning to shed unwanted pounds.

Since this man tended to work six days a week, he exercised only once a week on Saturday afternoons. He learned

Kids know better than grown-ups that what we do is more important than what we say.

— Pete Seeger

that he needed aerobic exercise three times a week for forty-five minutes each time in order to keep his heart healthy. He scheduled in two more exercise routines each week. Although it was difficult at first, he felt so invigorated after each workout that he began to look forward to his exercise time.

The most challenging area for our friend to make a change concerned learning to relax. He tended to be rushed, overworked, frequently worried, and often tired. He usually slept six hours a night during the week, and up to eight hours on weekends. He began to experiment with his sleep schedule, and he discovered that seven hours was his magic number. With the extra hour of sleep, he felt more alert and had much more energy. He began to demand less of himself at work and at home, and started allowing himself more time so that he wouldn't have to be rushing around.

Within three months, he seemed like a whole new person. He lost twenty-eight pounds and felt great about his new appearance. He stopped having two glasses of wine a few nights a week and decided to save wine for special occasions only, since he noticed a lag in his energy after having alcohol. He stopped working on Saturday mornings, as he had been accustomed to doing for years, and began to go on more outings with his wife and children. He was more serene and more relaxed, and he had developed a great sense of humor.

Most significant were the changes that took place in his family. His children were eating more nutritious food and less junk food, and they were doing their work around the house with less complaining. The family was spending quality time together and fighting less often. His wife had adapted some of his new eating habits and lost twelve pounds herself. "I attribute the improvements in my family life to a few of the major changes in my lifestyle," he said with certainty. "When my family saw what happened to me, leading a lifestyle of wellness became more appealing. I haven't felt or looked this good in years! I only wish I'd done this much sooner."

Learn to relax, and health will follow.

— Taoist proverb

Laughter is a softening influence which prevents the hardening of one's heart.

— Karen Kolberg

Teaching our children to lead a life of wellness is a skill that will reap benefits for a lifetime — physically, mentally, and emotionally. Here are some basic principles of wellness to teach your children about good nutrition, exercise, and managing stress.

Good Nutrition

According to the U.S. Department of Agriculture (USDA), Americans are changing their eating habits for the better and teaching their children to eat fewer nonnutritious foods and more nutritionally sound meals. Red meat is being replaced by poultry, fish, bean products, nuts, and grains, and fresh produce consumption is growing rapidly across the country. The USDA's latest guidelines recommend a low-fat diet, with grains as the foundation, or at least 40 percent of one's daily food consumption. The USDA has divided foods recommended for daily intake into six food groups.

Eat for strength, and not for drunkenness!

— Ecclesiastes 10:17

The USDA's Six Main Food Groups to Eat Each Day

1. **Grains:** This category includes breads, cereal, rice, and pasta. Six to eleven servings are recommended per day, depending on age and body weight. One serving is approximately one slice of bread, or one-half cup of pasta, cereal, or rice. Grains have been the dietary foundation for people living in the temperate zones of our planet for thousands of years.
2. **Vegetables:** When it comes to vegetables, the yellow, orange, or dark leafy green ones are the richest in nutrients. Three to five servings per day are recommended. One serving is approximately one cup of raw vegetables, or one-half cup of cooked vegetables.
3. **Fruit:** The USDA recommends two to four servings of fruit per day. One serving is approximately one medium-size piece of fresh fruit, or three-fourths of

a cup of berries, such as cherries, blueberries, straw-berries, and so forth.

4. **Protein:** This category includes meat (preferably lean meat with fewer than three grams of fat per ounce), poultry, fish, dry beans, tofu, eggs, nuts, and seeds (with a caution on the high fat content of nuts). Two to three servings are recommended per day. One serving is approximately three ounces of lean meat; three-fourths of a cup of tofu, beans, or low-fat cottage cheese; or one whole egg.

5. **Dairy:** This includes milk, yogurt, and cheese. The USDA recommends two to three servings per day. One serving is approximately eight ounces of low-fat milk or yogurt, or one ounce of cheese. For those who prefer an alternative to dairy, substitute soy or rice products.

6. **Fats:** Fat is found in two forms: saturated and un-saturated. Saturated fat is found primarily in the meat group, while unsaturated fat is found in poul-try, fish, and vegetable oils. To meet the need for essential fatty acid, choose from the unsaturated group. One to three servings per day are recom-mended. One serving is approximately one pat of butter, one tablespoon of oil or salad dressing, or two teaspoonfuls of mayonnaise.

A crust eaten in peace is better than a banquet partaken in anxiety.

— Aesop

Eight Ways to Help Your Child Develop Healthy Eating Habits

1. Plan your meals for the week with your child, adding flavorful dishes and variety, and make nu-tritional eating something to look forward to.

2. Serve a balance of foods from the six food groups each day.

3. Encourage children to drink at least eight glasses of water each day, including a small glass before each meal to help prevent overeating.

4. Teach children to eat snacks that are healthy and low in fat, such as fruits, vegetables, air-popped popcorn, low-fat yogurt, bread, or low-fat crackers.
5. Encourage children to eat slowly at each meal, chewing each bite of food thoroughly and putting the fork down between bites.
6. Teach children to eat until the appetite is reasonably satisfied, rather than overeating. Research has shown that those who eat moderate amounts of food, rather than overeating, live longer, healthier lives.
7. Make desserts low-fat and healthy, and save sugar and high-fat desserts (cake, ice cream, pie, pastries, or candy) for special occasions, such as birthdays and holidays.
8. Avoid additives, pesticides, and artificial flavor whenever possible, and eat food that is made with all-natural ingredients. Buy organic fruits and vegetables whenever available.

To do what you ought to do, when you ought to do it and be guided by your wisdom is the only real freedom.

— Paramahansa Yogananda

Five Benefits of Good Nutrition for Children

1. More energy.
2. More brain power for learning and thinking.
3. Better health.
4. Fewer illnesses.
5. Higher performance levels.

Exercise

One hundred years ago, scrubbing clothes in a washtub for twenty minutes burned about 140 calories and toned the upper torso and arms. Today, the same task involves putting the clothes into the washer and turning it on, which takes about two minutes and burns about 14 calories. With all of our modem conveniences, it's no wonder that so many American families are overweight. The U.S. Government's Council on Health and Fitness cites exercise as one of the most important aspects of a child's health. Here are a few ideas about how you can promote a more active lifestyle for your family.

Exercising Together

If you take care of the inches, you will not have to worthy about the miles.

— H. Coleridge

1. **Walk Together:** There are over seventy million walkers in the United States. Exercise walking has now become the number one fitness activity in America, with enthusiasts spanning all age brackets. When you are going on short neighborhood errands with your child, consider the benefits of walking rather than driving. A mother of a first grader began to walk her daughter to school each morning instead of driving her. "It makes such a difference in how I feel for the rest of the day, and we have a good time, too!" Taking fitness walks with your child to nature reserves, state parks, or interesting parts of town offers a fun adventure together as well as a good workout.

2. **Take Up a Sport with Your Child:** More and more parents are combining play and fitness with their children, teaching them how to lead active lives while having fun together. Biking, hiking, tennis, roller blading, running, playing Frisbee, swimming, baseball, basketball, or even kite flying are just a few of the ways that adults and children can keep fit and have some fun together. A mother and her seven-year-old son took up roller blading as a sport, and they now spend some time each week practicing their new skill. "I'm the only second grader with a mom who roller blades," her son Brian said, beaming. A father and his two teenage daughters recently signed up for an aerobics class together at a local gym. "We have a lot of fun going together, and we keep one another motivated," one of his daughters said.

3. **Take a Hike:** Hiking is one of the best ways to do aerobic activity together, since the scenery distracts you from the vigorous workout that you and your child will get in just one hour. A single father of five-year-old twin boys takes them on a hike every Saturday morning before lunch. "It's playtime, quality time, and a workout, all rolled into one for us," he said.

Five Benefits of Regular Exercise for Children

1. More energy.
2. More motivation.
3. Better health.
4. Trim appearance.
5. Greater self-esteem.

Managing Stress

Children cope with a certain amount of stress each day, depending on their age and upon circumstances at home and at school. Two questions children often ask when they experience stress are, "How will I get through this?" and "Will it ever end?" The following list of stresses children may experience can be used as a springboard for discussion and to help offer reassurance that, with support, they will get through their stress, and at some point the stress will end.

The difference between the words healthy and holy is only the distinction that has been made historically between the physical and the spiritual.

— Polly Berrien Berends

Twenty-One Ways Children Experience Stress

Ask your child to rank the following list of twenty-one stresses, with 1 being the most stressful, and 21 being the least stressful. Note that this checklist covers only some of the most common fears and stresses that children may experience and is intended for discussion only.

- Moving to a new location and going to a new school.
- Being teased or put down by friends and classmates.

- Losing a parent through divorce or death.
- Getting poor grades in school.
- Fighting or arguing with Mom or Dad.
- Getting lost.
- Going to the doctor or dentist.
- Hearing Mom and Dad quarreling.
- Being suspected of lying.
- Fear of death.
- Being spanked.
- Being left out.
- Getting sick.
- Losing a game.
- Having nightmares.
- Being embarrassed in front of other people.
- Being yelled at.
- Fighting with friends.
- Being harassed, attacked, or molested.
- Being held back a year in school.
- Having a new brother or sister.

Twelve Ways for Children to Reduce and Manage Stress

*How do you like to go
up in a swing,
Up in the air so blue?
Oh, I do think it the
pleasantest thing
Ever a child can do!*

*— Robert Louis
Stevenson*

1. Talk to an adult you can trust about your feelings.
2. Work off tension with physical play or exercise.
3. Breathe slowly and relax your whole body from head to foot when feeling tense.
4. Write about your feelings in a diary or journal each day.
5. Talk to a good friend who listens when you're having a rough time.
6. Ask for some extra attention from your family when you need it.
7. Get plenty of sleep each night, drink lots of water, and eat healthy food.
8. Have a hobby, such as drawing or playing a musical instrument, for relaxation and relief.

9. Learn to laugh at yourself when you make mistakes.
10. Get your tension and anger out in ways that don't hurt anybody — go for a run, yell into a pillow, punch a punching bag, jump on a trampoline, or throw pillows.
11. Agree with people who tease you when it makes sense to do so. If you drop a ball, for example, say, "You're right, I did drop the ball," in a carefree voice. When the teasing or put-downs are more cruel, learn to walk away, telling yourself, "I don't have to listen to this."
12. Don't keep secrets inside that are hurting you. Reach out to someone who can help.

Help your child to lead a lifestyle of wellness that includes good nutrition, regular exercise, and skills in managing stress by encouraging the above ideas, and by leading a healthy and active wellness lifestyle of your own.

22

Using Affirmations

Develop the skill of positive affirmations in thought, spoken word, and written word with your child, and learn to create messages that free you rather than limit you.

In Tibet, there is an ancient rite of passage that occurs as a young baby begins to communicate with words. The entire extended family gathers together and encircles the child, singing out positive blessings, words of praise, and wishes of hope and love for several hours. Even after the baby falls asleep, the ritual continues, until the family is satisfied that they have satiated the child's mind with affirmations. They believe that the child is now positioned for confidence and success as he or she learns to talk.

I am wiser,
better than I thought.
I did not know
I held so much
greatness.

— Walt Whitman

Affirmations are a very basic tool of self-management, through the choice of thoughts and words. The best way to teach affirmations is to model them for your child. If you lock yourself out of your car, try saying, "I am going to learn a lot from this," rather than "How could I be stupid!" When you fall short of a goal, say, "I have unlimited potential. I know I can do it," rather than "I'll never get it right!"

Certain words seem to evoke feelings of negativity and shame and can be considered junk food for the mind. Here are a few of the most common to be avoided:

- have to
- can't
- never
- impossible

- should
- always
- put-downs

- only
- not enough
- name-calling

Learning to use affirmations is a vital tool that will build self-esteem and encourage children to be self-accepting. Here are a few guidelines to help you and your child.

Principles for Making Affirmations

1. *State your affirmations in the present.*
   "I am a winner," rather than "I will win the game tomorrow."
2. *Say what you want, rather than what you don't want.*
   "I am calm and relaxed," instead of "I don't lose my temper anymore."
3. *Include feeling words that add positive emotion.*
   "I feel energetic and alive getting up on time!"
4. *Be specific about what you want, rather than vague.*
   "Today I feel great running three miles," instead of "Today I feel great running."
5. *Make the words simple and easy to remember.*
   "I am super smart," instead of "I am getting smarter and smarter all the time."

Only one thing registers on the subconscious mind: practice. What you practice is what you manifest.

— Grace Spear

When Julia was a baby, I drew some animals on index cards, each stating an affirmation that I wanted her to learn to say as she was learning to talk. Hilda Hippo said, "I am full of joy," and Mona Monkey said, "I am lovable!" They were simple and easy to remember; before long, there were twenty-four animals for her to look at, each with its own positive phrase. She loved to point to the cards, and before long, she was saying, "I am kind" or "I love to learn," as the cards stated. This idea worked so well that the animals were later named "The Lovables in the Kingdom of Self-Esteem," which is now a popular children's book.

Saying affirmations is like exercise. It must be done

Every child is born a genius.

— R. Buckminster Fuller

regularly in order to stay fit. Here are some sample affirmations from the Lovables to help you to get started.

Sample Affirmations

- I am lovable.
- I am courageous.
- I am gentle and strong.
- I am special and unique.
- I am proud to be me.
- I trust myself.
- I am peaceful inside.
- I am thankful.
- I love to learn.
- I love to play and have fun.
- I am capable.
- I take care of my body.
- I take care of the world around me.

Practice affirmations each day with your child, and watch your self-esteem grow. When you find yourself feasting on any of the "mental junk words," use humor to get yourself back on track. We know a father who playfully makes the sound of a siren when he puts himself or someone else down and says, "Emergency — I need a shift, quick!" He then uses an affirmation to change his thinking. Consistent efforts at affirmations will convince you that "shift happens!"

23

Super Study Area

Make an efficient and pleasing study area for your child in the corner of a bedroom or in a separate room, and create an environment that promotes organized, clear thinking.

I was visiting a friend's house recently and enjoying a "home tour" with him and his eight- and ten-year-old sons. When we got to the boys' bedroom, I was surprised and impressed by the efficiency of the boys' study areas. They each had their own desks with two-drawer file cabinets next to the desks. There were bulletin boards above the desk areas and small Rolodex files on their desks for phone numbers. A yearly calendar hung on each wall, along with a few plastic crates stacked with vital tools, such as paper, pencils, erasers, rulers, a calculator, pencil sharpener, colored markers, and so forth. They both had bright halogen lights on their desks for maximum light while studying.

If you employed study, thinking, and planning time daily, you could develop and use the power that can change the course of your destiny.

— W. Clement Stone

Both boys were particularly proud of their "offices" as they called them. Jim, their father, said that he had been a very scattered, disheveled student with "subminimal" study habits as a child. He wanted to give his boys what he didn't get — some direction, organization, and an efficient area to study in. It seemed to be working, since they were both excellent students.

I was inspired to go home and improve my own home office, as well as to help my own child to do the same. Over time, we have developed a very pleasing and organized system. Here are a few vital tips.

Seven Steps to a Super Study Area

1. Provide your child with a good desk and a comfortable chair.

2. Make sure that there is plenty of light in the room. Besides a ceiling light, consider putting an additional light on the desk.

3. Use a file cabinet or a few inexpensive cardboard file boxes, and provide some files for your child to organize letters, papers, projects, special documents, pictures, information, or report cards.

4. Provide some shelves, stacking baskets, or crates for homework and books.

5. Help your child to organize supplies, such as glue, pencils, erasers, paper, tape, a calculator, and so forth.

6. Provide a special calendar for homework, projects, and special events to be posted above the desk area, or use a weekly homework sheet and keep it posted on the refrigerator so that you can check off the homework assignments with your child.

7. If it's possible within your budget, consider providing a computer for your child. Used computers are now more reasonably priced than ever, and they are becoming as common to our children's generation as telephones and typewriters were when many of us were children.

The most important thing to acquire now is learning how to learn.

— John Naisbitt

A fifth grade girl was failing two courses and hated going to school. Her mother decided to do three things — set regular homework hours, encourage any sign of progress, and create an efficient study area. Her mother said the results were amazing. The regular homework hours gave her daughter consistency, the encouragement increased her motivation, and the study area gave her a sense of confidence and competence. Within a few months, her daughter's grades were up, and her attitude about school was improving significantly. When her teacher asked her what had helped her the most, she answered, "My new study area — it's just like a real office." Help your own child by creating a study area designed just for him or her.

24

Setting Goals

**Teach your child to turn dreams into reality
with the practical magic of goal setting.**

Goal setting is the process of making a dream come true step-by-step. The desire to meet a challenge and succeed has been a part of many cultures throughout history. The ancient Peruvians used to draw out their goals in symbols and paint them in primitive colors on the walls of caves. The Egyptians used to create elaborate rituals to move from the state of desire to actualization. They believed that writing out a dream in advance would assure a positive outcome.

Here are a few simple steps to follow to help your child set goals successfully.

*If you don't know
where you are going,
you will probably end
up somewhere else.*

— Laurence J. Peter

Seven Principles for Setting Goals

1. **Listen First:** Encourage your child to become quiet and listen to the wisdom within before setting a goal. Many goals are born out of competition or excessive striving rather than from one's own integrity. A healthy and solid goal follows listening to one's inner wisdom, rather than the reverse. Go over these vital questions before setting goals:

   • Is this goal something I really want?
   • Does this goal serve me in my life right now?
   • What will I need to bring this dream into reality?

Once these questions have been answered to your child's satisfaction, you can begin to create a game plan.

2. **Create Smart Goals:** Getting clear and specific about goals will help your child to create a personal map to success. The more realistic the goal, the more likely it is to take place, as long as the goal is something that your child truly wants rather than something force-fed by a well-intentioned adult. Consider these five key questions when helping your child to set "smart" goals:

Sensible	Does it make *sense* to do this?
Measurable	How will I *measure* when I've arrived?
Attainable	Can I actually *attain* this now?
Realistic	Is it possible and *realistic* at this time?
Time line	How much *time* will it take me?

3. **See It and Believe It:** Once the goal has been set, encourage your child to begin to see it as though it had already occurred. Drawing out goals in pictures, writing them down in vivid detail, or describing the desired end result on tape are great ways to keep the energy flowing in a positive direction. Once your child has set the goals, this will be the most important step to focus on each day.

4. **Set Monthly Goals:** Setting one or two monthly goals is a good way to practice the principles and see results quickly. A family of four selects one main goal per month each, along with a chart for marking down their progress on the refrigerator. Each person places a star on a winning day. They don't believe in failure, and they claim that they only have two kinds of days — "I did it" days and "Give it all you've got tomorrow" days. At the end of the month, they have an Excellence Dinner to celebrate their successes. (Usually all four of them succeed, since they enjoy keeping one another motivated.)

The world has a habit of making room for the person whose words and actions show that he knows where he is going.

— Napoleon Hill

91

5. **Set Yearly Goals:** Make yearly goal setting a family affair. Consider creating goals for the year in the following categories:

- Business or school
- Family and friends
- Money
- Vacation
- Learning
- Spirituality
- Physical health

Break these down into bite-sized pieces by creating goals for the month, and read over the yearly goals at least once a week.

6. **Reward Your Progress:** Rewards can provide a fun lift along the way. Create small weekly or monthly rewards to stay motivated, since every step along the way is a step toward success and worthy of acknowledgment! Give one another hugs, pats on the back, cheers, and encouragement. If someone slips, support that person in getting back on track.

7. **Be Willing to Let It All Go:** Sometimes something unexpected appears, and signs indicate that a change is needed. Being willing to drop a goal in favor of something more timely is a mark of courage and wisdom. Encourage your child to remain open to changes, and practice the art of detachment. There is a Zen saying that offers wise counsel during times of unexpected change: "Face change by resisting the current and perish. Move with change, resilient to the flow, and flourish."

Everything has a gestation and then a bringing forth.

— Rainer Maria Rilke

The Winner's Goal Chart on page 93 provides a simple and creative way to record your successes each day of the month.

The Winner's Goal Chart

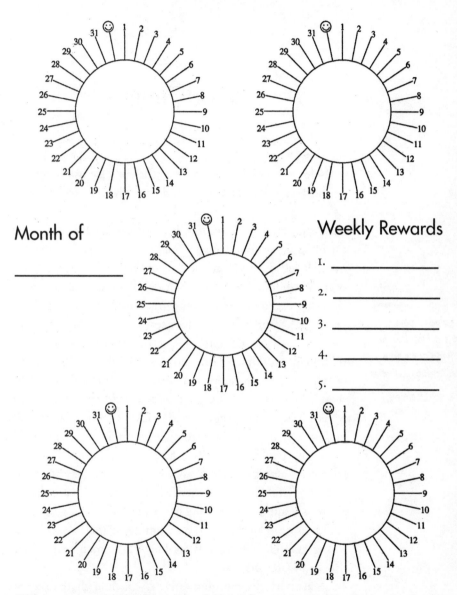

Month of

_____

Weekly Rewards

1. _____

2. _____

3. _____

4. _____

5. _____

Write one monthly goal in each of the circles. For each Win Day, color in the number line with a colored marker. Give yourself a reward for each Win Week (achieving at least 80 percent of your goals). © 1994 Diana Loomans. This chart may be duplicated for free, noncommercial use.

25

Good Timing

Help your child manage time efficiently by using time charts and learning to clock daily activities accurately.

Seventeen-year-old Jason told his mother that he needed the car to do a few errands that would take about forty-five minutes. He left the house at 3:30 P.M. and returned at 5:45 P.M. — over two hours later! Nine-year-old Rebecca was asked to clean her bedroom before company arrived. A fifteen-minute task took her forty-five minutes because she got distracted and interspersed cleaning with play. A mother of three children told them to do homework and promised that she'd be home by 5:30 P.M. to fix supper. At 6:20 P.M., she walked in disheveled and stressed. Two of the three children told her they weren't hungry, since they started snacking about 6:00 P.M. All of these scenarios have something in common — poor timing!

> *We need...a sense of the value of time — that is, of the best way to divide one's time into one's various activities.*
>
> — Arnold Bennett

Many people have only a hazy idea of how long it will take to accomplish needed tasks, which is why they are often rushed or late. Great leaps forward in performance are almost always a result not of working harder, but of working smarter! Children need to get a sense of timing in their system at a young age. How else will they know how to manage their time, and later their lives?

Start with the morning tasks. Use a time chart to write down a list of things that need to be done each morning with your child. To the right of each task, write down the suggested time that each task will take, along with a blank line to fill in how long the task actually took.

Time Chart

Tasks	Suggested Time	Actual Time
1. Bathroom time	10	_____
2. Dressing	10	_____
3. Making the bed	5	_____
4. Eating breakfast	15	_____
5. Gathering books & lunch	5	_____
6. Second bathroom time	5	_____
7. Farewell time	5	_____
8. Miscellaneous	5	_____
	60 minutes	

Time will vary with the age of the child since older children may have additional things to do, such as lunch making, household tasks, helping younger children, or driving to school. Although you need to invest some initial time to establish a routine with your child, if it's done in a cheerful spirit, it will create a happier home for everyone. If you are often rushed in the morning yourself, you might want to use a time chart along with your child. Here are a few more ideas to help your child to manage time.

People need responsibility. They resist assuming it, but they cannot get along without it.

— John Steinbeck

Three Ideas for Managing Time

1. **Extra Time:** Leva, a seven-year-old girl, found herself rushed and unhappy using a time chart with her mother, since she was used to spending time "putzing" between each task. They decided to give her one and a half hours each morning, rather than one hour, so that after all of her tasks were done, she would still have up to one full half hour each morning to play before school.
2. **Time Guessing Games:** If the thought of using a time chart initially seems overwhelming, start with

a bite-sized activity in time management. Play the "What's Your Guess?" game. When going shopping for food, show your child the list and say, "We're going food shopping. What's your guess? How long do you think it will take?" Or "I'd like you to clean up your toys in the den. What's your guess? How long will it take?" You can also place bets with your child on how long something will take, and offer a small reward for the winner. Whatever is required, time management will pay off in more time and less worry. Although it's true that love makes the world go 'round, good timing makes the day run smoothly as we go 'round!

3. **Backwards in Time:** When there is a deadline to meet, try calculating how much time will be needed starting with the deadline and moving backwards to the present time. For example, if your child has piano lessons at 4:00 P.M. and it is 1:00 P.M., start with the following:

4:00–3:30: Drive to the lesson.
3:30–3:15: Gather books for the lesson.
3:15–2:45: Clean the bedroom.
2:45–2:00: Help Dad outside in the garden.
2:00–1:30: Free time.
1:30–1:00: Eat lunch.

Although this might seem strange, we have found it remarkably helpful in getting things done and keeping us on time.

26

The Weekly Plan

**Teach your child to manage time and get things done
by using an efficient weekly "To Do" sheet
and a master calendar.**

Corporate presidents, teachers, entrepreneurs, parents, doctors, and lawyers all share something in common — they must learn to manage their time well. "Planning your work and working your plan" is an art and a skill essential to a successful life. Young children often have very little sense of time and need to learn as they grow up to manage tasks and get them accomplished within a time frame. Here are a few tips that we have found most useful.

Three Vital Tips for Planning the Week

1. **Master Calendar:** Use a master calendar for all of the monthly, weekly, and day-to-day meetings in the household. Fill it in by the month, giving each family member a different marker color on the calendar. This will save hours of chaos and confusion. Younger children can look up on the calendar and see that Mom has her board meeting on Thursday night, which means the babysitter will be coming, and older children can plan their schedules accordingly, if, for instance, they need to find a ride for an event. Post the calendar in a highly visible area, such as the kitchen, and keep it as current as possible.

Let our advance worrying become advance thinking and planning.

— Winston Churchill

2. **Weekly Lists:** Teach children to use an ABC list at the beginning of each week. After we spent years experimenting with various time management ideas, this format has turned out to be one of the most efficient for children to use. (See the ABC chart included on page 99.) Have your child fill in all of the "Most Important Tasks" for the week in the A column — such as study for the Wednesday science test, do the dishes on Monday, Thursday, and Saturday, and make a lunch each night. The B column is for "Important Tasks," such as clean the bedroom before Friday night sleepover, send a thank-you note to Grandma for the gift, and call the Boy Scouts' number to find out about the camp schedule for summer. The C column is for "Maybe Tasks" — things that might not ever get done if they aren't put on a list since they are optional, such as framing the painting that has been in the closet for a year, reading the first two chapters of a novel, or clearing some of the old junk out of the closet.

3. **Daily Lists:** For the more adventurous and industrious, complement the ABC list with a daily calendar as well (to fill in the actual day and time that the A, B, and C tasks will be accomplished). Although it can seem tedious to sit down and plan for the whole week, the twenty to thirty minutes it takes each week will pay off in time saved. The more specific you get, the more likely you are to achieve your goals.

> *The reward for work well done is the opportunity to do more.*
>
> — Jonas Salk, M.D.

Planning and managing time are essential skills for children to learn. The key to teaching them these vital tools is a triple P formula: patience, positivity, and persistence!

The Winner's Weekly Plan

A (Most Important Tasks)	B (Important Tasks)	C (Maybe Tasks)
1.	1.	1.
2.	2.	2.
3.	3.	3.
4.	4.	4.
5.	5.	5.
6.	6.	6.
7.	7.	7.
8.	8.	8.
9.	9.	9.
10.	10.	10.
11.	11.	11.
12.	12.	12.

**Reward for Completing
Top Five Tasks for Week:**

Affirmation:

27

Project Planning

Teach your child to break any project down into small, bite-sized pieces and turn feeling overwhelmed into a sense of step-by-step accomplishment.

Many people, old and young alike, wince when they hear the word project and run the other way. Deadlines, details, and fear of failure plague many of us when it comes to starting and completing projects. We often pass this dreadful drudgery along to our children unwittingly, and we produce a generation of "task dodgers."

Nothing is particularly hard if you divide it into small jobs.

— Henry Ford

The ancient Chinese philosopher Lao-tzu said, "The journey of a thousand miles begins with one step." Likewise, the completion of a task begins with one small accomplishment. Most projects involve more time, money, or resources than we may have initially thought, although, on occasion, we can blow a project up and make it so much larger than life that we fear it will take forever to complete. For all of these reasons, teaching children to plan out a project is an important and significant contribution to their future success.

The child who can set a plan into motion and move from start to finish successfully will take more risks, set more goals, and realize more dreams. Here are some simple steps to follow to help your child in project planning.

Ten Steps to a Super Project Plan

1. Use a chart (such as the sample chart provided on page 103) to map out your journey to success.

2. Describe the project — what it is and how you plan to achieve it.

3. Brainstorm with your child and write out a list of each of the steps it will take to accomplish the project.

4. Write down approximately how long each step will take, to begin to get a sense of the time needed overall to complete the project.

5. Number the steps in a sequence that is practical and makes sense.

6. Write down when each task will be accomplished on a calendar. Be specific (e.g., #1 — Tuesday, 4–5 P.M.; #2 — Thursday, 7–8 P.M.).

7. Write down who will help if assistance is needed (such as Mom, Dad, a teacher, a librarian, a friend, or a neighbor).

8. Check off each single step as a winning step towards the goal. Put your focus on each and every accomplishment and not on any of the setbacks.

9. If you lose momentum or unexpected obstacles arise, decide what is needed and change the plan accordingly. The plan is not set in stone. It serves one purpose only — to help get the job done with more ease and less stress.

10. Plan how you will celebrate when the project is achieved. Taking the time to honor yourself for a job well done is a hallmark of high self-esteem!

A terrace nine stories high begins with a pile of earth.

— Lao-tzu

Any project can become manageable and enjoyable when you follow the above ten steps with consistency. Try taking these steps with your child when you have a household project, such as a garage sale, fixing up an old car, painting or redecorating a room, clearing out a cluttered closet, donating junk to a charity, having a party, or doing major yard work. You will be amazed at the sense of accomplishment you will have when you use a step-by-step approach.

Your child can use a project planning chart for school

A short cut is often the quickest way to some place you weren't going.

— Anonymous

projects and achieve a sense of direction and accomplishment instead of the usual cycle of avoidance, procrastination, and cramming that many of us have experienced. A project planning chart is a tool that will save your child years of needless stress, and help to establish an "I can" attitude.

The Winner's Project Plan

Project:			Completion Goal Date:		
Results Expected:					
#	Step-by-Step To Dos	People or Resources Needed	Hours Needed	Start Date	Finish Date
My Reward for Successful Completion:			Actual Completion Date:		

© 1994 Diane Loomans. This chart may be duplicated for free, noncommercial use.

28

Journaling

Keep an ongoing journal of feelings, thoughts, questions, and ideas, and encourage your child to do the same.

There are universities in Australia that offer journaling as an accredited college course, claiming that a personal journal has the potential to evoke more wisdom than all the books one could read in a lifetime. Many great thinkers over the centuries have kept journals, including Socrates, Theodore Roosevelt, and Anne Frank.

Encourage your child to keep a journal and make entries several times a week. Journals can serve a variety of purposes — to record the day's events, to evoke feelings and opinions, or to create short stories, poetry, and interesting ideas. Here are a few simple tips for setting up a journal.

There is continuous astonishment at what your deep well contains if you just haul off and shout down it.

— Ray Bradbury

Seven Tips for Successful Journaling

1. Find a notebook or hardcover book with blank pages and a cover that is very pleasing. Keep it in a place where it is easily accessible.
2. Use a special writing pen that is just for journaling time.
3. Whenever possible, write in the journal at the same time of day (e.g., before bedtime or after school) to develop a habit.
4. Keep it private, and read from it to someone else

You learn as much by writing as you do by reading.

— Eric Hoffer

only on occasion. A journal is a place to write one's personal feelings and thoughts.

5. Don't date the pages in advance, so that there is no pressure to have to "catch up" if a few days are missed. When an excerpt is entered, date it at the end of the piece in case you finish it on a later date from when you started it.

6. Consider a theme for your journal, or combine several themes in one, such as a feelings journal, a dream journal, a "What I Did Today" journal, a creative writing journal, or a travel journal.

7. We know a family that keeps what they call an open journal. Each family member contributes experiences and feelings. It remains in a place that is accessible to all and is often read aloud after meals.

I like to write when I feel spiteful. It's like having a good sneeze!

— D. H. Lawrence

Which kind of diary or journal would interest your child? Young children might enjoy a scrapbook, combining artwork, feelings, and special events. Older children, especially teens, will enjoy exploring feelings in more depth in a notebook or hardcover blank book.

We have kept a variety of journals over the years. Currently, we each use a hardbound book with blank pages. Keeping a journal provides a great adventure in self-discovery. Begin to tap into more of your own unlimited potential by journaling, and help your child to do the same.

29

Creating Clear Agreements

Use preventive discipline by creating clear rules and agreements that both you and your child feel good about.

We often think of discipline as a form of punishment to change a child's behavior after an unacceptable action. But preventive discipline — creating fair rules that have logical consequences — prevents the need for punishment, which doesn't really work. Punishment sets up an "overdog-underdog" relationship. The overdog is an authoritative watchdog that barks out the rules and hounds the underdog to be responsible and get things done. The underdog is the "I'll show you" rebel who is angry, resentful, and often living a separate life that goes "underground."

Coming together is a beginning, keeping together is progress; working together is success.

— Henry Ford

Julia and I went through an "overdog-underdog" phase during part of her freshman year in high school. She was now a teen, and some of the agreements and rules from her childhood years were no longer valid. We struggled over homework hours, getting housework done, the phone, curfew, and going out with friends. It wasn't until we created some new agreements that had logical consequences that we began to restore peace. Here are a few examples from a clear agreement list, which we wrote out and signed together.

Sample Agreement List — Julia

1. I will take a one-hour break for myself after school. After that, I will do my homework so that

I have some time to be creative and relax in the evening.

2. I will let the answering machine pick up any calls during homework time. I agree to do this in order to feel good about getting my homework done, and so that I can call my friends back feeling relaxed.

3. I will honor my curfew, or call within a half hour of my curfew time when I have a valid reason for being late. I agree to do this so that my parents will know where I am when it's late.

4. I will write down my housework for the week on Mondays from the family job chart. I will fill in when I plan to accomplish these jobs on my weekly calendar. I agree to do this to do my part to keep harmony in the house.

What do we live for, if it is not to make life less difficult for each other?

— George Eliot

Sample Agreement List — Diana

1. I will approach Julia in a respectful and positive way when something needs to be done or changed. I agree to do this to keep respect and harmony in the household and to keep the lines of communication open.

2. If I begin to act like the overdog, I agree to write a note to Julia with some ideas on how to improve and ask her to sign it if she is in agreement.

3. I will acknowledge small successes, and I will be encouraging about mistakes. I will let go of unrealistic expectations and expect improvement rather than perfection.

4. I agree to one half hour meeting with Julia each week to acknowledge our successes, as well as to brainstorm ideas for improvement.

Fair rules with logical consequences can cover a wide range of areas, so that everyone can be in clear agreement.

Fifteen Areas to Create Clear Agreements

1. Going to bed and getting up in the morning.
2. Table manners.
3. Eating habits.
4. Answering phone and taking messages.
5. Getting homework done.
6. Doing housework.
7. Curfews and being late.
8. Cleanliness, dress, and self-care.
9. Language and communication in the house.
10. Handling disagreements.
11. Car safety and driving rules.
12. Telling the truth.
13. Politeness with family, friends, and neighbors.
14. Picking up after oneself.
15. Dating, sleepovers, and being with friends.

Help thy brother's boat across, and lo! thine own has reached the shore.

— Hindu proverb

When fair rules are created with clear agreements, comments such as "Nobody told me," or "I didn't know" can be bypassed. Clear boundaries are created, and everyone shares a common understanding. There are several ways to create fair rules and keep them updated as your child grows and changes. Here are a few ideas.

Ideas for Creating Fair Agreements

1. **Rules in Rhyme:** For very young children, consider creating the rules in rhyme, such as those four-year-old Carlos received in a hand-printed book from his mom. (For example, "When I'm hungry and want a treat, I reach for some fruit or a vegetable to eat.")
2. **Rules and Agreements Book:** Create a rules and agreements book for the whole family to discuss and then sign in agreement. This will save many hours of stress.

3. **Weekly Family Meeting:** Have a family meeting once a week to go over rules, consequences, and agreements, and to make any needed changes. Keep the meeting to an hour or less, and finish with something fun, such as playing games or sharing popcorn and a movie.

4. **Other Resources:** Take a class in effective parenting, read a few good books on using logical consequences with children, or seek the help of a professional. The time and money spent may be one of the best investments you will ever make.

30

Successful Money Management

**Instill some good ideas on spending
and saving money, and give your child a jump start
on successful money management.**

Money is one of the most alluring, feared, and misunderstood concepts in our culture today. We've been told, "Money is the root of all evil," and "Money talks." Girls are sometimes told, "It's just as easy to marry a rich man as a poor man," or "When money goes out the door, love flies out the window." We've heard that "All that glitters is not gold," and "Being rich isn't everything but it's a nice substitute!"

Despite all of the contradictions, there are some basic money management principles that most will agree upon as sound suggestions to teach our children. Here are a few rungs to help your child to climb up the ladder of successful spending and saving.

Nine Steps to Successful Money Management

1. **Allowance:** Give children an allowance each week to give them an opportunity to manage a small amount of money on a regular basis. Children over twelve are usually ready to handle a separate clothing or school expenses allowance in addition to their regular allowance. This gives them an opportunity to make choices and learn to budget money.

2. **Savings:** Open a savings account for your child and encourage saving 10 to 25 percent of all income

from allowance, babysitting, or a part-time job. Deposit the money in a savings account in your child's name. Most children take great pleasure in watching their savings account gradually grow.

3. **Donations:** Teach your child to give money back to the community. To do this, put aside 5 to 10 percent each month from all earnings. At the end of the year, donate the money to a religious, community, or charity group of your choice. Include your child in the process of deciding which donations you will make, and allow him or her to share in the joy and pride that come from giving to others.

4. **Budgeting:** Teach your child to budget money. The best budgeting system we have used includes a column for projected spending each month and a column for actual spending to the right of it. This system encourages responsible spending, since at the end of the month, you can compare the two columns. If you have never budgeted your money, pick up a good book on money managing and share the basic principles with your child.

5. **Smart Shopping:** Consider some basic concepts to teach your child about shopping.

- Look for good quality and a fair price, especially on significant items.
- Read the labels, look at the list of ingredients, and know what you are buying.
- Do some comparative shopping on big items.
- When money is tight, learn to shop for bargains.
- When money is plentiful, learn to ask, "Do I really need and want this item, and will I use it?"
- Teach your child the basic principles of paying interest, getting loans, and making investments. If you don't know yourself, take a class together, or read a book together on basic financial management.

Wealth is the product of man's capacity to think.

— Ayn Rand

6. **Gratuities:** Teach your child about gratuities and tipping — 15 to 20 percent for restaurants, a few dollars for taxi drivers, valet parking, airport baggage check-in, or hotel assistance, and so forth. Whenever Julia and I are away on a trip, I let her pay the tips and figure out the restaurant tip (giving a little more if the service is excellent).

7. **Money Goals:** Encourage your child to set money goals, such as "I will earn fifty dollars a month babysitting and save five dollars a month," or "I will earn one thousand dollars working this summer and put five hundred dollars toward my car next fall." Even the very youngest can be taught to set money goals, such as "I will save two dollars a month from my six dollars a month allowance," or "I will buy my first CD in four months!" I will never forget the thrill and pride that I felt at seven years old when I bought my first 45 record with my own money.

8. **Beliefs about Money:** Teach your child some positive affirmations about money, such as "I joyfully write out checks to pay my bills in thanks for the services I have received," or "I am responsible, clear, and prosperous with money." Talk about the faulty beliefs you were taught about money as a child, and let your child remind you when you begin to slip into old thought patterns about money. Instead of saying, "We can't afford that," try saying, "We are spending our money on other things right now," or "We'll put that on our prosperity list!"

9. **Prosperity Principles:** Talk about a few of the basic principles of wealth and prosperity with your child. Here are six of the basics.

   • We live in a world of infinite possibilities. The universe is full of abundance. We are already wealthy because we have life and freedom of choice.

- Wealth is a state of mind. A million dollars in the bank without peace of mind is poverty, whereas a hundred dollars in the bank with a sense of being carefree is wealth.

- Excelling in service to others by offering a service that holds great interest for you is the key to true wealth. A person with a prosperous attitude asks the question, "How can I enjoy serving?" rather than "How can I make a lot of money?" Making money is fun, but it's secondary to enjoying the way you make money.

- In every failure lies the seed of success. The truly prosperous person sees each fall as grist for the mill and learns from each mistake.

- Money is like water — it must flow. Receiving is as important as giving. The prosperous person is able to keep money circulating with generosity and gratitude.

- True prosperity always takes into consideration the good of the whole as well as the good of the individual.

There's a big difference between "making a living" and making a life.

— Joe Dominguez

Michael Malloy, a California therapist who specializes in marriage and family counseling, recently said, "In my practice, fear and confusion about money is one of the most common problems families face today." Help your child by instilling some solid and smart tips on successful spending and prosperity now. The investment will reap rewards for years.

"Esteeming" with Pride Chart

Read over the following chart of old beliefs and new beliefs, and help your child move from low esteem to full esteem while developing skills in self-management.

From Low Esteem	To Full Esteem
1. Children aren't dependable. They make many mistakes and need constant overseeing! If parents don't stay on top of them, their tasks won't get done.	1. Children need patience, guidance, and consistency when learning to manage themselves. Self-discipline is a life-long skill that takes time to instill.
2. Children are resistant to doing what needs to be done. They must be trained with authority.	2. Children have tons of energy and need consistent and clear direction as well as positive modeling.
3. Children are naturally lazy. They must learn to "go against the grain" to become capable and responsible.	3. Children are naturally ambitious. With frequent reinforcement, they become capable and responsible.
4. Children must be forced to do what needs to be done.	4. Children need structure and instruction, but most of all they need room to make some mistakes, along with reinforcement for small accomplishments.
5. Children should be punished when they don't do what they are told.	5. Children will learn from logical consequences that are set up in advance so that they learn that their choices have results in the world.

chapter
4

Learning Esteem

Learning is a lifelong venture that begins in the womb and continues throughout our lives. Instilling a love for learning in children will help them to use more brain power, develop their talents, and tap into more of their unlimited potential. Since brain research tells us that we use less than 5 percent of our brain potential, we know that it is our attitude, not our aptitude, that most determines our success in learning.

Chapter 4 will help you encourage children to flex their mental muscles by learning to study with purpose, sharpen their skills in memory and imagery, and begin to think in new ways. The cerebrally weak can become mentally sleek by finding heroes, learning fun facts, and appreciating art, music, literature, travel, and geography.

The following poem brings to light the most important ingredient that is necessary to instill a love for learning in children — an ability to teach with love.

Children Love to Learn when They Learn with Love!

by Diana Loomans

"I got an A," the young boy said. "All right, hooray for me!"
His teacher frowned and merely said, "You should have gotten three!"

"I cleaned the garage," the teen girl said, "and put your tools away!"
Her father scowled, and then he said, "That wasn't the right way."

"I've checked off everything on the list," the boy said with a smile.
His mother stated sullenly, "But it took you such a long while."

The children who lived nearby were learning so much more.
They were taught with lots of love, which helped each one to soar.

"I got an A," the young boy said. "All right, hooray for me!"
His teacher beamed and happily said, "You're proud of that, I see!"

"I cleaned the garage," the teen girl said, "and put your tools away!"
Her father grinned, and then he said, "You've helped a lot today!"

"I've checked off everything on the list," the boy said with a smile.
"Indeed, you have," his mother said, admiring him all the while.

Children need acknowledgment for what they're asked to do.
To learn to love and love to learn, so much depends on you.

Einstein the Second
by Julia Loomans

When I was in grade school one year, I had an "all drill, no frill" teacher who taught math in a dreadfully boring way. She gave us difficult tests and shamed students by writing their names on the board for all to see whenever they gave an incorrect answer. She often told us, "Shape up or ship out," and she liked to say, "If you can't pass this class, you'll never make it to high school."

I was not one of her star pupils. I had a hard time learning in such a controlled environment. The more rigid she became, the more my mental block grew. I started to do poorly on tests, and my name was appearing on the board more and more often. Instead of mastering math, I was becoming a master at writing notes — and passing them down the aisles to all of my friends. I wasn't the teacher's pet, but I was fast becoming the teacher's pet peeve! Earning this title didn't come without a price. I experienced extreme anxiety on Sunday nights just knowing that I had to face her on Monday mornings. My grades were going from bad to worse, and I was beginning to question whether I had any math ability at all.

In just two months' time, I went from being a smart kid who loved school to a frustrated student who dreaded going to school. I talked to my parents about it, and we came up with a few ideas. The first thing we did was to play "School" in the living room at home, with me starring as the drill sergeant teacher and my parents and some family friends posing as her sad and sorry students. I talked with squinted eyes and a scowl on my face, and I wrote names on an imaginary board while shaking a ruler at them. We laughed a lot, but more important, I was able to release some of my pent-up stress and get some empathy from the important adults in my life.

My mom talked to me about how many creative geniuses there were in the world who had done poorly at some point in their lives. I was amazed to learn that Isaac Newton did poorly in grade school, and Leo Tolstoy flunked out of college. I learned that Beethoven's first music teacher once told him that he was hopeless as a composer, and that Walt Disney was fired from a newspaper because his boss said he didn't have any good ideas. Even Albert Einstein had learning difficulties as a child. He didn't speak clearly until he was almost four, and he didn't read until he was almost eight.

My mom and I talked about how important it was to learn with positive encouragement. She told me creative genius doesn't usually flourish in a stiff or shaming environment. We made a short tape for me to listen to at night called "Einstein the Second." The tape helped me to realize that I had as much potential genius as good old Albert himself. The tape included phrases such as "I have a scientist and an artist inside," and "Look out, math, here comes Einstein the Second!" We made some math flash cards on colored index cards. At the bottom of each card was a fun phrase that I turned over and read after I had guessed the right answer, such as "Awesome! You've done it again! What a kid!" or "Hooray for you!" We used a glass jar and dropped a marble in it each time that I chose a correct answer on the flash cards. As the jar became full of marbles, my mom or dad would say, "Don't ever let anyone tell you that you don't have any marbles in math!"

Although my teacher didn't change her approach in the classroom, over time my grades improved. With the encouragement and support that I got from my family and friends, I was able to take a lemon and turn it into lemonade. Sometimes when I see kids who are in grade school, I remember what it was like to feel slow and stupid. I wonder how many of them are feeling the same way, and I just hope that there is someone in their lives to tell them, "Look out, math, here comes Einstein the Second!"

31

Homework Applause

Show interest in your child's learning process by encouraging good study habits and applauding all completed homework assignments and projects.

In Japan, there is a legend about a mother who guided her son up a mountain by breaking sticks into small pieces and throwing them up the mountain to serve as a guide for her son on his path through life. A Japanese mother of five grown children recently shared, "Of all the gifts that I gave my children, one of the most important was an active, enthusiastic involvement in their studies. Now they all love to learn!" If you need some tips about how to keep up with your child's schoolwork along with the myriad of other day-to-day tasks, here are a few "broken sticks" to help you guide your child on the path to knowledge.

All human beings by nature desire to know.

— Aristotle

Eight Ways to Show Interest in Your Child's School Activities

1. **The Parent-Teacher Connection:** Send a friendly note to your child's teacher(s) at the beginning of the school year, with a short description of your child. Let the teacher know that you look forward to the parent-teacher meeting and to working together as a team. Stay in touch, especially if a challenge arises.

2. **School News Check:** Read the school newsletter,

and note school events, exam times, and vacation periods on the family calendar. Talk to your child about school and stay in touch with your child's feelings about school at least once a week.

3. **Same Time, Same Place:** Help your child to develop excellent study habits by encouraging the "same time, same place" idea each day. Young children work best at a table in the kitchen or family room, where help is nearby. An older child will appreciate a quiet study area to work in. Several children might benefit from working in the same area, as long as it's quiet.

4. **Standing Ovations:** Since school is a child's full-time "profession" throughout childhood, receiving "applause" for a job completed is an important part of building self-esteem. Ask your child about homework assignments and take a few minutes at the end of the day to acknowledge the efforts that too often go unnoticed when the homework is done.

5. **Study Support:** If your child is discouraged or stuck on an assignment, offer support even if you don't know the answer yourself. One parent tells his son, "If we did know how to solve this problem, what would the answer be?" Then, they brainstorm together until they come up with a solution. If your child needs help beyond that which you can provide, look into peer tutoring or getting extra help.

6. **Mini-Breaks:** When there are several hours of homework to do, suggest a five- to ten-minute break every hour, since brain research has shown that the mind stays more alert with short, frequent breaks. Encourage your child to do the most challenging jobs first, saving the easy ones as a reward.

7. **Piece by Piece:** When there is a major project to do, turn deadlines into "livelines" by letting the

Self-education is, I firmly believe, the only kind of education there is. The only function of a school is to make self-education easier.

— Isaac Asimov

whole family share ideas and get involved. Consider using a chart or list and help your child to break the project down into bite-sized pieces, taking it one step at a time rather than cramming three weeks of work into three days.

8. **Self-Study:** The best way to teach respect for knowledge to your child is to continue in your own learning process through adult education courses or self-study. Model a love for learning, and your child will also love to learn.

32

Fun Facts
by Julia Loomans

Flex mental muscles and stimulate the mind by sharing interesting facts about the wonders of the world with your child.

The world abounds with surprises and mysteries. One of the greatest wonders of all is why we don't walk around in awe and amazement all of the time. Many of the great thinkers through the ages have invited us to keep alive the curiosity that we had as children. Albert Einstein said, "I don't think I am particularly intelligent, just passionately curious!" Playing the "Did You Know?" Game has been a fun way for my mom and me to learn together.

Here are some fun facts you can use to get started.

Sixteen Fun Facts

1. Did you know that the longest poem in the world is the *Mahabharata?* It is an ancient Indian masterpiece consisting of 100,000 stanzas.
2. Did you know that we are traveling around the sun at sixty-seven thousand miles an hour?
3. Did you know that some 62.5 million newspapers are printed in the United States each day?
4. Did you know that there are West African tribes who can chant back the history and knowledge of up to two thousand generations? This traces back much further than the entire Bible.

Talent is a flame.
Genius is a fire.

— Bern Willliams

122

5. Did you know that there are 86,400 seconds in twenty-four hours?

6. Did you know that honeybees must tap two million flowers to make one pound of honey?

7. Did you know that the Greek philosopher Epictetus said, "Nature has given us one tongue and two ears, that we may hear from others twice as much as we speak"?

8. Did you know that Winston Churchill failed sixth grade?

9. Did you know that some paper can be recycled up to seven times?

10. Did you know that scripted alphabets date back to about 6000 B.C.?

11. Did you know that only 2 percent of the world's population reads at least one book a month?

12. Did you know that one species becomes extinct on this planet every twenty minutes?

13. Did you know that less than 5 percent of the total land in the United States is wilderness?

14. Did you know that there are some 170 nations in the world today?

15. Did you know that approximately one million hours ago, humans still lived in caves?

16. Did you know that the Great Wall of China is the longest structure ever built, stretching two thousand miles across the northern plain?

Strange that I was not told that the brain can hold in a tiny ivory cell heaven and hell.

— Oscar Wilde

Playing "Did You Know?"

1. Put amazing facts into a family jar and take turns picking one each night after supper.

2. Go back and forth with "Did You Know?" facts while driving or walking. Whoever runs out of interesting facts first must come up with more for the next game.

3. Spring a "Did You Know?" question out of the

blue. It can even help to offset a bad mood. For example, my mom was frowning the other day, and I said, "Mom, did you know that it takes seventy-two muscles to frown and that the average heart beats twenty times more per minute when frowning?" "I didn't know that," she said with a grin, "but I do know that now I'm using only fourteen muscles to smile!"

33

Art Appreciation

**Enrich your sense of wonder and appreciation
for beauty by celebrating art together.**

The philosopher Plotinus said, "Art deals with things forever incapable of definition that belong to love, beauty, joy, and worship — the power and glory of which are ever building, unbuilding, and rebuilding in each man's soul and the soul of the whole world."

There are many ways to appreciate art with your child. Visit art museums and art galleries, go to art exhibits and shows, or read art history books from the library. Take an art class together for a "hands-on" experience, such as drawing, painting, pottery, crafts, or art appreciation. Buy some art reprints from an art store or museum, and hang some of the classics in your home, or send greeting cards with famous artwork on the cover to help your child become familiar with some of the classics of the ages.

A European family uses art greeting cards as flash cards to test one another on many of the most well-loved paintings. They do this as a game after their Sunday brunch. A Montessori teacher working with children ages three to six posts different art reprints each month in her classroom and teaches her students the titles and names of the masterpieces through music and song. If your child is very young, reading for ten to fifteen minutes at a time or half an hour of attendance at a museum or art show will be enough. As your child matures, sitting down for half an hour with an art book or attending an event

*Every child is an artist.
The problem is how to
remain an artist
once he grows up.*

— Pablo Picasso

*A talent is interested
in making money:
a genius is interested
in making art.*

— Arthur Schopenhauer

for up to a few hours will become interesting, especially if you are enthusiastic. Although the world is bursting with beautiful artwork from all corners of the Earth, here is a very brief list of some of the most beloved artists in the Western tradition to help you begin to explore the beauty of art with your child.

Beloved Artists

Hieronymus Bosch

Sandro Botticelli

Pieter Brueghel the Elder

Paul Cézanne

Leonardo da Vinci

Edgar Degas

Marcel Duchamp

Albrecht Dürer

Paul Gauguin

Vincent van Gogh

El Greco

Henri Matisse

Michelangelo

Claude Monet

Georgia O'Keefe

Raphael

Rembrandt

Pierre-Auguste Renoir

Auguste Rodin

Henri Rousseau

Peter Paul Rubens

Georges Seurat

If you would like to explore some of the major art movements with your child, start with these major categories.

Major Art Movements

Primitive

Egyptian

Far Eastern

Greek

Roman

Early Christian

Medieval and Gothic

Renaissance

Impressionism

Romanticism

Modern

Postmodern

Experiencing theater together is another lively and exciting way to celebrate creativity. Attending school productions is a good place to start with small children. As your child matures, you can "graduate" to high school and community productions, and, on special occasions, live theater productions with local theater companies.

A family who recently moved to the United States from Germany brought one of their wonderful German traditions with them — putting aside one night a month for theater appreciation. Some months, they attend a community event. Other evenings, they borrow a play from the library and assign roles to each of the five family members. They create their own play-reading sessions, followed by a discussion on the strong points and the weak points of the playwright. The following offers a "starter list" of playwrights.

Art still has truth; take refuge there.

— Matthew Arnold

Important Playwrights

Edward Albee	Eugene O'Neill
Maxwell Anderson	William Shakespeare
Bertolt Brecht	George Bernard Shaw
Anton Chekhov	Neil Simon
Euripides	Sophocles
Gilbert and Sullivan	Voltaire
Lillian Hellman	Oscar Wilde
Victor Hugo	Thorton Wilder
Arthur Miller	William Butler Yeats

For the more adventurous, consider creating your own family play and performing the production for a special occasion. When a single mother of four boys threw a big party for her oldest son Joshua's high school graduation, she surprised him with a twenty-minute play starring Joshua's three brothers and herself. They called it, "Joshua's Journey: A Future View." It was a hilarious skit all about Joshua's probable future — as a potential father, businessman, freethinker, and so forth. They had a relative videotape the entire play for him. When he went away to college the following year, it was one of the few items he took with him.

One ought each day, at least, to hear a little song, read a good poem, see a fine picture, and, if possible, speak a few reasonable words.

— Goethe

Theater and art link our children with many of their own hidden dreams, thoughts, and feelings. Through the appreciation of beauty, our children are transported from the real to the ideal, and, as Victor Hugo said, "The soul has greater need of the ideal than of the real."

34

Reading and Literature

**Instill a love for reading and the great classics
by reading aloud with your child and sharing
quiet reading time together often.**

I will never forget an English teacher I had in college. She had her first child at the age of forty-three, and she started reading Tolstoy, Samuel Clemens, C. S. Lewis, and J. R. R. Tolkien stories to her baby at two weeks old. By the time her child was one year old, he had been through more classics than the average adult reads in a lifetime. Her intent was to instill an early love for learning and reading into her son's growing mind. It certainly worked. At age four, he was an avid reader with an amazing vocabulary, and at the age of eight, he was reading the Charles Dickens classic *A Tale of Two Cities*. Although her efforts probably surpass most of our own interest levels by leaps and bounds, she was nevertheless passing on a great treasure to her son — a lifelong love for reading. Benjamin Franklin said, "What will change you most in five years will be the people you meet and the books you read." As your child is growing up, there will be many wonderful books to discover — picture books, schoolbooks, books chosen from the library, and books received as gifts. But the love for reading starts when a parent reads to an infant and nurtures a child with reading throughout the years. Literacy is one of the keys to a full, rich life. The child who reads is the child who thinks independently and asks questions.

How do you promote reading in your child? First,

A man will turn over half a library to make one book.

— Samuel Johnson

encourage reading by being a reader yourself. Your child will pick up everything you do. Second, keep a variety of good books in your home and take the time to read them out loud. Third, show an active interest in your child's school reading, and look through the books together often.

A good book is the precious life-blood of a master spirit.

— John Milton

Although reading a variety of books will be vital to your child, certain enduring books evoke so many pictures, ideas, and experiences that they are considered timeless classics. Encourage your child to read a few of them each year. The following list offers some popular Western titles to help you to get started.

Classic Books for Children

The Adventures of Tom Sawyer (Mark Twain)
Alice's Adventures in Wonderland (Lewis Carroll)
Anne Frank: The Diary of a Young Girl (Anne Frank)
A Bear Called Paddington (Michael Bond)
Black Beauty (Anna Sewell)
The Call of the Wild (Jack London)
Charlotte's Web (E. B. White)
A Child's Garden of Verses (Robert Louis Stevenson)
A Christmas Carol (Charles Dickens)
Heidi (Johanna Spyri)
Island of the Blue Dolphins (Scott O'Dell)
The Lion, the Witch, and the Wardrobe (C. S. Lewis)
Little House in the Big Woods (Laura Wilder)
The Little Prince (Antoine de Saint-Exupéry)
Little Women (Louisa May Alcott)
Mary Poppins (Pamela Travers)
Pippi Longstocking (Astrid Lindgren)
Rebecca of Sunnybrook Farm (Kate Wiggin)
Robinson Crusoe (Daniel DeFoe)
The Secret Garden (Frances Hodgson Burnett)
The Swiss Family Robinson (Johann Wyss)
Treasure Island (Robert Louis Stevenson)
20,000 Leagues Under the Sea (Jules Verne)
The Velveteen Rabbit (Margery Williams)

Voyages of Doctor Doolittle (Hugh Lofting)
Winnie the Pooh (A. A. Milne)
The Wizard of Oz (L. F. Baum)

Classic Books for Teens

The Adventures of Huckleberry Finn (Mark Twain)
Black Like Me (John Howard Griffin)
The Call of the Wild (Jack London)
Cry, the Beloved Country (Alan Paton)
Doctor Zhivago (Boris Pasternak)
Emma (Jane Austen)
For Whom the Bell Tolls (Ernest Hemingway)
Gone With the Wind (Margaret Mitchell)
The Good Earth (Pearl Buck)
The Grapes of Wrath (John Steinbeck)
The Great Gatsby (F. Scott Fitzgerald)
The Hobbit (J. R. R. Tolkien)
Madame Bovary (Gustave Flaubert)
1984 (George Orwell)
A Passage to India (E. M. Forster)
The Red Badge of Courage (Stephen Crane)
The Scarlet Letter (Nathaniel Hawthorne)
The Sun Also Rises (Ernest Hemingway)
A Tale of Two Cities (Charles Dickens)
To Kill a Mockingbird (Harper Lee)
Wuthering Heights (Emily Brontë)

Youth is not a time of life; it is a state of mind.

— Samuel Ullman

For some additional categories to explore together, try world history, mythology, black history, women's studies, fairy tales from around the world, or poetry.

Books are creative companions, guiding a child in the adventure of life. Books help us to develop an interior space of wonder and awe, and provide us with a connection to the past, as well as a bridge into the future. When was the last time that you curled up with your child and got lost in a good book together?

35

Music Appreciation

**Learn to appreciate the gift of music
by listening to a variety of musical styles,
and singing or creating music together.**

Beethoven once said, "Music is the mediator between the spiritual and the sensual life." The Hindus believe that sound through music is the voice of God speaking to us. Music can be a wonderful, uplifting, and energizing experience to explore and enjoy with your child. We can learn something from all kinds of music — ballads, ballet, blues, classical, choral, comedy, country, dance music, jazz, New Age, opera, pop, reggae, rock, and international music of all kinds.

*God speaks to me
and I write.*

— Wolfgang Amadeus
Mozart

When Julia was a baby, I played a wide variety of music in the house — different music for different times of day. We often started the day with classical, proceeded with jazz, pop, light rock, international, or reggae, and ended the day with some quiet New Age or classical music. She seemed receptive to each and every type of music and loved to dance, kick her feet, and move to the various tempos. Her taste as a teenager is very eclectic and runs the gamut from classical to rock. There is no doubt in my mind that exposing her to a wide variety of sound at a young age has instilled within her a deep appreciation for the majesty of music. Some of our most cherished memories are associated with music — such as juggling scarves together to the tune of "Humoresque" by

Dvořák, eating a relaxing meal together with Vivaldi's "The Four Seasons" playing in the background, dancing through the house while doing housework to the beat of '50s or '60s music, or playing Bach's "Air for the G String" while sitting by the fire. Music offers a potpourri of experiences for your child. Here are a few of the benefits.

Benefits of Music

- Music is a wonderful way to evoke self-expression.
- Musical expression stirs the imagination and helps to generate new ideas.
- Music helps to release energy.
- Music nourishes and soothes the emotions.
- Music can heal, energize, and balance us.

What the child learns in song will linger all day long.

— Diana Loomans

Although there are hundreds of truly great composers and music selections, you can't go wrong if you choose from the following lists as an introduction.

Famous Composers over the Last Four Centuries

Johann Sebastian Bach	Wolfgang Amadeus Mozart
Ludwig van Beethoven	Sergey Prokofiev
Johannes Brahms	Franz Schubert
Frédéric Chopin	Richard Strauss
George Handel	Pyotr Ilich Tchaikovsky
Franz Joseph Haydn	Antonio Vivaldi
Felix Mendelssohn	Ralph Vaughan Williams

Music That Paints a Rich Story with Sound

Out of Africa (motion picture sound track)
Chariots of Fire (Vangelis)
Star Trek (motion picture sound track)
Hungarian Rhapsodies (Franz Liszt)
E.T. (motion picture sound track)

An American in Paris (George Gershwin)
Field of Dreams (motion picture sound track)
Star Wars (motion picture sound track)

Music for Clear Thinking

Born Free (motion picture sound track)
Handel, *Water Music*
String music of Vivaldi
Corelli, Torelli, and Telemann
Brahms, Violin Concerto
Tibetan bells music
Weber, *Oberon* "Overture"
Pachelbel, Canon in D

Music is the invisible made visible.

— Leonard da Vinci

Music for Meditation

Paul Horn, *Inside the Taj Mahal*
J. S. Bach, "Come, Sweet Death"
Handel, "Largo"
Aeoliah, *Angel Love*
Daniel Kobialka, "When You Wish Upon a Star"
R. Carlos Nakai, *Canyon Trilogy: Native American Flute Music*
Selections from Steven Halpern, David Lanz, Michael Jones, Georgia Kelly, and Enya

Upbeat Lyrical Music with Positive Lyrics for Children

Try any of the selections available from the following artists.

Peter Alsop	Jerry Florence
Karl Anthony	Scott Kalechstein
Steven Bergman	Michael Mish
Stephen Longfellow Fiske	

Music from around the World

Africa: *Missa Luba: An African Mass,* Muungano Choir
Austria: Johann Strauss waltzes
Austria: Boskovsky, *Charm of Old Vienna*
Celtic lands: Stivell, *Renaissance of the Celtic Harp*
China: *The Yellow River Concerto*
England: Music of Vaughan Williams
France: Offenbach, *Gaîté Parisienne*
Japan: *Music for the Koto*
India: Ragas by Ravi Shankar
Italy: Gioacchino Rossini overtures
Hawaii: *Songs of the Island,* "Hawaiian Wedding Song"
Incan: Yma Sumac, *Harp Music of the Andes*
Spain: Joaquín Rodrigo, *Concierto de Aranjuez*
International sound from around the world: Tor Dietrichson, *Global Village,* music from Africa, India, Latin America, Persia, and the Far East.

Music gives soul to the universe, wings to the mind, flight to the imagination, a charm to sadness, gaiety and life to everything.

— Plato

This list suggests just a few from the many possibilities you will find at a local library or music store. Consider playing music as a part of your appreciation experience. If you don't play any instruments, start out by picking up some percussion instruments, a tambourine, bells, a recorder, or any other small instruments, and play along with some recorded music. If you feel inclined, take music lessons together, and before long, you'll be playing home concerts.

We know a family of four who each decided to take music lessons four years ago; they now play the piano, violin, flute, and cello together on Sunday evenings. They are getting quite skilled as a group and recently performed their first concert at a bar mitzvah. After their performance their youngest, the flute player, told me that he loved playing music with his family. "When we play together," he told me "we're all in harmony!"

36

World Travel, News, and Geography

Help your child to become globally literate by discussing world news and learning about other countries and cultures together.

We live in a time of technological explosion that some futurists equate with "the second discovery of fire." The nations of the world can now communicate instantly, and our children can watch news captured live via satellite from all over the world. Despite these amazing advances, tests of grade school and high school students show that our children have little sense about what is going on in the world, where other countries are, and what other cultures are really like. Teaching our children to relate to the community, the nation, and all the nations of the world is a necessity in our changing global culture. Here are some ideas to help you to instill a sense of global awareness within your child.

If you wish to embrace life, then embrace the globe.

— Arnold Atlas

Four Ways to Develop More Global Awareness

1. **Explore Maps Together:** Eight-year-old Yolanda already looks at a map of her city, Cincinnati, Ohio, with her father whenever they are in the car together. Since he had a poor sense of direction growing up, he wants to give his daughter a feeling of familiarity with her city. In their recreation room, a map is posted of their state, along with a map of the United

States. Above these two maps is an atlas of the world and a map of the Milky Way galaxy. After they play Ping-Pong, they look over the maps and talk about people, places, and things. Enrique, Yolanda's father, wants her to have a sense of connection with her world. "I came from a chaotic, poverty-stricken environment without any sense of direction about my city, the world, or my life! This is one way I can help Yolanda to grow up differently."

2. **Follow Newsworthy News:** Stay in touch with world issues and discuss global issues. A busy family of six subscribes to a weekly world news magazine. Each week, they rotate and choose a family member to read the magazine and summarize the important events in the news. On Sunday evenings, they get a "global rundown" after dinner from the reader of the week.

3. **Country and Culture Study:** Travel to distant countries, if not in person, then via movies, videos, television specials, and books. A retired Marine Corps officer who is now the grandfather of three has made a list of twelve countries for the year. Since his grandchildren visit frequently, he chooses a nation for the month and shows the children books, a movie, or photographs of that particular country and culture. Although he only covers twelve countries a year, over ten years this amounts to an impressive 120 nations! "I want my grandchildren to grow up globally literate," he explains.

4. **Finding International Friends:** Encourage your child to write to an overseas pen pal, consider joining an international community club or group, or open your home to a foreign exchange student. A middle class family of five decided it was time to become more culturally diverse when they each signed up for an overseas pen pal. Within eighteen months, they had sent their oldest child off to visit

She stretched her mind to its utmost extent, then traveled through books to each continent.

— Diana and
   Julia Loomans and
   Karen Kolberg,
   *Positively Mother
   Goose*

her pen pal in Uganda, and they were preparing for a visit from their father's pen pal — a businessman from Russia. "Our home now has an international flavor, and we are much more aware of cultural diversity," said the mother.

Sharing the world's peoples, places, and events with your child will bring a sense of connection and community — two important building blocks to world unity.

37

Finding Heroes

**Share respect and admiration with your child
for people who display acts of courage, develop
exceptional ability, or model great strength.**

*The hero is no braver
than the ordinary man,
but he is brave five
minutes longer.*

— Ralph Waldo
Emerson

Heroes inspire us to become all we can be. Although they are
our equals, we admire them because they mirror the strong
and admirable side of humanity. Never before in history has
there been a time when mentors, guides, and leaders were
needed more than now. Our children's generation will be responsible for making some of the most important decisions
ever regarding the environment, global politics, the economy,
and peace negotiating. To accomplish the monumental tasks
that we are passing along to them, they will need the influence
of strong leadership. Recognizing and appreciating the great
thinkers and leaders of the world is a skill that starts in childhood. Take the time to talk about heroes in your family, community, nation, and world. Include some of the great leaders
of the past, as well as those who will be needed in the future.
The following questions may be useful in your discussion.

Discussing Heroes

- Who has been a hero in your own life, and why?
- When have you been heroic in your life for yourself or someone else?
- Name three well-known leaders you admire. What
  is it that you respect about them?

- What do you feel are the most important qualities that a great leader can have?
- In what ways would you like to make a difference in the world when you grow up?

Here are some examples of heroes in various categories. You will probably have several to add to each one.

Heroes in Different Fields

1. **Adventure:** Neil Armstrong. On July 20, 1969, Neil Armstrong became the first astronaut to land on the moon. When he took his first step, he said, "One small step for man, one giant leap for mankind." What is one small step that you are taking now that may be one giant leap for your future?

2. **Civil Rights:** Rosa Parks. She has been called the mother of the Civil Rights movement. Her insistence on her right to a seat on a public bus in 1955 started a bus boycott that changed segregation laws and sparked an entire movement. Rosa's act of courage swept the headlines and changed the lives of millions of Americans. What is one way that you have taken a stand in your life?

3. **The Environment:** Chief Seattle. As a Suquamish Indian leader, he believed that the Earth was the most precious resource of all. He wrote these famous words: "The Earth does not belong to man. Man belongs to the Earth. All things are connected. Man did not weave the web of life; he is merely a strand in it. Whatever he does to the web, he does to himself." How can you, as one individual, care for the Earth more?

4. **Equal Rights:** Alice Paul. She was a trailblazer who wrote the first equal rights amendment in 1923. She continued to support the women's movement throughout her life. In the 1970s, she supported the later equal rights amendment, which still waits to be

Seize common opportunities and make them great... weak men wait for opportunities; strong men make them.

— Orison Swett Marden

ratified into the United States Constitution. What belief do you support that hasn't yet become accepted?

5. **Everyday Hero:** Eighteen-year-old violinist Frank Maaten. Maaten lost all four fingers of his right hand — the one he used to play the violin. The doctors told him it was impossible to ever play again. A few years later, he became the best concert violinist in all of Sioux City, Iowa, in their symphony orchestra. What obstacle would you like to overcome in your life?

6. **Inventions:** Thomas Edison. In his eighty-four years, he invented 1,097 things, including the phonograph and the light bulb. He once said, "Creativity is 90 percent perspiration and 10 percent inspiration." What area of your creativity would you like to develop more?

7. **Music:** Ludwig van Beethoven. Beethoven's first music teacher told him he was hopeless and had no musical talent at all. His passion was so great for music that he "followed his bliss," and became one of the most famous composers of all time. He continued to write brilliant music even after he was completely deaf. What is one of your greatest passions, and how would you like to develop it?

8. **Mythological Figures:** The Phoenix. In ancient Egypt, there was a myth about a great bird known as the Phoenix. It lived for five hundred years, and then was consumed by fire. Instead of dying, it rose from its own ashes and became even stronger than before. What is one difficulty that you would like to rise above in your life?

9. **Politics:** Abraham Lincoln. He was a man of great persistence. He failed in business, went bankrupt, lost his fiancée to death, had a nervous breakdown, and lost eight elections. Finally, he became the president of the United States and helped to abolish slavery. He didn't believe in failure. What area of your life would you like to be more persistent in?

If a man does not keep pace with his companions, perhaps it is because he hears a different drummer. Let him step to the music which he hears, however measured or far away.

— Henry David Thoreau

Towering genius disdains a beaten path. It seeks regions hitherto unexplained.

— Abraham Lincoln

10. **Service:** Mother Teresa. Mother Teresa was a small woman with a very big heart. When she realized that poor people were dying on the streets of Calcutta, she decided that she could help make a difference. She became one of the most renowned Sisters of Charity in the world. What is one way that you can be of service in your community?

11. **Space:** Sally Ride. She was America's first woman astronaut. When she returned from space, she was elated. She had realized a dream that she'd had for many years. She advised others, "Talk about your dreams with someone every day. You can do anything you want if you believe you can." What is one of your most cherished dreams?

12. **World Peace:** The Dalai Lama. He is a Buddhist teacher and leader who won the Nobel Peace Prize for helping to lead over 100,000 people out of Tibet when the Chinese invaded in the 1950s. In India, he helped form a democratic government for his exiled people. For over thirty years he has been a spokesperson for nonviolence. His commitment to living a life of compassion has inspired millions. What are you contributing to world peace?

The hero thinks of virtue — the common man thinks of comfort.

— Confucius

For further exploration, here is a small list of great leaders from various fields.

More Heroes

Susan Anthony	Helen Keller
Pearl Bailey	Martin Luther King, Jr.
Andrew Carnegie	Anne Morrow Lindbergh
Sir Winston Churchill	Margaret Mead
Marie Curie	Golda Meir
Albert Einstein	Eleanor Roosevelt
Mahatma Gandhi	Albert Schweitzer
Kahlil Gibran	Margaret Thatcher
Carl Jung	Martha Washington

38

Memory Games

Help your child to develop an excellent memory with the use of imagination, creativity, and memory games.

Memory is the mother of all wisdom.

— Aeschylus

When Julia was learning to spell, she often forgot to put an *e* on the end of words such as *airplane*. One day, I told her a story about Alex the Airplane, who took off on the runway and heard a faint voice shouting from behind, "Wait for e...wait for e!" It was the letter *e* trailing after the airplane. She never forgot to put the *e* on the end of the word again. Her imagination had grasped a previously boring concept in a fun new way that made it easy to recall. Here are a few of the memory techniques we have used over the years.

Memory Made Easy in Five Simple Steps

1. **Stacking and Linking:** When learning facts in sequence, we often used a method called stacking and linking. For example, when Julia was learning the seven continents, we used this short story, which stacks and links all seven continents.

   I took a trip to see my *aunt on an ark (Antarctica)*. After I landed, I went *south on a mare (South America)*. I used *your rope (Europe)* to steer my horse. I traveled in a *free car (Africa)* on the *Ost Trail* with *Lia (Australia)*. *A shah (Asia)* was with him. After that, I headed *north on a mare (North America)*.

Within five minutes, Julia knew the continents backwards and forwards. We used another stack and link story to learn the nine planets in order.

> Once there was some very *murky (Mercury)* water at the end of a river. A large white statue of the Roman goddess *Venus (Venus)* was immersed in the murky water from the neck down. In her hair, there were hundreds of *earthworms (Earth)* crawling all over her head. Each one of them was eating a small *Mars (Mars)* candy bar! Above her head, hanging from a tree was a large red *jewel (Jupiter)* spinning in a circle with the word *Saturday (Saturn)* written across the red jewel in large white letters. Suddenly, a ghostlike blue figure emerged from the clouds and descended towards Venus. It was the Roman god *Neptune (Neptune),* who was coming to save Venus from the torrid *rain (Uranus).* As it poured, Neptune lifted Venus out of the murky water, with the help of his trusty dog companion, *Pluto (Pluto).*

Because the story was so ridiculous, it was easy to remember. In fact, we still know the nine planets years later, backwards and forwards.

2. **The Use of Association:** This is also very effective. In fourth grade, Julia was giving her first speech. She associated all of her main points with images in the room, such as the door, chalkboard, windows, and flag. It was so effective, she remembered her speech for weeks. When we shop for food, instead of using a food list, we sometimes associate food items with our car — for example, a bumper made of bread, a steering wheel made of oranges, the front seat covered with milk, and so forth. This adds humor to the shopping, and it helps us to remember the unusual items, such as Band-Aids on

Memory is a painter; it paints pictures of the past and of the day.

— Grandma Moses

the windshield wipers. Remembering names by associating them with an unusual picture is a sure-fire way to help your child remember names. For example, the name Anna Brown could be visualized as a woman holding a *fan* that is *brown,* and Marcia Lennon could be associated with going to a *marsh* to look for a *lemon!*

3. **Using Rhymes:** This can be an excellent way to improve memory, such as "i before e, except after c." We have used rhymes for remembering many facts, such as "Columbus pulled through in 1492," or "On their first flight, two brothers said, "Whee!" — the Wright brothers way back in 1903."

4. **The Use of Rhythm:** This is another excellent trigger for the memory. Julia learned her social security number at a young age by putting it to the tune of *Yankee Doodle.* When she was learning the multiplication tables, we put each number sequence (such as 2 x 2, 2 x 3, 2 x 4, 2 x 5...) to a popular tune and created body movements to go along with it. She "graduated" from being the slowest to one of the fastest students to know her multiplication tables with the fun influence of rhythm and movement.

5. **Using Acronyms:** This can also be helpful in memorizing. For example, the musical notes EGBDF, when translated as "Every Good Boy Deserves Favor," become easy to remember in order. For the categories of the animal kingdom, try "Kind Pigs Care Only For Good Slop," which stands for kingdom, phylum, class, order, family, genus, and species. When you use memory games, or mnemonics (the Greek word meaning "to remember"), three main steps help your child to develop an ace memory.

One of the profound miracles of the human brain is our capacity for memory.

— Jean Houston

Action: Put action into the picture.

Color: Make it wild and colorful.

Exaggerate: The more unusual the picture, the
  more memorable it will be.

Help your child to remember more effectively by tapping into the most creative and effective way to memorize of all — using the imagination!

39

The Outrageous Exercise

**When creating a dream or goal, practice making
the vision big, bigger, biggest, and finally, outrageous!
Stretch the mind to its utmost extent, and
entertain a whole new realm of possibilities.**

A quotation by Oliver Wendell Holmes inspired the birth of this exercise. He said, "A mind, once stretched by a new idea, never returns to its original dimensions." I realized that when I was mentally stuck, I needed some sort of inner workout that could rejuvenate my lethargic perspective on life. I came up with the outrageous exercise and began trying it with those who were adventurous and willing.

I introduced it to my friend Anita, a graduating high school senior who was worried about an upcoming college entrance interview. **Phase 1** was to make the outcome bigger than life, so we imagined that the interviewer was calling her and "requesting the honor of her presence" to come to the college for just a short thirty-minute interview. This evoked some laughter, which was a good sign that the exercise was already beginning to have an effect.

Phase 2 was to make the picture even bigger, so we pictured all of the major universities in the country calling her and sending flowers and gifts to convince her to come to their college. **Phase 3** was to make it biggest of all, so we imagined that several of the most prestigious international universities were sending her Federal Express letters cordially inviting her

*It is not because things
are difficult that we do
not dare; it is because
we do not dare that
things are difficult.*

— Seneca

to an all-expense-paid trip to their country to consider enrolling at their school, free of tuition. At this point, she was laughing hard (at the same time, her wall of fear was breaking down and being replaced by humor and wild possibilities).

Phase 4 was to make the picture outrageous. She came up with it herself. She received a special telegram inviting her to attend the Ultimate University of the Universe, and the invitation included a large salary just for attending! Sound ridiculous? That's just the point! The more far-fetched, the better. The object of the Outrageous Exercise is to break through the spell of limitation and fear playfully, and open the mind to the field of all possibilities. Although it isn't intended to replace a compassionate listener who can help you to overcome fear, it provides a fun way to overcome the internal tightness that sometimes prevents us from dreaming big dreams.

Anita ended up going to her interview with a sense of lightheartedness and humor, and she was accepted. Her comment was, "After the outrageous game, it was hard to take it seriously! I realized that there would be other options if I didn't get in."

Here are the four phases of the Outrageous Exercise.

Phase 1: Make the outcome bigger than life.
Phase 2: Stretch the picture to make it even bigger.
Phase 3: Make the picture as big as you can.
Phase 4: Now, create an outrageous outcome — one that surpasses your wildest dreams.

Try this exercise with all ages to dispel fears, remove prejudiced thinking, build confidence, or reach a goal. If you need some assistance, go through the outrageous exercise with the most mentally fit segment of the population — anyone under seven years old.

40

Imagery Tools

**Teach your child to see with the mind's eye by
using visualization and practicing mental rehearsal.**

At the 1984 Olympic Games in Los Angeles, sixteen-year-old
gymnast Mary Lou Retton captured the hearts of millions of
people with her amazing performance. When she was inter-
viewed, she said that she had been imagining herself performing with super confidence for months — over and over
again. She was using mental rehearsal to gear herself up for a
successful performance.

*Imagination is more
important than
knowledge.*

— Albert Einstein

Fourteen-year-old Carlos Anatos was taking chemotherapy
treatment at a New York City cancer outpatient center when he
decided to use visualization along with conventional treat-
ments for his lymph cancer. He pictured his cancer cells being
carried off in red wagons by tiny little elves each day for fifteen
minutes. Within six weeks, his cancer had decreased dramatically, and within three months, there was no trace of it.

Nineteen-year-old Maxwell Endhelson, a London actor,
was becoming so fearful before live performances that his
throat would constrict to the point where he could not project his voice at all. He began to visualize his throat as a flowing waterfall — flowing freely and effortlessly as he projected
his voice. For a full half hour before going on stage, he
listened to waterfall music as he pictured the waterfall flowing. Within a few performances, he was feeling confident and
projecting with great gusto.

Visualization is primarily a skill of the imagination. It is a tool that facilitates the actualization process; it is one of the most underrated skills in the world. The inner mind thinks in pictures and therefore responds strongly to pictures. As a parent, I have used visualization with Julia at several stages in her life. When she was two years old and afraid of monsters under the bed, we created "the safe wand," which was a special wand that could shrink down the wild beasts to the size of a grain of sand. Often, after using the wand, the monsters would become "mini-monsters" that became her pets.

When Julia was ready to be potty-trained, her dad and I introduced her to Brutis, a great big invisible English sheepdog who would race her to the potty whenever she had the urge. A previously tedious task became a fun adventure. After Brutis came on board, Julia was potty-trained in just a few days. When she resisted new foods, such as pea soup, broccoli, or asparagus, I would tell her a story before her nap about the adventures of Deena and Dale — two imaginary friends who, inevitably, would try a new food in the story. She would wake up to discover that, miraculously, we were having the same food for dinner and voilà — like magic — she would accept the new food.

When Julia was up against the verbal harassment of a fellow student in second grade, she imagined that she was an Aikido master and put all of her attention on the point between his eyes as he spoke. She imagined all of his words going right past her as she offered no resistance. Within a few weeks, he developed a crush on her. It was quite a dramatic switch.

If you would like to use visualization tools with your child, here are a few suggestions to make the imagery exercise more powerful.

"Do you believe in fairies? If you believe, clap your hands."

— J. M. Barrie, *Peter Pan and Wendy*

Visualize this thing you want. See it, feel it, believe in it. Make your mental blueprint, and begin to build!

— Robert Collier

Six Steps to Using Mental Imagery

1. **See It:** Picture the desired outcome as though it's happening now, and not in the future.

2. **Sense It:** Use all five senses in the picture — sight, sound, smell, touch, and taste.

3. **Feel It:** Get emotionally involved in the picture, and get excited about it.

4. **Activate It:** Step into the picture and become actively involved, as though it is really happening.

5. **Repeat It:** Hold the picture in mind for at least ten minutes a day, up to three times a day.

6. **Sustain It:** Visualize in as much detail as possible to make an impression on the mind and to exercise more of the imagination.

The following imagery tools have been easy, fun, and effective for Julia and other children to use.

Six Imagery Tools

1. **Circle of Excellence:** Picture standing on a stage with a warm, flowing stage light shining down over you. You are standing inside your circle of excellence — a place where you feel strong, capable, centered, and talented. You can come here in your mind's eye anytime you need to energize yourself or feel empowered.

Star light, star bright,
First star I see tonight,
I wish I may, I wish I
might
Have the wish I wish
tonight.

2. **The Laser Light Mind:** Imagine your thoughts becoming light rays, moving in each and every direction. Now align all of the light rays in the same direction, and feel your mind moving into laser focus. You are now able to fully concentrate with ease on one thing at a time.

3. **A Shower of Flowers:** Imagine a shower of hundreds, even thousands, of flowers pouring down over someone who is scared, ornery, or out of sorts. He or she will begin to lighten up, loosen up, and laugh. Use this one with care — it really works!

4. **The Finger-Thumb Anchor:** Imagine that you are joining your right forefinger and your right thumb

together. You are holding an invisible grain of power that can bring a sense of peace over you and the entire room you are in. Use this finger-thumb technique whenever you need to feel better in any way.

5. **The Magnificent Magnet:** Visualize yourself as a strong magnet — attracting loving people, positive events, and happy experiences to yourself. You repel any undesirable experiences away from you, and use your magnetic ability to attract what you want.

6. **The Rainbow Bath:** Imagine walking through the colors of the rainbow, feeling refreshed and cleansed. Go through each color slowly — red, orange, yellow, green, blue, and violet. Step out feeling great — as though you've just been through a "mental" car wash.

Encourage your child to use imagination to rehearse for upcoming events, change moods, develop confidence, or relate better with others. Before long, your child will be directing his or her own movies of the mind, and playing producer, director, actor, and audience rolled into one.

Imagination continually frustrates tradition; that is its job.
— John Pfeiffer

Learning Esteem Chart

Read over the following chart of old beliefs and new beliefs, and help your child move from low esteem to full esteem while learning.

From Low Esteem

1. Children would prefer to play all day and must be forced to learn.

2. Learning is supposed to be tough. If they don't do hard work, children aren't learning enough!

3. Sometimes learning is boring, but that's just the way it has to be. It was boring for us, and it will be boring for them.

4. Measuring performance through grades is the best gauge for success in learning. Attaining good grades is true success.

5. Making mistakes is embarrassing and painful and should be avoided at all costs.

6. A college education is necessary for success in the world today. A Ph.D. is one of the highest forms of success.

To Full Esteem

1. Children have a natural instinct to learn when they are in a positive, stimulating environment.

2. Learning is supposed to be challenging and exciting. When the process is relevant and experiential, true learning takes place.

3. True learning is creative and alive. Even mundane learning or rote memory can be brought to life with play and creativity.

4. The purpose of learning is to prepare children for the future and to instill a love for lifetime learning. Attaining this is true success.

5. Making mistakes is a natural part of learning. If we aren't making any mistakes, we probably aren't learning much.

6. Finding one's greatest passion and living it are some of the highest forms of success.

chapter
5

Playful Esteem

A prominent psychologist was once asked if he had any advice that might help families get closer. He replied, "Laugh fifteen times each day. The family that plays together stays together." Chapter 5 offers ideas to help you exercise your mirth muscles together and overcome the dreaded CPT (Can't Play Today) Syndrome. It will help you to use the three bones of life more often — the backbone, the wishbone, and, especially, the funny bone. Create a laughing board, use amusing mascots, have more fun with meals, and turn humdrum tasks into adventures. Set aside a play night once a month, and let the whole family experience the fun of questions from the wild, the hats in the house, and fun interviews.

The following Playful Bill of Rights was written for the child in all of us. You now have the right to let your hair down and let your inner kid out to play whenever you want.

The Playful Bill of Rights

All Children Deserve:

1. The **right** to move freely and expressively;

2. The **right** to safe, loving touch;

3. The **right** to positive mentors and teachers;

4. The **right** to wonderful, inspiring playmates;

5. The **right** to free time for daydreaming and play;

6. The **right** to be creative and artistic;

7. The **right** to full expression of all feelings;

8. The **right** to loud, uncontrollable laughter;

9. The **right** to be outrageously imaginative;

10. The **right** to be appreciated and fully enjoyed.

Is Froggie Home?
by Diana Loomans

When Julia was young, she was absolutely fascinated with the new phone answering machine. "Can I call and leave messages on it?" she would ask pleadingly. "No," her dad and I would say, "it's for *real* messages from callers." A few days later, I came home from work to find eighteen messages on the machine counter. Who in the world would leave so many messages? I wondered. The first one was Julia's voice disguised as a lady frog. "Hello, is Froggie there? This is Auntie Leap. Please tell him I've called. Thank you." The next one was similar, only this time, it was a male frog. "Hello, this is Froggie's Great Uncle Lumpy. I'm calling from a lily pad, so I can't leave a message. Please tell Froggie I called. Thank you. Ribet..."

On and on the messages continued — from Froggie's cousins, grandparents, toad friends, and even Froggie's schoolmaster! Since each message was rather lengthy, I found myself becoming more and more irritated with Julia's lack of cooperation with our request. After going through seventeen of the eighteen "Froggie messages," I considered rewinding and erasing all of them. I'd certainly had enough, and I was already thinking of some consequences that might help Julia keep agreements in the house.

I decided to listen to the eighteenth and final message, just in case it was legitimate, but I should have known better. "Ribet...hello," a raspy frog's voice said. "This is Froggy. I'm sorry to be using your phone, but my frog parents won't let me use their answering machine. I was wondering, have there been any messages for me today?" I started to giggle under my breath. What a kid! This was too much, even for me. Julia had broken the agreement, but at the same time, her underhanded creativity was quite hilarious. Now I was locked in the horns of a dilemma. How could I teach her to abide by the rules and encourage her creativity at the same time?

When Julia came home from her friend's house that night, we hashed the situation over and came to a great solution. Since the answering machine was for our home phone only, we'd put Julia in charge of changing the message greeting each week. That way, she could exercise her creativity in a constructive way. She loved the idea. For the next few years, we took turns coming up with funny poems, songs, riddles, and one-liners for her to recite into the machine. Those greetings kept our callers thoroughly entertained, and, as a side benefit, they were more motivated to leave a message. More important, it was a win-win solution for everyone. I have learned that finding win-win solutions lies at the heart of true discipline in parenting. Practicing this has brought a big leap of awareness for all of us.

41

Play Night

Choose a night to watch comedy movies, play games, or creatively express with paints, crayons, clay, or whatever inspires you.

We were visiting some friends and noticed that each morning the entire family of five would smile and say, "The walls are gonna shake and Mom's gonna bake on Sunday night!" We were told that if we wanted to know what they were talking about, we'd have to stay and find out. By Sunday, the suspense had mounted enough to keep us in town an extra day to attend their infamous night!

After supper, "Dad" started playing blues on the piano and wailing out a tune while wearing a clown wig. "Mom" did a little jig and baked some delicious homemade bread, and everybody started singing and playing small instruments. The evening proceeded with some hilarious charades and a game of hide-and-seek, and then ended with a funny movie and popcorn. It was so much fun, our faces actually ached from all the laughter.

We now have Play Nights once a month or so, sometimes including relatives and friends. We usually start with a potluck, sing or play some games, and end with our favorite part, playing improvisational theater games. Here are some of the ways that other families have enjoyed play nights.

The true object of human life is play. Earth is a task garden; Heaven is a playground.

— G. K. Chesterton

Play Night Ideas

1. **The Toy Closet:** A family of four reserves a closet in the hallway for their once a week play evenings. The closet is filled with fun props, unique toys, small musical instruments, and a number of games. Each week, one of the family members decides on the evening events, and the rest of the family joins in on the fun.

2. **Sing-Alongs:** A father of three children learned to play the guitar for enjoyment a few years ago and began teaching his toddlers to sing old folk and blues ballads. Now that they are a little older, they have sing-alongs by the fire a few times a month. Several of their friends and neighbors often join them for a good old-fashioned night of singing folk tunes and wailing out the blues. Sometimes his children accompany him with harmonicas, bongos, a flute, or even an electric organ.

3. **Creative Expression Night:** When four-year-old Matthew, a kindergarten student, brought home some clay to work on a class project, his mom and two sisters couldn't keep their hands off the clay. His mother decided to buy some clay for the whole family, and they had a sculpting party. Everyone enjoyed it so much that they decided to share in the arts together one night a week. They have dabbled in watercolor, chalk, acrylic paints, and even T-shirt decorating. "None of us thought we had any artistic talent," Matthew's mother said. "Wow, were we wrong! I guess we just had to give ourselves a chance."

4. **Games People Play Night:** A couple with two children decided to learn to play some non-competitive games with their sons, along with games that children play from around the world. They now enjoy a wide range of indoor and outdoor

God respects me when I work, but he loves me when I sing.

— Rabindranath Tagore

games that they have learned from picking up a few books on the subject (see the resources list in the back of the book). "It's not that we are against competitive games," said the father. "It's more that we want our children to know that there are many fun ways to play without having to compete." As a side benefit, they claim that their boys are able to come up with more creative game ideas on the playground than ever.

Taking time to get playful and silly together will convince you that "the family that plays together stays together."

It takes a long time to become young.

— Pablo Picasso

42

The Laughing Board

**Create a fun laughing board and post it
in a common area. Post various photos, cartoons,
and notes for all to enjoy and cackle over.**

*Childlikeness has to be
restored with long years
of training in the art of
self-forgetfulness.*

— Suzuki

The first bulletin board we put up in the kitchen was posted with bad photos, just to give us a good laugh. We never dreamed that it would become such a "showpiece" in the house. Friends and neighbors would check the board on a regular basis to see what the latest photos were. We have created other themes over the years, and we continue to enjoy them.

A laughing board is a fun way to keep smiles, new ideas, and creativity in the atmosphere. Create a different theme every few months, or whenever the creative urge strikes. Here are some ideas to help you get started.

Nine Ideas for Creating a Laughing Board

1. **Fun Memories:** Post vacation, holiday, or family photos. Show them off and relive the good times over and over.
2. **Wild and Crazy Poses:** Try something different. Take a risk and pose wearing a wig, a banana nose, or anything else that's memorable.
3. **Oops Photos — The Best of the Worst:** These usually draw the most attention of all! Be prepared to make reprints for your friends!

4. **Cartoons and Jokes:** Clip entertaining words or playful quips to cheer up those who read them.
5. **Playful Notes or Fun Messages:** Leave affectionate, silly, or fun messages for one another on a magnetic marker board.
6. **Fun Invitations:** Post any fun invitations you receive on your laughing board. If you haven't received any lately, create one for yourselves.
7. **Quotes for the Shots:** Place famous quotes, or your own nimble lines underneath your favorite photos.
8. **Baby Face Photos:** Put up baby pictures of the whole family, and ask friends to donate a baby picture as well, for amusement and merrymaking.
9. **Silly Smorgasbord:** Post a little bit of everything!

Laughter is the shortest distance between two people.

— Victor Borge

The laughing board will become a rollicking refuge from the small storms of everyday life, entertaining you and all who come to visit.

43

Questions from the Wild

**Ask one another unusual or outlandish questions
that expand the mind and stimulate the imagination.**

We were driving on a half-day trip with a group of friends when our friend Jim said to his two children, "Hey, we've been in the car for a couple of hours and nobody has asked me a wild question!" Both children began to shout out unusual questions at once. "How many monkeys with wooden legs does it take to kick the seeds out of a watermelon?" one asked. The other added, "Dad, would you rather travel on an airplane in a hammock or a swing and why?"

Jim sat up straight in his seat and retorted with, "It would take twelve rhesus monkeys about fifteen minutes for the watermelon, and I'd take a swing seat on the plane so that I could swing through the air with the greatest of ease!" The rest of the drive flew by as we all took turns asking a wild question and hearing each person retort with a unique answer. Since then, we have played many versions of this game while doing everyday activities, such as driving, cooking, cleaning, or walking. We have often passed a few wild questions around the table when we have guests, much to their delight and surprise.

Here are twelve sample questions to help you to wander into the wild side of the mind.

We are all filled with a longing for the wild.

— Clarissa Pinkola Estés

Twelve Wild Questions

1. Would you rather show up to have a peek before the beginning of the world or after the end of the world, and why?

2. Which animal won the jogging race — the toad wearing Nikes or the rabbit on roller blades?

3. If you could choose between wearing a clown nose, a cone head cap, or Groucho Marx glasses to your next fancy restaurant, which would you pick and why?

4. Would you rather be a walking hand, a singing foot, or a runaway head?

5. Which color tastes better — aqua or fuchsia?

6. If you could invent a cure for AIDS, an end to world hunger, or a universal language that everyone could speak, which would you choose and why?

7. Would you rather go through life being a T, an X, or a V, and why?

8. Who would you rather spend a whole day with — Einstein, Mozart, or Joan of Arc?

9. If you had to be just one age for the rest of your life, what age would you pick, and why?

10. What is the sound of an infant gazing?

11. If you didn't know how old you were, how old do you think you'd be?

12. Would you rather be the stripes on a zebra, the warts on a toad, or the horn of a unicorn?

Questions take us on a deep quest into the unknown regions of mind.

— Sally Renneau

For added fun, you can create wild side questions by categories, such as history, animals, food, adventure, sports, risks, surprises, and so forth. Experiment for yourself. This game is a great bridge builder between the young and the old and can be enjoyed by all. The next time you want to expand your mind and stretch your linear limits, abandon the common thought and take a walk on the wild side of your imagination.

44

The Hats in the House

**Express your feelings or ask for what you want
in a playful, nonverbal way by putting on a hat
that best expresses your mood in the moment.**

*All people have the
same feelings,
whether they are
two or ninety-two.*

— Virginia Satir

It all started when Julia came home from school wearing a colorful crown on her head that she had skillfully crafted in her art class. For weeks, we left it out so that we could put it on whenever we wanted to get some attention or be "treated like royalty!" We discovered that the playful act of putting on a crown made it easier to express our feelings and ask for what we wanted. Since being in touch with feelings and needs is vital to self-esteem, we began to collect hats and label them to represent some of the most basic feelings, such as sadness, excitement, anger, fear, and happiness. Over time, other hats found their way into our repertoire. Here are some of our favorites.

Some Hat Ideas

1. **I Need a Hug Hat:** Wear this hat when you feel sad or discouraged and want some comfort and support.
2. **Hooray for Me Hat:** Wear this hat when you feel excited or proud of yourself and want acknowledgment, applause, or celebration.
3. **Handle with Care Hat:** Put this hat on when you feel angry, ornery, or out of sorts and want others to know that you need some empathy and understanding.

4. **Silly Me Hat:** Wear this hat to let others know you're feeling foolish, goofy, or wild and would like to get playful or outrageous with those who are willing.

5. **Silence Is Golden Hat:** This hat means business — quiet time needed! Wear it when you want some quiet time to yourself.

6. **Lend a Listening Ear Hat:** When you feel scared, overwhelmed, or confused, this hat lets others know that you need empathy and some tender, loving care.

7. **Notice Me! Hat:** This hat lets others know that you are feeling lonely or sad and want some attention and affirmation.

To make hats, try drawing on colored baseball hats or visors, collecting unusual hats from rummage sales or resale shops, using straw hats, or making the hats wild and creative with construction paper. Wearing hats can be a fun, non-threatening way to teach your child to get in touch with his or her feelings and express needs without shame. If hats don't appeal to you, try scarves, masks, sunglasses, colored shirts, or even signs that can be worn around the neck. Use your imagination to find ways to express emotion in a playful, creative way, and teach children a communication skill they will carry with them for a lifetime.

Tell me what you think, and I'll know your mind. Tell me what you feel, and I'll know your heart.

— English proverb

45

Amusing Mascots

**Use a toy, puppet, or stuffed animal as a
mascot to pass along messages, ease conflicts,
and bring a humorous tone to any atmosphere.**

*An adult is just a
deteriorated child.*

— Max Wertheimer

Several years ago, Julia had a small plastic pink panther that
became a favorite toy. One day, she misplaced him and was
frantic, searching everywhere for her little bendable buddy.
Since her closet had slowly become a "creative chaos zone," I
had propped the pink panther on top of the pile, and placed
a piece of paper between his pink paws. When she discovered
him, she read the note. It said:

> *This cool cat you would surely impress*
> *By cleaning up this jungle of a mess!*

Within a few hours, her closet was immaculate. It was a
small miracle. The next morning, I found the little pink rascal
on top of my paper pile on my desk, sporting a pink glittery
scarf around his neck (undoubtedly something he'd found in
the closet the day before). He held a note that read as follows:

> *From whisker to whisker, this cool cat will smile*
> *When you get to the bottom of this paper pile.*

It was the start of a preposterous pink panther message
marathon that lasted more than five years. Since then, we

have amused each other with other mascots, including a unicorn stuffed toy, a plastic black widow spider, and a Chinese beanbag bear.

Here are a few examples of how others have enjoyed musing over mascots.

Popo the parrot lives in a kitchen with a family of five. He holds notes for various family members in his beak, and often has a single sock in his beak to let everyone know that the matching sock is missing and Popo probably ate it. Popo never seems to mind, since he has a voracious appetite for the unusual.

A local spiritual center has a statue of a dog placed next to the entrance who wears a sign hanging around its neck that boasts, "Be aware of God." The dog never fails to get a smile and often receives a pat on the head as people enter.

Pedro Panda is a three-foot-high white bear who sits on a pedestal to greet guests in the hallway of a large community center. He has become quite a conversation piece and often holds signs for visitors, such as "One thing is clear — you are always welcome here!"

A third grade teacher uses an owl puppet to open discussions and bring up problems that students might be intimidated to raise on their own. The owl has become an integral part of the classroom and is frequently requested when a conflict arises.

It is a happy talent to know how to play.

— Ralph Waldo Emerson

Amusing mascots provide a lively and sportive way to bring out the kid in everyone. Use them with your child to enhance communication and play.

46

Food Fun

Take time to get creative with food. Serve it in playful shapes, feed each other, eat with your nondominant hand, or, for the more adventurous, eat with no hands.

When Julia was seven or eight, she used to beg me occasionally to let her bypass the utensils and eat with her hands. I resisted at first, being concerned with manners, etiquette, and following the rules. As serendipity would have it, soon after Julia's father began to prepare Indian cuisine and to eat it in traditional style — you guessed it, with his hands! The first time Julia came back from the feast, she was ecstatic. "My wish came true, Mom! I really got to taste the food when it was all over my hands!"

Nothing digests food quite as well as a happy disposition.

— Diana Loomans

Julia's enthusiasm was contagious. Before long, we were experiencing food in a whole new way. We tried spaghetti, rice casseroles, and even stew with our hands. The results were amazing. We laughed more, ate more slowly, and tasted the food in a whole new way.

Here are some scrumptious ideas to help you add more fun to your food time.

Fun Food Ideas

1. **Designer Plates:** Take the time to design the food in unusual shapes, colors, and sizes on the plate. Make faces out of raisins to top off oatmeal, create animal shapes out of vegetables, make designs out

of toppings or sauces, or write the names of diners on each plate out of food. For added fun, place a small fortune under each plate, or use unusual place settings for special effects.

2. **Sticking to It:** At least three cultures in the world eat with chopsticks regularly. The Chinese use chopsticks that are thick and have a blunt end; Korean chopsticks are thin and often made out of metal; and Japanese chopsticks are slender and pointed at the edges. We know a number of American families who eat with chopsticks on a regular basis. If you haven't tried eating with chopsticks, you will enjoy adding a whole new ritual to your eating habits. If anyone in the family has a tendency to eat too fast or overeat, chopsticks are a perfect solution, especially for beginners.

3. **Sweet Spoonfuls:** You haven't really tasted food until you let someone else feed you an entire meal. You might be surprised by how much less food you will need when someone else feeds you. A mother-daughter team tried feeding each other the evening meal, taking turns giving each other spoonfuls to help each other learn to eat slower. Both of them were amazed at how much slower they chewed their food, savoring each bite. For the daring and the adventure seeking, don't miss trying this exquisitely simple and nourishing way to eat. Children of all ages love it, too.

4. **International Cuisine:** Create an international fun meal, with samples of food from another country. Rice is by far the most common food, eaten each day by over half of the world's population. Corn is a main filler in Central America, where it is often made into tortillas. Potatoes are eaten in large quantities in many European cultures. Ethiopians eat a lot of millet and pancake bread. Create a meal around one of these international staples, and

A truly great man never puts away the simplicity of a child.

— Chinese proverb

enjoy a taste of culture while you dine. For added effect, play music from the same country in the background.

5. **Creative Cooking Night:** When a mother of two grade school children got divorced and lost her gourmet cook husband, she despaired that her son and daughter would be sentenced to peanut butter and jelly sandwiches and frozen foods forever. She decided to try one recipe a month to get herself acquainted with the kitchen and invited her children to do some experimental cooking along with her. Over time, they became so adept in the kitchen that Monday nights have become creative cooking night. They try a new recipe and cook a few tried-and-true ones so that they are set for the whole week. They lighten up the evening with music, jokes, and laughter. Mondays have become fun nights when they look forward to good food and good company.

Having fun with food is bound to bring your family closer as you share good humor as well as good nutrition.

If you are prone to eating fast, swallowing your food whole, ignoring each other as you eat, or doing two things at once while eating, we encourage you to "feed the urge" and begin to have some fun with your food now and then. If it happens to be spaghetti, make sure you have film in the house — it could provide another photo for your laughing board!

When I am older, I shall never be a "grown-up"!

— Julia Loomans

47

"Mirthwhile" Messages

**Use creative quotations, humorous quips and
questions, or entertaining words to make your written
or spoken messages more memorable and fun.**

When we began to leave unusual messages on our phone answering machine, we had unexpected side benefits — many of
our callers left creative and sometimes hysterical messages in response. One of the more memorable messages we created was:

> *"Hello, the tricky two of us are fixed on being all mixed-
> up; getting our sick kicks playing tricks on this
> mixed-up machine. So please leave a mirthwhile or
> mixed-up message at the sound of the tricky tone."*

The funniest part of the message was the way we recited
it. We each took turns, reciting a single word at a time back
and forth. The effect was a "medley of voices mingling in
mixed-up amusement."

A few days later, we received a message from a very serious
and sober neighbor, whom some of the neighbors had nicknamed "Stoneface" (since he often yelled at the children in the
neighborhood). He was, in fact, calling to make a minor com-
plaint about children in his driveway again. Here is what he said.

> *"My, oh my, I'm marvelously amused by your mixed-up
> message, but no longer mindful, but instead, mixed-
> up and miserable. Would you mind calling me to re-
> mind me of what it was I had in mind before the tricky
> two of you mixed up my mind?"*

*It is better to be a
young June bug than an
old bird of paradise.*

— Mark Twain

Our relationship was never the same after this. Our rapport improved, and he even began to make paper airplanes for the neighborhood kids.

We have left a number of creative or unusual messages on the machine since then, and we have noticed that we receive more messages. Here is one of my favorite messages, which Julia created.

> *"Hello! Benjamin Franklin once said, 'The heart of a fool is in his mouth, but the mouth of a wise man is in his heart!' Although you'll have to use your mouth to leave a message, if you speak from your heart, the message will go a long, long way!"*

Here are a few examples of other "mirthwhile" messages.

More "Mirthwhile" Messages

1. **Laughing Letters:** A friend of ours who is a long-distance father sends regular letters to his two sons, and occasionally sends a fictitious letter, written on parchment paper, from "Confucius." Recently, his sons were slacking off on writing, so he sent a note from Confucius that said, "Confucius says, 'He who writes to his father each week will live long and prosper!'"

2. **Amusing Mug Shots:** A photographer friend takes pictures of his friends making goofy faces and then sends them a surprise copy for a birthday, holiday, or wedding gift, with a funny caption underneath.

3. **Rhyme without Reason:** One of our highly creative friends sometimes leaves an entire phone message in rhyme.

Since you probably leave several messages each week on paper and by phone for family and friends, try adding the ingredient of humor and watch the fun multiply.

Love may make the world go around, but laughter keeps it from getting dizzy.

— Don Zochert

48

From Humdrum to Fun
by Julia Loomans

**Come up with clever and playful ways to
make everyday jobs come alive and turn mundane
tasks into wonderful memories.**

My mom and I were shopping in a food store on a busy Friday afternoon when we ran into my high school theater teacher and her son. They were chatting with each other in the frozen food section with heavy New York accents. When we said hello, they introduced themselves as visitors from the Bronx. They kept a straight face even as we grinned from ear to ear. We later found out that each time they shop for food, they pick a character and an accent for the day. The next time we went shopping, my mom and I became Sophia and Esmeralda from Spain. I don't remember much about what we shopped for, but I do remember how much fun we had talking with Spanish accents. Here are more fun ideas to try.

*I never did a day's work
in my life. It was all fun.*

— Thomas Edison

Eight Ways to Turn Humdrum into Fun

1. **Three Cheers for Chores:** Play games when driving, such as "Questions from the Wild" (see pp. 162–63), guess the song games (humming a small portion of a song while your partner guesses the song), or talking games, such as "Fun Facts" (see pp. 122–24) or "Creative Storytelling" (see pp. 50–51).
2. **Swing Cleaning:** Sing songs together while working, or blast "oldies" in the house and dance while you vacuum, sweep, mop, or dust, and josh as you wash.

3. **It's Done, Go Have Some Fun:** Surprise each other occasionally by doing the other person's chores for him or her. Rather than provide an explanation, just say, "The work is done. Have some fun!"

4. **Clean the Sink and Be Merry:** Hold interesting debates or discussions while cooking, chopping food, cleaning, or doing any other mindless tasks.

5. **The Whoops Box:** Instead of starting arguments over who left something out, create a whoops box. Throw everything that is out of place into the whoops box, and offer small rewards for whoever gets to the whoops box first to put the runaway items back where they belong.

6. **Treasure Map while You Mop:** Create a housework treasure map for your child to help make the work exciting and fun. Plant small notes or trinkets along the way, or create clues that can only be solved when the work is completed.

7. **The Crazy Kid Closet:** Keep a variety of zany masks, wigs, and silly toys that can only be worn when doing housework or chores around the house. Take the opportunity to create some jollity and provide unforgettable entertainment while you labor in laughter.

8. **Rip-roaring Reminders:** Use off-the-beaten-track notes to remind children of the myriad of small details that are sometimes overlooked, and add wit to the message. When you see a wet towel lying on the floor, for example, instead of creating a scene, post a comical note on the towel that says, "I may be all wet right now, but I do have a dry sense of humor by nature, so please hang me back on the rack where I belong!"

Concoct your own original ways to transform humdrum into fun, and watch the household mood swing from static to ecstatic.

Work is love made visible.

— Kahlil Gibran

Creativity, like love, requires a soft focus — an ongoing flirtation with the unknown and the irrational.

— Anonymous

49

Fun Interviews

Conduct a fun interview with someone special at family gatherings, on birthdays, or for any special occasion.

When Julia was three months old, I conducted a taped interview with her, asking her questions such as "So, what do you think of life so far?" and "What's your favorite time of the day to nap?" Her answers, all in gurgle of course, were remarkably well suited to the questions. Since then, it has become a tradition to tape a fun interview with her once or twice a year. The young can also tape interviews, audio or video, with their parents or elders, to learn more about their family history. Here are some questions that might help you get a jump start on the idea. Keep in mind that they must be adapted according to age.

Seek to know another and you will find yourself.

— Taoist saying

Sample Interview Questions

1. What is your favorite color, food, game, animal, hobby, sport, or thing to do? (Note: This could actually be a series of questions.)
2. What would you like to say to someone special? (Pick a person whom both of you know.)
3. What do you wish you could do more of? (And then remind him or her that wishes still do come true.)
4. What is one of your secret wishes? (That is, one of those secrets you are willing to share.)

5. What is one of the biggest scares you ever had? (And how did you deal with it?)
6. What is one of the best gifts you have ever received?
7. What is something most people don't know about you?
8. Imagine that your face is on the cover of *Time* magazine. What have you achieved?

The following are some great questions to ask someone for a fun birthday interview.

Ten Top Birthday Questions

Sometimes, the question is more important than the answer.

— Plato

1. What is one of the funniest things that happened to you last year?
2. What is one of the most frightening things that happened to you last year, and how did you overcome the fear?
3. Whom did you get closer to last year? (Or whom did you want to get closer to?)
4. What is one of the most important lessons you learned last year?
5. What was one of the biggest risks you took last year?
6. What goal would you most like to achieve this year?
7. Where would you like to travel this year?
8. If you could go back and live one day over again from last year, which day would it be, and why?
9. What hobby would you like to take up this year?
10. If you could learn from any teacher in the world, past or present, whom would you study with this year?

Fun interviews are a wonderful way to get closer to family and friends, and the "interviewee" is bound to feel important and cared for.

50

Letting Out Your Own Playful Child

Find ways to let out your own playful child as you share quality time with your child each day.

When Julia was in third grade, I made a list of forty things we could do together to have fun at home. The list ranged from reading library books, drawing together, baking, and planting new plants. I asked her to rate each activity from 1 to 10 by holding up her fingers. Five fingers meant okay, eight fingers meant fun, and ten fingers meant a lot of fun. We went over the list together, and she rated each activity. When I got to the bottom of the list, I said, "Playing and wrestling on the floor." She stopped for a moment and looked up toward the ceiling, as though she were adding something up. Then, she looked at me and flashed all ten fingers, four times in a row! "Do you give it a 40, Julia?" I asked incredulously. "Yes" she said, "because when you wrestle with me on the floor, your face looks just like mine!"

I pondered over her comment for a long time, and I realized that she was right. When I was wrestling on the floor, I was inviting my inner child to come out and play with her. All of the day's responsibilities and worries were cast aside, and I was simply having fun with her. I looked again over the list of forty ways to have fun together at home. I noticed that all the ideas she had rated as a 10 had something in common: I was in my element — abandoned, carefree, and letting out my

The great man is he who does not lose his child's heart.

— Mencius

playful child. Almost all of them included some degree of laughter.

After that, I made a promise to myself to show her more spontaneity and even more of my playfulness. I began to realize that one of the greatest gifts we can give our children is our own aliveness.

It is the childlike mind that finds the kingdom.

— Charles Fillmore

Our list of fun activities has changed over the years. When Julia was eight, she enjoyed it when I chased her around the house acting like Big Bird from *Sesame Street*. As a young teen, she loved it when I danced to music with her, especially when I turned a spoon upside down, pretending it was a microphone to lip-synch a tune on the radio. The games have changed, but the principle remains the same. Recently, I was singing in what I call "Oops Opera" through the house, and Julia burst through the door and said, "Oh, Mom — I'd like to see you get silly like this a lot more often!" I decided to write down a few fun agreements for myself, to help keep my "gleequilibrium" intact more often.

Ten Fun Agreements for the Playful Child in Me

1. I'll play in some way at least three times a week (dancing, hiking, roller blading, or biking).
2. I'll sit down to enjoy each meal and take my time.
3. I'll get plenty of sleep each night.
4. I'll have "a fun friend" over at least once a week.
5. I'll give and get at least three hugs a day.
6. I'll keep crayons, paints, and clay in the house, and play music more often.
7. I'll laugh more of my laughter and cry more of my tears.
8. I'll enjoy a few special treats each week, such as a massage, bubble bath, or special dessert.
9. I'll take myself on a half-day adventure each week.
10. I'll be spontaneous and do the unexpected more

often, such as complimenting a clerk or hugging a friend.

Experiment by writing your own fun agreements to help bring out your own childlike spirit. Also ask your child to name ten irresistibly fun activities that he or she would like to do more often with you. You might be surprised by how many of your child's choices invite your spontaneous inner child to come out to play. Why not say yes!

To attain high art and a pure mind is absolutely indispensable.

— Suzuki

Playful Esteem Chart

Read over the following chart of old beliefs and new beliefs, and help your child move from low esteem to full esteem while playing and having fun.

From Low Esteem

1. Work before play. This teaches children responsibility.

2. Raising children is a serious responsibility.

3. Children are too silly as it is. They need to learn to obey and settle down more.

4. Play is frivolous. It's for kids, not adults.

5. Parents can't afford to have much of a sense of humor; there's too much to do.

6. How can parents get their children to respect them if they act like clowns? Children must be disciplined in a serious way.

To Full Esteem

1. Work and play go hand in hand. This motto teaches children to enjoy their responsibilities.

2. Raising children is too important to be taken so seriously.

3. Children are naturally playful. Their joy can bring candor and life to many otherwise ordinary moments.

4. Play is necessary for everyone each day.

5. You may be rusty, but inside there is a playful child waiting to come out. Start by letting the little things become more fun!

6. Knowing how to play is a tremendous gift we can give to our children. They will appreciate our ability to direct them with joy.

"Letting Off Esteem": Creative Conflict Resolution

There are two ways to approach our children when we are in conflict. The first is to seek to gain *control* and overpower our children, and the second is to seek to maintain *connection* and empower ourselves and our children.

Chapter 6 offers hands-on ideas to creatively "let off esteem" and stay in connection with your child, even while in conflict. Suggestions range from artwork, puppetry, games, role-playing, reversing roles, conflict resolution skills, and creative ways to spare the rod and love the child.

The following Ten Commandments of Control take a playful look at a very serious subject — that of being in control and the high price that must be paid to adhere to the age-old creed.

The Ten Commandments of Control

(How to Be a Serious, Unhappy Person Most of the Time)

1. Thou shalt wear a grim expression at all times.

2. Thou shalt hold thy body in a stiff and rigid posture.

3. Thou shalt stuff and store all of thy feelings in thy gut.

4. Thou shalt remain logical and analytical whenever possible.

5. Thou shalt be in control at all times, no matter what.

6. Thou shalt dwell on the feebleness, faults, and fears of others.

7. Thou shalt blame and shame everyone around thyself for everything.

8. Thou shalt expect the worst in all situations.

9. Thou shalt never get too close to anybody for any reason.

10. Thou shalt inflict upon others that which was once inflicted on thyself.

The London Ladies
by Diana Loomans

Julia had done it again for the third time in two weeks! My blue shirt was gone, and she hadn't asked me if she could wear it. I stood by my closet, feeling my irritation rising to anger. How could she be so oblivious, I wondered. Why couldn't she follow such a simple request? I stomped down the hallway to her bedroom door. I could hear the radio playing in her room as she accompanied the song, singing her little heart out in blissful oblivion. With my fist ready to pound on the door, I was revving up to let her know just how I felt about it. Almost despite myself, I found myself pausing to catch my breath. "Keep it light, be easy on her, and remember that you were a teenager once, too," an inner voice reminded me. And then, I asked myself a question that would turn it all around: "If I did know what was funny about this, what would it be?"

I took a deep breath, paused for a moment, and knocked on the door. Julia emerged, bright eyed and singing, with my shirt on, of course. "Dahling," I suddenly said, taking on the role of a proper English lady, "I just cahn't believe that you are ahctually wearing my bloody shirt without ahsking for my pehmission again! You must go and take it off straightaway since you haven't followed your Mumsey's pehfectly logical request." I stood with my nose held high in the air and my arms crossed, tapping one foot on the ground with an indignant expression on my face.

Julia looked puzzled for a moment, and then a smile broke out over her face. Without skipping a beat, she jumped on the English bandwagon, retorting with, "Oh, Mumsey, you simply muhst be patient with me. Now that I am ohlder, I am just pehfectly caught up in all the more important things in life. Surely you do understahnd, don't you, dahling?"

The mood had already taken a dramatic turn for the better. We were both grinning through our roles and beginning to delight in the unexpected. "Now you simply muhst listen to me," I said. "Just because your life is in a whirl doesn't mean that my wahrdrobe will be changing without my pehmission. From now on, it's ask Mumsey first, or else you'll get a good old-fashioned English scolding — ahl right, dahling?"

"Oh, ahl right, Mumsey," Julia said with a theatrical smirk on her face. She took off the shirt and hung it back in my closet. On her way back, she caught me off guard as she threw her arms around me and said, "Oh, Mom, you're really starting to get the hang of having a teenager! Thanks for not yelling about it." She retreated into her room with a look of gratitude and relief on her face.

I went to sleep that night savoring a small sense of victory. I had broken through the stubborn barrier of parenting with disapproval and shame and instead had enjoyed a jolly good time correcting my child's behavior. Julia hasn't confiscated any of my clothes out of the closet since (knock on wood), and we've affectionately named our characters "The London Ladies." They make an appearance every now and then when we need to improvise our way through a small everyday challenge. This practice always lightens the load and definitely keeps our visiting friends on their toes.

51

Spare the Rod and Love the Child!

Teach your child to live and communicate nonviolently by finding positive alternatives to spanking, hitting, and verbal abuse.

When Julia was in fourth grade, she had a friend named Anna who lived in the neighborhood. Anna was delightful to be around but, at times, very difficult. She was highly imaginative and humorous in her play, but she was also prone to sudden mood swings that included verbal outbursts, hitting, and verbal accusations. One day, I drove her home from school and dropped her off in front of her house. "Will you wait here?" she said in a distressed voice. "I need to see if my mom is home before I can go in the house." We agreed to wait, and a minute later she rushed toward us with a panic-stricken look on her face. She jumped into the back seat of the car, slammed the door, and said, "Please, I have to go back to your house! My mom isn't home yet, and she protects me from my dad." I drove Anna back home with us, feeling a wave of deep sadness about the terror that she lived with each day. The incident shed new light on Anna's behavior, and I felt empathy for her pain and fear.

When I spoke with her mother, I found out that Anna's father had a history of physical and sexual abuse from his own childhood that he was now repeating with Anna. He was sporadically going to get professional help for his problem, and Anna's mother was still hoping that things would turn

Example is not the main thing in influencing others. It is the only thing.

— Albert Schweitzer

around. Unfortunately, while Anna's mother was sitting on the fence hoping that her husband would change, Anna was desperate for some relief from the madness and collecting emotional scars that would be with her for a long time.

The history of parents punishing or abusing their children almost always bears the same facts — the parent who abuses was once abused in a similar way and hasn't allowed the residual feelings to come up to the surface. Author and therapist Alice Miller explains that abusive parents often carry with them as adults an unconscious belief that enables them to justify their behavior: "If I inflict on others what was once inflicted on me, I don't have to feel the pain that the memory would bring."

Adolf Hitler's childhood is a prime example of this theory. He was treated like a dog by his father and whipped almost daily. On one occasion, he claimed that he managed to stop himself from crying and felt nothing as he counted the thirty-two lashings he received from his father in one of his routine beatings. "The result," says Miller, "was a primitive human being, incapable of empathy for other human beings. The feelings of hate and revenge latent in him constantly drove him to new acts of destruction." Hitler needed a tremendous amount of empathy and understanding from a loving mentor who could guide him through his searing childhood memories of abuse and help him to reconcile the war that raged within him. That did not occur; instead, his repressed desire for revenge drove him to instigate one of history's most vengeful plots — the massacre of millions of innocent human beings. Interestingly, Hitler experienced frequent nightmares throughout his life, waking up in a cold sweat and frantically counting aloud. Perhaps this was the voice of his abused inner child, still trying to scream out the words that were once frozen in his throat as he endured the beatings.

Although most of us were not raised in a home as violent as Adolf Hitler's, many of us carry emotional scars from the wounds of verbal abuse (threats, shaming, or put-downs), spankings, sexual abuse, or severe punishments. Author John

Bradshaw once said, "What gets repressed gets repeated." In order to break the chain of family violence from repeating itself, we need to take the time to heal our own wounds with compassion and care. To build self-esteem in our children, it is vital that we find alternatives to physical and verbal abuse. Here are just a few of the reasons to spare the rod and love the child.

Nine Reasons Not to Use Physical or Verbal Violence

1. **Violence Begets Violence:** All too often, children who are raised with violence repeat the same patterns of abuse in their significant relationships as adults. Even those who are convinced that they will never repeat that which was done to them discover that repressed rage is often more powerful than logical reasoning. Without expert help, the physical or emotional violence is likely to be repeated.

2. **Loss of Self-Esteem:** When children are physically or verbally shamed, the message that will most likely register is "I am not acceptable or lovable." Over time, such children lose confidence and may carry deep feelings of unworthiness into adulthood.

3. **Loss of Trust:** Children who are hit or verbally abused lose trust in significant others and often feel alone in the world. The environment no longer feels safe, and such children are likely to become rebellious or aloof, or adopt a hypervigilant attitude in response to their surroundings.

4. **Fear of Making Mistakes:** Children who are hit or reprimanded for making mistakes become fearful of learning and avoid taking risks whenever possible. Instead of seeing mistakes as rungs on the learning ladder, they see them as something to be avoided at all costs.

Like a forgotten fire, childhood can always flare up again in us.

— Gaston Bachelard

5. **Loss of Connection with Self and Others:** Physical or emotional violence often causes children to lose touch with personal feelings and needs, and they may develop a "secret underworld." Often such children comply with the rules and behave well on the surface to gain approval, but a deep inner rift may form within them and between adult and child.

6. **Lack of Creative Problem-Solving Skills:** Children who are spanked, hit, or put down frequently are deprived of the experience of learning to manage stress and deal with conflicts in a positive way. If they want to approach problems differently, they will have to "unlearn" the old negative patterns and then start from scratch, learning skills in cooperation and conflict resolution as adults.

The way to improve the world is first in one's own heart and head and hands.

— Robert Pirsig

7. **Bottled-Up Emotions:** Children who are hit, shamed, or frequently yelled at often store tension and anger in the body, resulting in poor health, depression, and an inability to feel and express a full range of emotions. They may learn to repress feelings and needs, and begin to live in the intellect, with no way to deal with pent-up stress, other than through repression or outbursts.

8. **Loss of Ability to Know and Express Needs:** Children's misbehavior is often a cry for help. Often, children who are acting out have feelings and needs that are not being heard or addressed; they may be sending out an SOS in the form of inappropriate behavior. When spanking, hitting, or verbal abuse is the response children receive, children may internalize this as a punishment for having needs. Such children are likely to feel shame for having needs and may learn to repress feelings and stop asking for things.

9. **Physical Injury:** Children's health may be endangered when they are hit or verbally abused, especially

over a period of time. Children who are physically hit or emotionally harassed often have chronic digestive ailments, headaches, stomach problems, or other stress-related diseases. Frequent spankings or beatings can cause damage to the spinal column, neck, or head area. In severe cases, the damage can cause permanent injury or death.

Fall seven times,
stand up eight.

— Japanese proverb

For the above reasons and more, it is vital to come up with alternatives to the old tradition of controlling a child through coercion, punishment, or violence. If you were raised in a physically or verbally violent household, getting counsel and support may offer the empathy and relief that you need. There is no greater investment you can make in your child's future than to begin to heal some of your own childhood wounds. The following suggestions provide alternatives for parents who want to stop the destructive cycle from continuing.

Thirty-Three Alternatives to Physical and Emotional Violence

1. Honor your own feelings and needs as being most important, because you can't give to your child out of an empty cup.
2. Get empathy from those willing to listen to you without judgment.
3. Seek the help of an expert if you have painful, unresolved memories from childhood.
4. Join a support group, such as Parents Anonymous or Adult Children of Alcoholics.
5. Take a parenting class and begin to reeducate yourself.
6. Take a ten minute time-out when you feel yourself losing control.
7. Take a drive alone and yell or scream in your car when you feel your temperature rising.

8. Write your angry feelings in a notebook or journal, rather than acting in ways you'll regret later.

9. Call a friend and ask for support when you feel an outburst brewing.

10. Go outside and take a brisk walk to gain perspective.

11. Use humor or role-playing to laugh at yourself when you start playing the authority figure.

12. Ask for a hug from someone when you feel the tension coming on.

13. Acknowledge to someone you trust that you are feeling scared about repeating some of your old patterns.

14. Read books on positive parenting.

15. Observe parents that you admire and ask them questions about their approach to dealing with conflict.

16. Write notes or letters to your child instead of yelling or spanking.

17. Give yourself one dollar every time you choose an alternative to hitting or yelling. Save the money and go out and celebrate your positive parenting with your child.

18. Do something fun alone each week to recharge yourself.

19. Reach out and hold your child's hand when a conflict begins.

20. Post agreements that you and your child feel good about regarding how to deal with conflicts. When you're slipping, go back and read the agreements out loud and recommit to them, or re-sign the contract.

21. Save small grievances for once-a-week family meetings, which will give you time to think about how you'd like to express your feelings.

22. Express your regret and apologize to your child as soon as you realize you have expressed your frustration in a violent or inappropriate way.

"If you tame me then we shall need each other. To me, you will be unique in all the world. To you, I shall be unique in all the world."

— Antoine de Saint-Exupéry, The Little Prince

23. Draw or scribble out your feelings in marker, chalk, or crayon on paper.

24. Let yourself cry if you need to instead of lashing out at your child.

25. Do a five-minute spiritual check-in and ask for guidance.

26. Ask yourself the question, "If I did know what to do right now, what would the answer be?"

27. Exercise for five or ten minutes — racewalk, run, dance, jump rope, or jump up and down on a trampoline to release some stress.

28. Practice catching yourself and your child "doing something right" and acknowledge the progress.

29. Use a goal chart and reward yourself for each day of positive parenting.

30. Know your hook areas, hot buttons, and tender spots, and plan ahead for how you will react when you are feeling "hooked in." Also, recognize that these hook areas may be the places within yourself that most need some addressing and empathy.

31. Throw some rocks outside, scream into a pillow, or throw some pillows to help release physical tension when it builds up.

32. Ask yourself, "Has what I am about to do ever happened to me?" and "How did I feel when it did happen?" This might help you to realize that you are about to repeat an old pattern.

33. Be gentle with yourself and acknowledge each step of progress along the way.

You are one of your child's greatest teachers. The best way to teach nonviolence is by having patience and compassion with yourself and by taking the time that you need to restore wholeness within yourself. Consider this to be one of your primary tasks in parenting, and great things will follow.

Mistakes are merely steps up the ladder.

— Paul J. Meyer

52

Reversing Roles
by Julia Loomans

**When things get tense and you start to fall
into familiar patterns, stop and reverse roles.
Carry on with the conflict, and see what happens.**

Native Americans knew the value of reversing roles when they came up with the phrase "Walk a mile in the other person's moccasins." Reversing roles can be a lifesaver. My mom and I first tried it when we were both feeling ornery and tired. We were begrudgingly unloading boxes from the trunk of the car on a hot day. I was complaining about how heavy the boxes were, and my mom was coming up with zinger comments such as, "Why can't you be more positive about this? Maybe I should just do it myself."

My shoulders were getting tense, and I was beginning to roll back my eyes, feeling more resistant than before. I let out a loud sigh, and my mom paused. "Okay, it's role reversal time, Julia," she suddenly said. "You stand over there and act like me, and I'll stand in your place and pretend to be you, okay?" I didn't know if it would work, but I was willing to give just about anything a try. We got into position and began to mimic each other with amazing accuracy. We stood, walked, and gestured just like the other, and the lines that came out of both our mouths were classic.

It felt so good to watch my mom go through the motions of being me. And it felt empowering to act out her part. It helped us to understand and be understood. Before long, we were laughing so hard we could hardly carry the boxes. We now have given permission to each other to call a "reverse roles" whenever we feel like it. I want to do this with my own children when I grow up.

The definition of insanity is doing the same thing over and over again and expecting different results.

— Anonymous

53

Catch That Feeling!

Play catch — throwing a fun object back and forth — and take turns sharing your feelings while having some fun.

I was attending a workshop several years ago, and I became entranced with the teacher's use of a large ball. At the end of each session, the participants would take turns catching the ball, expressing what they had learned, and then throwing the ball to another eager player. The results were incredible. People expressed their feelings, demonstrated mastery of the material, and enjoyed themselves, all at the same time.

Since then, I have used the game to get in touch with feelings in a lighthearted way with Julia on several occasions. When we moved across the country to California a few years ago, we had many adjustments to make in a short period of time. After a few weeks passed, although we were delighted with our move, unexpressed feelings of tension and fear of the unknown were mounting.

One day, I took a large round pillow off the couch and said to Julia, "Let's play with the ball and see if we can catch up with all of the feelings going on inside about our move. I'll start with one, then I'll throw the ball to you, and you can tell me what you heard me say. Then it will be your turn to do the same, okay?" She agreed reluctantly.

"I'm scared you won't like it here, but I'll want to stay," I said, as I tossed the pillow ball to her. "You're scared I might want to go, but you'll want to stay," she repeated as she

When we are safe enough to bounce our feelings back and forth without fear of harm, then we shall have peace.

— Tori Ugunda

caught the ball. I nodded emphatically. "Well, I'm scared that I won't find the kind of friends here that I had back East," she said with a few tears while throwing the ball to me. "You're scared of feeling like the new kid on the block, missing all your good friends back home." "Yes," she answered wistfully.

Be patient toward all that is unsolved in your heart, and try to love the questions themselves.

— Rainer Maria Rilke

Our feelings continued to surface as we threw the ball back and forth — questions about the decision, concerns about adjusting to the new city, and worries about losing our connection together due to the new demands. Fears rumbled as the ball tumbled, and it was an incredible feeling of relief. The physical element of throwing the ball back and forth kept the energy moving, eased us out of our heads and into our feelings, and set a playful tone. Once we were able to hear all of the feelings on both sides, we were able to come up with some good ideas to help us feel more at home in our new city.

We have "caught many more feelings" since then by playing this simple game. It has helped us to toss repression and catch more expression! Try it!

54

Power Play

Become aware of the power dynamics in your relationship with your child, and learn to use empathy and play to move from overpowering each other to empowering each other.

Behind most human conflict lies a struggle for power and a lack of training in empathic listening. Most of us learned when we were very young to *overpower* one another with intimidation and control, rather than to *empower* one another with compassion, honesty, and acknowledgment. Many of us were raised by parents who believed that whoever had the control had the power, instead of realizing that whoever had connection with his or her own power could empower others. Because of this, many of us spend a lifetime fighting with one another, looking to "get our power back," rather than tapping into our own limitless supply. Being able to acknowledge our own power plays with honesty and humor marks true wisdom and genuine relating.

It is not powerful people who rob others of their rights. It is those who feel powerless inside who must oppress.

— Danaan Parry

One of the greatest revelations I have had as a parent has been learning to understand the subtle differences between empowering Julia and overpowering her. I came to realize that every moment I tried to gain power over my daughter rather than connecting with her, I was freezing my potential to become the parent I longed to be! Even more tragically, I was losing opportunities to relate to her in an honest and real way. We began addressing this issue through the use of puppets. We started with two puppets — a jackal and a giraffe (both characters adapted from international peacemaker Marshall Rosenberg's work entitled *Compassionate Communication*). The jackal was the fearful puppet who had a deep underlying need for empathy to get relief from the belief that "It's a dog-eat-dog world out there!" The giraffe was the non-judgmental puppet who told the truth, listened from the heart, and offered empathy rather than an argument.

We made an agreement that whenever we were moving into a power struggle, we'd use the puppets. The person struggling for power would put on the jackal puppet, and the other person would play the role of the giraffe, offering an ear and giving empathy by simply listening to the jackal and repeating what was said without judgment. The results were amazing. One night, we were arguing over Julia's increasing tendency to go to bed late and wake up tired the next morning. We were clearly locked in a power struggle, with me in the intimidating role and Julia in the aloof role. We called a break, and I put on the jackal puppet. Our dialogue went as follows:

Jackal: You are staying up later and later, and you're not getting to bed on time, and I want to see this stop!
Giraffe: You want me to stop getting to bed so late.
Jackal: Yes, I do! You're not getting enough sleep.
Giraffe: You are concerned that I'm not getting enough sleep.
Jackal: Yes. How will you keep your eyes open with so little sleep?
Giraffe: You are worried that I will be tired all day tomorrow.
Jackal: Yes! I'm concerned that you will feel tired and run-down tomorrow.
Giraffe: You want me to feel awake at school tomorrow.
Jackal: Yes! And I want you to have a good day instead of a tiring day.
Giraffe: You'd like me to feel good at school.
Jackal: Yes, that's it. That's exactly it.
Giraffe: You'd like to see me wide awake and alert.
Jackal: Yes.

Any child can tell you that the sole purpose of a middle name is so he can tell when he's really in trouble.

— Dennis Fakes

No one can make you feel inferior without your consent.

— Eleanor Roosevelt

Giraffe: Okay, I'll go to bed earlier tomorrow night.
Jackal: Good. That would be a big relief to me.

Although the dialogue was simple, the puppet play pulled us right out of the power struggle, and the added element of the giraffe's empathy made it easy to get to the feeling that I had underneath the power struggle. Once Julia realized that I had a genuine concern about her well-being rather than a need to be in control, it was easy for her to agree to go to bed earlier. Since then, we have reversed roles many times, playing jackal or giraffe for each other to move through a power struggle and get to the underlying *feeling* or *need* in a situation. Even when we don't see eye to eye on a subject, understanding each other makes the whole process of coming to an agreement much easier.

One is always in the dark about one's personality. One needs another to get to know oneself.

— Carl Jung

If puppets don't appeal to you, try using hats, wearing signs, or role-playing. One family of five uses humorous masks when they begin to get into a power conflict. The person in distress wears an Indian chief mask and acts out the part of a controlling leader. The rest of the family members put on tribal masks and play the role of the listening Indians, giving the chief empathy. Within a short period of time, they are usually laughing, and their listening skills help them to come to a new level of understanding.

The next time you are experiencing a power struggle, try role-playing and practicing the powerful skill of empathy. (For more ideas on empathic listening, see "Empathy Each Day," pp. 12–17). These tools might help you move from tug-o'-war to hug-o'-more!

55

Freeze!
by Julia Loomans

The next time you find yourselves lost on the path of clash and gnash, call a Freeze! Finish the argument in animal sounds, gibberish, song, or in slow motion, and watch the drama transform before your eyes.

The first time my mom and I played Freeze! was during a debate about whose turn it was to labor over a big pile of dirty dishes. We were getting nowhere, and I was about to do some serious pouting in my room, when my mom suddenly called out, "Freeze!" Before I could speak, she turned around and continued the argument with, "quack-quack-quack, quack-quaaack," while waddling around in the kitchen in circles. "Quack-quack, quack-quack QUUAAACK!" I squawked back without skipping a beat.

Laughter opens not only people's mouths, but their minds as well, and allows some rays of reason to strike home.

— Franca Rama

The duck squabbling went on a few more minutes in loud bursts of squeaks and quacks, until we were worn down and began to laugh. We ended up doing the dishes together, mumbling an occasional "quack-quack, quack" under our breath. It was amazing how much better we felt. Who would have ever thought that something so corny and so simple could bring so much comic relief! Since then, we have come up with more ways to play Freeze! Here are a few of our favorites.

Five Ways to Play Freeze!

1. **Say It in Slow Motion:** Gesture v-e-r-y s-l-o-w-l-y while grumbling in a low voice, trying to keep a straight face.

2. **Singing Squabble:** Sing through the rest of your disagreement back and forth in opera, country western, rock, blues, ballad, folk, or pop to the tune of a popular song, or make up your own song.

3. **Animal Argument:** Finish your conversation in animal language, posing as ducks, frogs, wolves, dogs, cows, chickens, lions, or goats. The sky is the limit on this one!

4. **The Silent Scream:** Gesture, yell, and scream at the top of your lungs back and forth — without making a sound.

5. **The Battle of Gibberish:** Garble your words or mimic another language, such as Dutch, French, German, Russian, Spanish, or Swahili, or make up your own. This is an especially good way to finish an argument in a restaurant or on a bus.

Argue for your limitations, and sure enough, they're yours.

— Richard Bach

Following a couple of ground rules helps when playing Freeze!

Ground Rules for Freeze!

1. Play the game only when all parties are in agreement and want to play.

2. Agree to use it as a playful way to reduce seriousness and gain perspective rather than a hurtful way to mock each other or make fun of each other's feelings.

3. Agree that it's not a cure-all but, instead, a way to break the ice and begin to see the humor in the situation. Sharing empathy or creating clear agreements may also be necessary later.

The next time you need some perspective in the middle of a tense situation, try calling a Freeze! You won't really appreciate the fun until you are willing to come out of the cold and try it for yourself.

56

Moving Right Along

When you find yourself repeating the same old arguments and want to create some new possibilities, try moving and physical exercise.

What happens when you are upset or angry and you start to move? The mood shifts, you gain perspective, and you get some exercise — three for the price of one.

If you're alive, you've got to flap your arms and legs, you've got to jump around a lot.

— Mel Brooks

One father has an agreement with his family whenever there is a conflict. If the issue can't be cleared up in fifteen minutes, they all go outside to walk it off and talk it out. "The first few minutes are usually tense, but as we breathe in the fresh air and walk together, we are able to begin to listen to one another," he said.

A woman with three children under ten years of age bought a small trampoline to get some exercise and was amazed to discover how effective it was in dispelling struggles among the kids. When the children were arguing, they took turns jumping and talking about their feelings. "Most of their spats turn into laughter once they get on the trampoline. I guess it's pretty hard to jump up and down and stay angry at the same time!"

A couple with two teenage children used to fight at the dinner table. "We took up biking together, and it changed our whole approach to resolving conflicts. We biked before supper and pedaled off some of our stress."

Try movement for yourself: Dance through a difficulty, jog through a jam, or hopscotch through a hassle. You'll discover that you can't stay stuck in the same old groove when you turn off the broken record and start to move!

People should follow their own energy.

— Will Schultz

57

Character Play

**When things get tense and the pressure is on,
finish your fight posing in a character role, and
see if you can keep a straight face.**

I was attending a dinner party for twelve people at the house of a friend, thoroughly enjoying the conversation when, suddenly, a quibble started between the host and hostess. He began to interrupt her story with critical remarks such as, "No, no... you don't have it right — it was 1965, not 1966!" The guests became fidgety as the argument continued to escalate.

The host stood up abruptly and excused himself. He soon returned to the room sporting a top hat and a round magnifying glass in his left eye. "Good evening, Madam," he said. "I am Detective Knows-It-All, and I am here to straighten out any memory difficulties you may be having. I am a detail specialist," he added, as he examined the top of her head with his magnifying glass. He was talking in a heavy Swiss accent and had a twitch on the left side of his face.

"Oh, I'm so glad to see that you make weekend calls, too, Detective," she said. The guests began to chortle as they continued their conversation. "Since my wife doesn't care much for details and I am overly fond of them, I arrive on the scene occasionally to set her straight and iron out the tension, too!" The couple modeled a brilliant alternative to the typical bickering that can drag on half a century between people with differences in perception. Within ten minutes, the guests shifted from discomfort to delight, and Detective Knows-It-All was hugging his wife.

Our greatest glory consists not in never falling but in rising every time we fall.

— Ralph Waldo Emerson

Here are a few more examples of fighting in character.

A father of four children under twelve has a tendency to get authoritative and controlling at bedtime. To help himself kick the habit, he developed a character named "Sergeant Stiff" who talks in a monotone voice, has a rigid stride, and demands that all children must be in bed by the nine o'clock hour. As he walks them up the stairs, he mumbles, "Gallop, two, three, four..." He claims that this eases the tension and demonstrates to his children that he can laugh at himself.

Settle one difficulty
and you keep a
hundred away.

— Confucius

Two ten-year-old twin brothers were going through a period of relentless sibling rivalry when their sixteen-year-old brother named them "Muhammad and Big Bruiser." Now when they begin to squabble, they playact their character roles and have a slow-motion boxing match, including all the gestures. This process makes them laugh while giving them a chance to vent some steam.

A seventeen-year-old high school senior girl had a tendency to become aloof with her family when something was bothering her. Now she becomes a silent mime actress to exaggerate her tendencies to be sullen and silent. She acts out her feelings while her family guesses what she is doing. "It has helped me to see the humor in my silent tactics," she says, "and it's making it safer for me to express my real feelings!"

Playing a character role teaches children and adults to see the humor amidst the drama, which usually breaks the serious spell of an argument. This process isn't intended to replace the anger and grief that sometimes need to be expressed outright, but it can offer an inventive alternative to "mindless acts of senseless argument." Trying out a different role provides a refreshing lift from the monotony of an old, worn-out part and offers the opportunity to explore new perspectives.

58

Picture This!
by Julia Loomans

Use artwork of all kinds — crayons, finger paints, watercolor, or clay — to express feelings when in a conflict, and see what emerges.

We talk too much; we should talk less and draw more.

— Goethe

My mom and I were having a difficult time one morning. We decided to take a break and do something creative, just to get a breather from the stress. I started to doodle with crayons on a piece of paper. "What are you drawing?" my mom asked with curiosity. "I'm drawing a picture about our argument," I said, which surprised even me, since I hadn't realized it. She decided to join me, and half an hour later, we were talking about our artwork. I had drawn a mountain and a gopher hole. My mom was standing on the mountainside with her arms folded, and I was inside the gopher hole with a hat pulled over my ears. "When you're angry and you aren't listening to me," I said, "I go to a hideaway inside and tune you out." Showing her the picture, I explained, "If you can stop talking and listen to me, I'll come out of the hole and we can go up the mountain together."

She had drawn a picture of herself stuck in between two rocks out in a field, with me off in the distance, far away and blurry. "When I start to act like a critical parent, I get stuck between a rock and a hard place, and I know that I'm repeating some of the same old patterns that I felt when I was little," she told me. "When I felt criticized or scared, I used to go into my gopher hole, too." That surprised me, and it helped me to feel closer to her. It also helped her to see that she was doing the same thing to me that was done to her because she hadn't realized how scary it felt to be in the gopher hole all alone when she was little. We put our drawings up and talked more about them. Since then, we've used crayons, paints, watercolor, and clay to express what's going on inside that is hard to put in words.

One of the most unusual drawings I ever made was a picture of me with a grin on my face, with my arms folded neatly in my lap, sitting up straight in a chair. Inside my stomach, there was a strange-looking squiggly caterpillar doing somersaults. Her name was "Tiggyboomp," and she loved to sleep. In fact, it was her dream to weave a cocoon and someday become a beautiful butterfly. But she'd wake up and start wiggling around whenever my mom was acting like everything was okay but was feeling sad or angry underneath the surface. We talked about the picture and what could be done so that Tiggyboomp could get some sleep. "If you keep feeling one thing and acting out another, then Tiggyboomp will eventually have babies, and I will have lots of caterpillars in my stomach when I grow up," I told her. "But if you're honest and tell me what you really feel, then Tiggyboomp will be able to fall asleep. If she sleeps for a long time, she'll weave a cocoon, and when she wakes up, she'll be a butterfly that can fly inside my whole body!"

"I wonder how many caterpillars I have in my stomach," my mom said. "I suspect I have more than one!" I didn't argue with that, but I did share a thought with her that she enjoyed. "Just think, Mom, if your caterpillars go to sleep, when they wake up, you'll have lots of butterflies flying inside of you."

After that, we both drew pictures of the caterpillars inside of cocoons fast asleep, since that would mean that we'd made progress. They haven't come out of their cocoons yet, but we know they will soon. When they do emerge fluttering their wings, we're going to paint a butterfly mural to celebrate.

Art inspires us to the fullest expression of self.

— Leonardo da Vinci

Use the creative arts to explore feelings with your child. Who knows what might emerge?

59

Teaching Children
Conflict Resolution Skills

When there is tension or disagreement in a group of three or more, follow some simple conflict resolution principles and move from conflict to connection together.

Let the ideas clash, but not the hearts.

— C. C. Mehta

Every organized group of living creatures experiences some moments of conflict. Guinea pigs in a cage will roll and tumble together one moment and grapple over a piece of lettuce the next. Children in day-care centers frolic and play together as well as volley for attention or struggle over the latest toy. Children on playgrounds may fight over the rules when playing games, and families sometimes bicker over small everyday conflicts that arise in the household. Schools often experience conflict regarding curriculum and administrative decisions, businesses may have employees that dispute company policy, and governments frequently debate international issues.

Since most adults didn't attend schools offering courses such as Conflict Resolution 101, many small fires that could be put out with the aid of a few negotiation skills turn into bonfires that rage out of control. Teaching children to resolve conflict provides a skill that will carry them through many of the difficulties they may encounter with others throughout their lives. Futurist John Naisbitt says that effective communication is one of the most valuable skills we can teach our children to prepare them to live in the world of tomorrow. Here are a few basic principles to follow when creating a conflict resolution group.

Seven Steps to Creating a Conflict Resolution Group

1. **Set an Agenda:** Gather together in a place where you won't be disturbed, and determine what will be talked about and how much time you will take, with the understanding that there may be future meetings set up. Pick someone who will act as the focus person to keep the group on track and to be the timekeeper. One family of four has a group meeting twice a month to discuss anything that needs addressing. Their appointed person blows a whistle when the group is losing its focus, which always gets a laugh from family members.

2. **Believe that Resolution Is Possible:** Focus on finding win-win solutions for everyone. If a group of dedicated people of any age come together with the intent to resolve a conflict, holding the belief that it is possible, the sky is the limit! A teacher who teaches skills in peacemaking to her seventh graders starts out each session by saying, "There is a solution that can work for all of us. Let's venture to find it." Sometimes, it takes more than one meeting to come to a resolution.

3. **Give Everyone a Chance to Speak One at a Time:** Let each person express his or her feelings and needs without interruption or judgment of any kind. A teen support group in San Diego uses a small heart-shaped pillow, passing it around the circle to each person one by one. Whoever holds the heart receives complete attention from everyone in the room, and only the person with the heart speaks. The entire group listens intently, with each receiving an opportunity to respond and express feelings when the heart is passed in the circle. This allows the person speaking to express feelings freely, without fear of being interrupted, judged, or

The man who removes a mountain begins by carrying away small stones.

— Chinese proverb

evaluated. They have adapted this from author and seminar leader Cliff Durfee's book *Heart Talks* (see "Resource Guide"). For many of the teens, it's the first time they have ever been listened to with respect rather than criticism. Other support groups have used a variety of props to pass around the room, such as a wand, a stick, a stuffed toy, a flower, or a hat. The skill of good listening cannot be emphasized enough in learning to resolve conflict. Most conflicts arise because people are not really listening to one another.

Be patient with everyone, but above all with yourself.

— St. Francis de Sales

4. **Give Empathy rather than Advice or Opinions:** When children or adults feel strongly about something, they need to be heard rather than advised or judged. Giving empathy is one of the most effective ways to respond to another when in conflict since it acknowledges the other person's feelings and needs. Dr. Marshall Rosenberg's empathic communication model is an excellent tool to use in a conflict resolution group (see "Empathy Each Day," pp. 12-17, for more complete information). In a recent circle of students and teachers that I worked with, I witnessed a remarkable turnaround as each person received empathy for his or her feelings and opinions instead of opposition or intellectual feedback. One student said, "It was great to hear the group repeat what they heard me say without adding their own two cents to the conversation. When I felt that I had really been heard, it was much easier to give empathy to the others when it was their turn. We probably got more accomplished today with the empathy model than we have in the previous five meetings!"

5. **Be Honest:** Take the plunge and let others know your feelings without being accusing or making

anyone else wrong. At a family meeting, a father of three teens addressed the possibility of selling the house and moving into a condominium. He started out the meeting by saying, "I am feeling confused about moving and scared that we won't be able to agree on an outcome. What I'd like to do today is to listen to everybody without making any decisions. Maybe after we have heard from everyone, a decision will 'make us.'" He set the tone by talking honestly about his feelings and concerns.

Express your feelings creatively, and all will sit up and take notice!

— Michael Melbrooks

6. **Use "I" Statements:** If someone did something that triggered a certain reaction in you, let him or her know about it by expressing your feelings rather than addressing that person's faults. A ten-year-old girl was participating in a CRC (Conflict Resolution Circle) and needed to express her anger to a ten-year-old peer. Instead of saying, "You were mean and awful to yell at me that way in front of all my friends," she said, "When I heard what you said, I felt really angry because I wanted to talk to you in private and not with all of our friends around." This approach made it much easier for her peer to respond without getting defensive.

7. **Use the Sandwich Method:** Start and end with something positive. A sixteen-year-old boy addressed his boss by acknowledging some of his positive qualities before he went on to express his feelings of frustration with the payroll policy. He ended the meeting by acknowledging his boss for being concerned enough to take the time to attend the meeting. This approach puts the problem in perspective and helps others realize that there are still some things that are going right.

Teaching children to communicate effectively in situations of conflict will help them avoid misunderstandings and prevent potential disputes. Children who can resolve conflicts in a respectful way will grow up with the capacity to teach others how to resolve conflicts nonviolently and to understand themselves more.

60

Becoming Real

**Share more of the real you with your child,
and discover a new level of intimacy together.**

Being honest and real with your child helps foster self-esteem
for you both. Here are some of the basic principles.

Five Ways to Become
More Real with Your Child

1. Be honest.
2. Be willing to learn from your child.
3. Be vulnerable and share more of your feelings.
4. Be willing to not know.
5. Share your dreams and your sorrows.

Some of our most endearing memories together stem
from those times when pomp and circumstance have been
swept aside in favor of being real. I remember being on the
beach with Julia when she was four years old. We were having a great time building sand castles and wading in the
water. The hours flew by, and when it was time to go, Julia
began to display a rare strain of resistance. She threw her
towel into the water, claimed that she had to hunt down a toy
that she hadn't even brought, and proceeded to commit
the worst of all "beach crimes" — she started to run on the
beach, sprinkling pebbles and sand over unhappy sunbathers
while I followed closely behind. I was angry and embarrassed

*All of us are human
becomings,
rather than human
beings.*

— Sky Schultz

by her behavior. She began to whine and cry, and I became more frustrated by the minute.

"You know, a lot of parents would spank their kids for this," I said, in the hopes that it would shake her up enough to get her to stop resisting. "And a lot of parents would punish their children if they acted like this. . . . Do you know what I'm going to do to you right now?" I asked loudly and with authority. "Do you have any idea what I am going to do right now this very moment?" "No" she answered with trepidation. "Well, I don't either!" I said quite honestly.

Julia was stunned and started to giggle. We both began to laugh, and as we packed up to leave, she gave me a big hug. "Thanks, Mom" she said. I knew what she meant. She was glad that I had told her the truth rather than lashing out mindlessly in anger. On the drive home, we created some new beach agreements. We were able to drive home relaxed instead of raging.

When Julia was ten years old, one morning I was unusually out of sorts. I questioned her choice of clothes, criticized her for insignificant things, and gave her a hard time for not finishing her homework. "Mom," she said, "I'm not going to let this get to me. I know this is about you and not me." I stood back, surprised for a moment, and responded, "You're right. I'm having a rough morning, and I'm glad you're speaking up for yourself." It was a candid moment of honesty for both of us. In the face of her angry mother, Julia was able to step back and recognize that the frustration I was expressing had nothing to do with her. As a parent, I was able to acknowledge her courage. It was a moment when both of us swapped rift in favor of real.

As we were finishing this book, with publisher deadlines right around the corner, the pressure was on. One day, we were on the computer together and I started to create a "mountain out of a molehill." Julia went to her room to get some relief, and I sat down and became aware of how much pressure I was feeling. When I could relax a little, I asked myself, "Why am I writing a book about self-esteem anyway,

Generally, by the time you are Real, most of your hair has been loved off, and your eyes drop out and you get loose in the joints and very shabby. But these things don't matter at all, because once you are Real, you can't be ugly, except to people who don't understand.

— Margery Williams,
The Velveteen Rabbit

when I'm being such a poopy parent right now?" The answer came to me: "So that I can learn to enjoy being a poopy parent and see the humor in it all!" I went back to the computer. I found myself typing out "The Five Stages of Poopy Parenting." I was on a roll, so I filled in the five stages with typical scenarios that parents go through in their struggle to drop the old and establish the new.

I realized that I was struggling in Stages 3 and 4 at times, so I printed up the five stages and slipped them under Julia's door, along with a note that said, "Julia, I guess we've done a poopendous job of parenting today. Read over the following five stages and check which stage you think we're in today." A half hour later, she slipped a note through her door that said, "I'd say we're struggling in Stage 4, Mom, but I sure do a-pooh-ciate your admitting it!"

Read over the Five Stages of Poopy Parenting for yourself, and determine your own "poohisition."

Nothing is as hard to do gracefully as getting down off your high horse.

— Frank Jones

The Five Stages of Poopy Parenting

Stage One: I'll never pass along to my child any of the old, stinky ideas that I was raised with!

Stage Two: Poops! I'm doing it! I'm acting out some of the same old patterns. My demands on my child are sometimes out of pooportion.

Stage Three: Whew! I've done a poopendous job of repeating some of the old patterns. It's time I get some empoohthy and support for the poohisition I am in.

Stage Four: There's impoolivement, but it's a challenge learning to poopervise without acting poope-rior. I want to relate honestly with my child and not pooperficially.

Stage Five: Poohray! I'm making some poopherb improvements. From now on, I will strive for progress, rather than poolifection.

"Letting Off Esteem" Chart

Read over the following chart of old beliefs and new beliefs, and help your child move from low esteem to full esteem while learning skills in creative conflict resolution.

From Low Esteem	To Full Esteem
1. Children should be seen and not heard, and they must always listen to adults.	1. Children need to be seen and heard again and again. When adults listen to children, children's self-esteem grows.
2. Children must be trained to behave and obey, because they are naturally unruly.	2. Children are eager to cooperate, and they need the positive influence of a strong role model.
3. Adults must appear strong and in control at all times.	3. No adult has all the answers. Sometimes vulnerability is true strength.
4. Children must be punished when they misbehave. How else will they learn?	4. Children need to be approached with honesty and love when they do something that isn't working, so that they can learn self-acceptance.
5. Children must be punished or shamed when they disobey so they learn to stop acting out.	5. To err is human. To correct children with patience and love is divine.
6. Children should follow the rules no matter what — no questions asked.	6. Children need simple logical explanations and some freedom of choice (for example, Would you rather do your work before or after lunch?).

chapter

7

Esteem Extras

Some parents and educators believe that self-esteem is a bonus — something to build in children after the basics of life are taken care of, such as housework, homework, responsibilities, and discipline. Self-esteem is an extra all right, an *essential extra!* Those who have it often *ask for the extras, go the extra mile* in life, and *take extra time* to appreciate those they love.

Chapter 7 offers ideas that will help you to act on the extras more of the time. The ideas presented will encourage you to create history out of your moments and to savor more moments out of your history.

The following poem was written after talking to hundreds of parents about what they would do differently if they could raise their children all over again. Their number one wish was to honor the old Latin phrase "Carpe diem," which means, "Seize the day."

If I Had My Child to Raise Over Again

by Diana Loomans

I had my child to raise all over again,
I'd finger paint more, and point the finger less.
I'd do less correcting, and more connecting.
I'd take my eyes off my watch, and watch with my eyes.
I would care to know less, and know to care more.
I'd take more hikes and fly more kites.
I'd stop playing serious, and seriously play.
I'd run through more fields, and gaze at more stars.
I'd do more hugging, and less tugging.
I would be firm less often, and affirm much more.
I'd build self-esteem first, and the house later.
I'd teach less about the love of power,
And more about the power of love.

Painting with Love
by Diana Loomans

I will always remember a teacher I had the good fortune to know when I was a young adult. Her name was Beverly. She was a slight woman with a big heart, a brisk walk, and a capacity to see the big picture. She had a passion for creativity and the healing power of love, and she believed that today's children were the gateway to a better tomorrow. She had a reputation for helping people to open up their hearts and tap into more of their potential. From the moment I met her, I knew that Beverly was someone who would live up to the fascinating stories I'd heard about her. When she looked at me, I had the uncanny feeling that I was being seen from the inside out. She listened to me with such attentiveness and reverence that I felt truly seen and heard. She was someone who believed that the little things really do make a difference in life, and that each person has unique gifts to contribute to the good of the whole.

One day Beverly told us about a "little extra" that she was doing with some bilingual grade school children she was teaching. She called it "Painting with Love." At the close of each class, one child was chosen to be the Student of the Day. The rest of the class would encircle the selected student and begin to dip imaginary paintbrushes into great big imaginary paint cans that were filled with golden paint. As they painted the Student of the Day (which they did by making long sweeping brush strokes about six inches from the student's body), they imagined that they were painting that student with love as the child stood with eyes closed, taking it all in. As they painted, they showered the child with words of appreciation, affirmation, and good wishes. "I like playing with you." "Thanks for being such a fun friend." "We wish you a great day." "You are a special person." "We're glad that you're in our class." Other good intentions that came to mind were shared spontaneously by students and teacher alike.

Although this activity took only five minutes, Beverly believed that it was one of the most important activities of the day. She said that for many of her students, it was their first experience receiving acknowledgment from others. But her real goal was simpler than this, and much more profound. She wanted to give her students an opportunity to experience the power of giving and receiving love in a simple, nonthreatening way. It worked! As students became familiar with the exercise, they looked forward to it, often asking as they walked into class, "Will we have time to do Painting with Love today?" Her answer was always the same: "When it comes to love, there's always enough time!"

During the semester, one of her students became ill and missed a few weeks of school. Beverly was told that the boy had leukemia and wouldn't be back to school at all. When she informed her class about Carlos, they asked if they could put him in their circle and paint him with love that day. She agreed that it would be a good idea. As they formed a circle, they imagined that Carlos was standing in the middle of the circle, and they painted him with love. When they were done, one of the students said, "Can we go to the hospital and paint him with love in person? I think he'd like that!"

One week later, a number of students traveled by bus together, heading for the hospital to visit Carlos. They brought him colorful artwork, told him stories, and painted him with love before they left. His father, a quiet widower who didn't speak much English, sat in a chair and skeptically observed. But Carlos had a different response after his friends left. He sat up feeling energized and alert, and he had one of the best evenings he'd had in weeks. Word traveled back to his classmates, and before long, there were small busloads of students going to paint Carlos with love each week. Carlos looked forward to their arrival and often watched the clock every hour on the day of their visits, asking the nurses repeatedly, "Is it 3:30 yet?" Even as his condition worsened, the nurses noticed that after the children visited, Carlos needed less pain medication and slept more soundly.

One week, some eager students arrived to find an empty bed. Carlos had gone into a coma and was in the intensive care unit. A few days later, he died. When his classmates heard the news, they put him in their circle of love and "painted" him with their affirmations, blessings, farewells, and tears for the last time. The following week, his father contacted Beverly to express his gratitude for bringing so much joy to his son's final days. "I'd like to thank you, especially for the Painting with Love," his father said in broken English. "You see, I came from a family that wasn't very expressive or affectionate, and although I thought it was silly at first, I learned a lot watching you give Carlos the special attention and kind words. In his final hours, when he was in a lot of pain, I felt helpless and asked Carlos if there was anything I could do for him. He nodded and began to make a feeble motion. I knew what he meant. He wanted me to paint him with love. I felt awkward, but I was determined to give him what he had asked for. As I began to paint him with love, I was flooded with emotion, about his death, and about my strong love for him that I knew would grow even more after his passing. As I painted Carlos with love, I was able to tell my boy I loved him for the first and last time.... How can I ever thank you?" It was a poignant moment of truth for Beverly and her students, and they realized how many ripple effects their painting with love exercise had set into motion.

A few years ago, word reached me that Beverly had died. Although I hadn't seen her in many years, I felt as though I had lost one of my best friends. She had shown me through her actions how important the little things really are. Because of the example she set, I had become a more creative teacher and parent, and a more compassionate human being. She had believed in me before I believed in myself. After she heard me speak to the class on building self-esteem in children, she once said, "You have some great ideas. Some day, they will be written in books — important books!" As I write this story, I am finishing my fifth book and starting a sixth. It's going to be dedicated to her and to the healing power of love.

61

Star Gazing

Get into the habit of gazing with wonder at your child. See him or her as if for the first time. Seize the moment to appreciate and revel in your child's uniqueness.

In Yiddish, there is a word that describes the trembling joy and awe that parents feel while beholding a child's beauty and rarity. It is called *kvelling*. The child who feels noticed and adored is a child who will grow up feeling confident and important. The child who feels like a star in the home growing up will lead others to the stars as an adult. And as a child is blessed when an adult admires him or her, so is the adult blessed, for *kvelling* will later return to the parent in the form of respect and devotion.

To gaze at a child is to gaze into the heavens of humanity.

— Maria Fuller

Some of the happiest times that Julia and I have experienced together are the times when I am *kvelling*, or really "seeing" her. Here are some of the everyday moments that can be transformed into memorable events by taking a few extra moments to notice your child's uniqueness.

Seven Ways to Star Gaze

1. **I Appreciate You:** In the morning before school, take a few extra moments to verbally appreciate your child just for being alive!

2. **I Like You:** While attending an event together, be extra affectionate. Letting your child know that

you like him or her can be as valuable as saying "I love you."

3. **I Enjoy Talking to You:** After dinner, while still at the table, take some relaxation time to sit and enjoy your child, talking about anything your child wants to talk about.
4. **I Admire You:** Before bedtime, stroke your child's hair and spend some time just admiring your child. The child who is admired is the child who feels precious and valuable.
5. **I Delight in You:** While doing errands, take the time to delight in your child's mannerisms and uniqueness. There are few things that could mean more to children than knowing someone delights in their existence.
6. **I Acknowledge Your Efforts:** While cooking, cleaning, or doing a project together, compliment your child, acknowledging your child's efforts to help you. This is the most effective way to receive more of the same behavior from your child.
7. **I See Your Uniqueness:** While relaxing together, become totally present, as if your child were the only living person on Earth. Let your child know about the unique gifts that he or she brings to others.

We find delight in the beauty and happiness of children that makes the heart too big for the body.

— Ralph Waldo Emerson

One of our friends recently experienced the death of her mother. Through her tears, she managed to say that her greatest agony was the regret that her mother had never really "seen" her. She had never experienced the nourishment of *kvelling* from her mother. The new physics teaches us that when we look at a star, we change it by the simple act of observing. Likewise, when we truly see our children, we change them by the simple act of stargazing.

62

Five Things

Sit down with your child and write down the five things you most want from each other at this point. Before reading the lists aloud to each other, guess what the five things might be on the other's list, just for fun.

The idea for "Five Things" came about one night in a restaurant after we had been having a few strained days together about getting jobs done in the house. Our intention was to go out and give each other empathy, which meant that we would take turns listening to each other, and then repeat what we heard the other person say without judgment until the other person felt satisfied and understood. It worked so well that we were able to break the spell and attain a better understanding before the main dish ever arrived. One of our teachers has often said, "We must learn to ask for what we want very specifically, to give the other person a good chance of succeeding when trying to meet our needs."

While we ate dinner, we marveled over how unaware each of us had been regarding the other person's needs. Julia, for example, had a need for less direction and more room to make mistakes and do things for herself. I had a need for her to get more done on her own, without having to check in with me every few steps along the way. Since we weren't clear on the other person's needs, we were actually "rubbing each other the wrong way" without even knowing it. We decided to play a game to further explore our current needs. We took our napkins, since they were the only paper we could find, and

Be careful about what you ask for... it just might show up!

— Yule Gettit

decided to write down the five things we most wanted from the other person, specifically. So, for example, if we wanted more attention, then we might say, "I'd like to spend more time talking together a few nights a week after dinner," or "I'd like to do something fun together once a week for a few hours," rather than simply asking for more time in general.

We each wrote down the top five desires that we would like to receive from the other person (Julia included her dad on her list), and then, for added fun, we took turns guessing what the other person had written down. Surprisingly enough, we were both able to guess most of each other's desires, but the specifics made all the difference. Here is what we wrote down.

Our life always expresses the result of our dominant thoughts.

— Søren Kierkegaard

Julia's List: What I Most Want from Dad

1. When you ask me how I am, really listen to me and what I am saying.
2. Play and wrestle with me more. Take some time to just laugh and play with me each time we visit (for fifteen to thirty minutes).
3. Talk to me about what I am doing at school once a week or so. Look at my books and my homework when I see you, and tell me when you feel excited about something I'm doing.
4. Take time to talk to me about how you feel about your dreams, fears, and life, and not just about being in school and your job.
5. Take me on a small trip (one to three days) once or twice a year so that we can be alone out in nature and explore together.

Julia's List: What I Most Want from Mom

1. Plan special projects with me once a month, like sculpting, making a video together, exploring nature, or painting.

2. Be really goofy with me more often — almost every day, even if it's only for a few minutes.
3. Talk to me about my jobs at the beginning of the week and then let me take it from there. Trust more that I will get them done.

4. Play and have fun with me at least a couple of hours a week without any interruptions, and without any other thoughts on your mind about your work or other people.
5. Ask me about my feelings a couple of times during the week about school and other things, and give me compliments whenever you can — a few each day would be great!

Diana's List: What I Most Want from Julia

1. Tell me one thing you appreciate about me each week, or more often.
2. Do your list of jobs in the spirit of cooperation each week on your own.
3. Help out in little ways a few times a week; for example, if you see garbage that needs to go out or a plant that hasn't been watered, pitch in and do it.
4. Share your important feelings and needs with me and ask for what you want from me each week.
5. Be open to trying new things that you've never done before that I invite you to experience — an unusual restaurant, a new book, a different church, a play — at least twice a month.

The results of this exercise have been quite amazing. Although making the lists by no means guarantees the outcome, the lists have given us a blueprint so that we know how to nurture and love each other more. Our five things have changed over time, but our strongest needs from each other remain quite similar. Try playing the Five Things Game with your child and open a window to a new world of caring together.

63

The Story of You

**Chronicle the story of your child's life
through photographs, stories, myth, poetry,
music, or any other form of creative expression.**

What story could fascinate a child more than the story of his or her own life? Within a few weeks after Julia's birth, I wrote a story called "The Birth of Julia Faye" that described my experience of the pregnancy and an in-depth story of her birth. It has become a ritual to read her the story each year on her birthday. Although she's heard it many times, she still listens with wide eyes and both ears open.

When she was four, I created a poster for Julia with the title *My Life So Far*. I posted various photographs along with captions beneath, all in poetry. She read it countless times, and she took it to school for her special show-and-tell day in kindergarten. A few years ago, we each wrote a fairy tale about our lives in a writing seminar that chronicled the dark and light sides of our life journey thus far — complete with swamps, dragons, castles, and magic. It was a wonderful way to appreciate our lives as stories-in-motion, rich with drama, mystery, and adventure.

We have also started a life scrapbook that commemorates various cycles in Julia's life, such as babyhood, her toddler years, early childhood, junior high years, and now teenage years. It includes special cards, photos, her artwork over the years, poems, and letters her dad and I have given her. She currently has a collage on her wall of important people and

Our attitude toward the newborn child should be one of reverence that a spiritual being has been confined within limits perceptible to us.

— Maria Montessori

places — filled with photographs of her friends, relatives, trips, and special memories to savor.

Chronicle the story of your child's life and give your child the gift of self-reflection and an appreciation for the continuity of life. Make a scrapbook, write out a script and act it out together, create a song about your child's life and sing it together, create a special myth or story, or hang a series of pictures on the wall from birth through your child's current age. Here are some other ideas families have put into practice.

The Universe is made of stories, not of atoms.

— Muriel Rukeyser

> *When a young man of eighteen went off to college, his mother gave him a special photo album—filled with photos of him at all ages that she had duplicated from the originals and gathered together in an album that he could take along as a keepsake of his childhood.*

> *A retired father wanted to give his daughter something special for her fiftieth birthday, so he pulled fifty years of photographs together and put them on video, along with a touching lyrical song that had the whole family in tears.*

Look at your whole life as one long story, trying to find a higher meaning. Begin asking yourself this question: why was I born to this particular family? What might have been the purpose for that?

— James Redfield

> *A mother of three grown children decided to share special memories and stories about each of her children on cassette tapes and present one to each child on his or her birthday. She never did deliver the tapes in person, since she died suddenly from a heart attack, but her children later came across the tapes — each labeled, "To my children with love." They were deeply touched by her thoughtfulness.*

> *A father of two children keeps a blank book in the house for each of his young daughters, slowly filling the pages with poetry, stories, fond memories, words of wisdom, and loving thoughts. Both of the girls cherish their books, handwritten by their father.*

Each child's story is a unique and precious ripple in the ocean of life. Catch a few of the waves by taking the time to creatively celebrate the story of your child's life.

64

Creative "I Love Yous"

Get creative with your expressions of love by creating custom-made "I love yous." Tell your loved ones often and specifically of the many ways you love them.

The "ordinary" way to say "I love you" to a child is simply to say, "I love you!" We discovered this quite accidentally a number of years back. As I tucked Julia into bed one night, I capped off our big hug with, "Good night, I love you." Julia responded with, "No, that's the regular way to say it. Tell me what you really love about me, Mom, and tell me a lot of things, okay?"

I began to tell her a number of things I loved about her: "I love your playful spirit. I love to hear you laugh. I love spending time with you. I love to watch you grow and learn. I love the way your hair smells. I love your thoughtfulness." The list went on for some time. Finally, she said, beaming, "And I love you for all of the ways that you love me!"

Our creativity was launched from there, and our "I love yous" continue to catch each other off guard. Sometimes we play "I love you tennis," bouncing far-fetched claims back and forth while playing catch, such as, "I love you all of the atoms in all of the galaxies," or, "I love you all of the sand on all of the beaches." Other times, we gesture our "I love yous" or say them in mime.

Here are five ideas to help you to say "I love you" more creatively.

Love is a dance that doesn't begin until you get out on the dance floor.

— Scott Kalechstein

Five Ways to Say "I Love You"

1. **Specific "I Love Yous"**: When you want to say a simple "I love you," instead tell your child something very specific that you love about him or her for a much more memorable effect.

2. **The Morning Question**: Ask your child when you wake up in the morning, "How would you like to be loved today?" You might be surprised by the answers you receive.

3. **Expressions of Love**: Read a story or poem out loud, or play a special song, and ask your child to listen very carefully to each word. When you are finished, let him or her know that the words and melody express sentiments that you feel about your child that cannot be put into words easily.

4. **Artistic "I Love Yous"**: Create your own poem, painting, story, or song in honor of your love for your child. Present it to your child at an unexpected moment.

5. **Loving Questions**: Ask yourself on a regular basis, "What is one way that I can express my love to my child that he or she would enjoy?"

While a good old-fashioned "I love you" will always warm hearts, a custom-made "I love you" will set hearts aglow.

The way is not in the sky. The way is in the heart.

— The Buddha

65

The Hobby Habit

Find a hobby of some sort that you can enjoy with your child so that you can share recreation, play, and quality time together.

A friend of ours who moved to a Polynesian island with his family a few years ago recently lost his seventeen-year-old daughter in a car accident. At the family funeral, he had beautiful seashells, gems, and stones displayed on a table for all to see and admire. He explained that when he moved to the island, it was a big adjustment for everyone. His daughter, fourteen years old at the time of the move, was particularly disturbed by all the changes.

New habits basically ask for three weeks of perseverance. After that, it becomes a new thought pattern.

— Diana Loomans

"I used to take her for long walks on the beach just to let her air all her feelings," he said. Before long, they were collecting beautiful shells and stones on the beach. This eventually led to a semiprecious gem collection. "We spent many wonderful times together sharing this hobby, and it has become a very precious memory for me now. In fact, having a hobby with my daughter was the one way I could count on spending a little quality time with her."

Here are some other ways that parents and children have developed a "hobby habit" together.

A forty-five-year-old father and his twelve-year-old son collect old steel parts from discarded utility items such as sinks, refrigerators, washing machines, and bicycles, and they make sculptures together in the garage. They recently won an award at a local fair.

A family of four collects stamps from around the world and displays them in framed cases for all to enjoy.

A fourteen-year-old-girl took a weaving class and became so enthusiastic about weaving that she was able to convince her two sisters and her mom to take up the hobby with her. Last Christmas, they presented her grandmother with a stunning wall hanging that was crafted by all four of them.

An eight-year-old boy and his uncle (his surrogate father) both love motorcycles. They have decided to completely rebuild the engine of an old Harley 45 and go on a motorcycle trip on the bike when they achieve their goal.

If your reaction to the idea of creating time for a hobby is, "You must be kidding," you may be living out an "all work, no play" life script. Ask yourself if this is what you really want to be modeling to your child. Hobbies aren't just for young children and the elderly. They add creativity, interest, and enjoyment to life, and they will help you to live in the present rather than the past or the future.

First we form habits, then they form us.

— Rob Gilbert

If you need ideas, visit a local hobby shop, and start with something easy, like paint-by-number kits, puzzles, T-shirt designs, model airplanes, photography, or ink stamp designs. If you already share a mutual interest, seize the moment more often. Developing the hobby habit will help you to transform ordinary hours into memorable hours.

66

Self-Poetry
by Julia Loomans

Discover more of your feelings, needs, and dreams by going through self-poetry exercises together.

"I am *me!* I need *to be out in nature.* I plan to *follow my dreams."* These are just a few of my answers from a self-poetry exercise. My mom has led me through this fun way to get in touch with myself several times since I was little.

We usually do self-poetry one of two ways. The first is to take turns being the reader and the responder. The reader reads each phrase out loud, and the responder says the first thing that comes to mind. Then, when the responder is finished, the roles are reversed. The second is to fill in the blanks with written words and then let the other person read them.

I love to do the self-poetry exercise. It helps me to explore myself, and I like getting the attention from my mom. Over time, we have created the following five exercises, and we've been amazed at how much they stir up. Share a self-poetry exercise with your child and discover more of your own world within.

Writing free verse is like playing tennis with the net down.

— Robert Frost

All about Me

1. I am_____.
2. I need_____.
3. I love_____.
4. I fear_____.
5. I miss_____.

6. I plan to_____.
7. I want_____.
8. I believe_____.
9. I wonder_____.
10. I know_____.
11. I really_____.
12. I question_____.
13. I will not_____.
14. I dream_____.

Appreciating You

1. I love your_____.
2. Whenever you_____.
3. What's really great_____.
4. You sure do_____.
5. Thank you for_____.
6. Sometimes when you_____.
7. I feel so_____.
8. Do you realize_____?
9. I want_____.
10. I appreciate_____.
11. At times_____.
12. I enjoy_____.
13. I like_____.
14. I'll always_____.

Poetry is the language in which man explores his own amazement.

— Christopher Fry

Make a Change

1. I can decide to_____.
2. I'd like to ask for_____.
3. I will practice_____.
4. I can change my_____.
5. I want to understand_____.
6. I can be more_____.
7. I can keep my_____.
8. I'd like to start_____.
9. I really want_____.

10. I know that I_____.
11. I can stop_____.
12. I now see_____.
13. I'm sure_____.
14. I'm going to_____.

Resolve a Conflict

1. I feel_____.
2. I'd like you to hear_____.
3. I need to_____.
4. I'm still_____.
5. I often_____.
6. I want to_____.
7. I'm ready to_____.
8. I see that_____.
9. I don't_____.
10. I just_____.
11. I wish_____.
12. I sure do_____.
13. I know that_____.
14. I understand_____.

Poetry is the spontaneous overflow of powerful feeling.

— William Wordsworth

A New Adventure

1. Let's go_____.
2. How about_____?
3. We could_____.
4. Have you ever_____?
5. Why not_____?
6. And then let's_____.
7. I'd love to_____.
8. It would be_____.
9. Let's take_____.
10. I sure would_____.
11. When we_____.
12. Someday soon_____.
13. Imagine_____.
14. I'm hoping to_____.

We all write poems; it is simply that the poets are the ones who write it in words.

— John Fowles

67

The Greetings Box

**Keep a twelve-month file box with preaddressed
birthday and holiday cards, postcards, and thank-you
notes for friends and relatives. Make a joint effort
to stay in touch with those you love.**

In Africa, certain tribes drop stones in a river and hope that
as the river carries the stones downstream, their distant
beloved friend or family member will receive the intention
that was left in the stone. Luckily, our postal system is more
direct, and we are fortunate to be able to take up a pen for
just a few moments and then mail our friendly greeting directly to our beloved's door.

*Small service
is true service.*

— William Wordsworth

A sixty-five-year-old grandmother we know has six children and twenty-six grandchildren. She sends all of them
regular birthday cards, holiday cards, and even friendly
"thinking of you" postcards. Her secret is an organized system. Once a year, usually the first week of January, she buys
her cards, stamps, and postcards, and she begins to address
them and file them by the month. Then, at the beginning of
each week, she writes personalized notes on each card to be
mailed that week and sends them off. "It is amazing how
great all the kids feel about being remembered," she says with
satisfaction. "I've learned that it's the small things more than
the big things that let others know we care."

We were inspired by her loving efficiency and decided to

create our own greetings box for the year. We've missed a few dates, but we are remembering far more than we are forgetting. And it's a great feeling to mail off small affirmations of love to those we care about. This project took only a few hours to set up, but the payoff in good feelings will last all year long.

68

Changing Family Mind-Sets

Become aware of the faulty beliefs and limited thoughts that crop up in the household, and learn to pull up the mental weeds and plant fruitful seeds together.

When patterns are broken, new worlds can emerge.

— Tuli Kupferberg

The mind is much like a garden. It will grow anything that is planted, whether it's food, flowers, or weeds! Mind-sets are actually mental weeds, and they need to be tended on a regular basis to keep the garden of the mind beautiful.

All of us have various strains of mental weeds that crop up, depending on our backgrounds and current influences. We all have some blind spots and might overlook certain weed clusters, which is why we need one another to help us compassionately sort out the flowers from the weeds.

The chart on page 237 lists some of the most common family mind-sets.

One of the greatest gifts we can model for our children is the ability to recognize and change our thoughts. Consider creating your own list of mind-sets and playfully encourage one another to pull the weeds and plant fruitful seeds. Soon, you'll have a house full of lush mental gardens like Monet's famous garden at Giverny in France.

There is nothing either good or bad, but thinking makes it so.

— William Shakespeare

Cultivating the Garden of the Mind

Old Weeds	New Seeds
1. I'm all alone, and nobody knows how I feel or what I need.	1. I can share my feelings and needs with others.
2. I can't count on anyone to come through for me.	2. I can count on me to be there for myself and to ask for help.
3. There are some secrets that should be kept in a family to protect the family name and privacy.	3. Every family needs some privacy, but secrets usually involve shame. We can learn to trust one another only by being honest.
4. Parents have all the power, and kids have none.	4. We all need a sense of power, even if our roles are different.
5. Families that do things differently from us are strange.	5. We learn by staying open-minded to other lifestyles.
6. Sarcasm is a good way to express feelings and have fun.	6. Sarcasm hurts. Honesty works better.
7. Calling names is okay when there's a fight.	7. Expressing feelings is important, but name-calling doesn't work.
8. We have to stick together. It's a rough world out there!	8. We like to feel close, but we also like to explore the world.
9. We have to learn to put up with one another — the good, the bad, and the ugly.	9. We need to be patient with one another while continuing to share ideas for improvement.
10. It's not possible to live with the same people every day and not butt heads. Everyone wants his or her own way.	10. Perfection isn't possible, but harmony is! We can get along if we respect and honor one another's needs.
11. Nobody ever listens to me. Everyone is just too preoccupied. I feel lonely in this family.	11. We all need to be heard. I will listen to others and ask them to listen to me.
12. In a family, sometimes you learn to go without so that others can get what they need.	12. In a healthy family, everyone comes into agreement on big decisions. No one plays the martyr.

69

For No Reason At All

Create "romance" in your relationship with your child by doing loving things for each other for no reason at all!

Everyone loves to get surprises, especially children, since they live in a world that is constantly teaching them something new. One of the best ways to generate "romance" in your relationship with your child (a sense of being creatively alive in your relationship together) is to do the little extras for no reason at all. I remember putting one dozen beautiful roses in a vase when Julia was seven or eight and watching her face change from surprise to delight when I told her that they were for her. "Who are they from?" she asked me curiously. "From the angels," I said. "They just wanted you to know how much they love you!" A week later, there was a letter addressed to me in crayon without a stamp that Julia had put in the mailbox. It was a note from the angels thanking me for delivering the flowers on their behalf. Here are some other ideas.

If one is to do good, it must be done in the minute particulars.

— William Blake

That best portion of a good man's life, —
His little nameless, unremembered acts
Of kindness and of love.

— William Wordsworth

A fourth grade teacher puts aside seventy-five dollars each year for her "lovable child fund!" She buys twenty-five gifts that cost about three dollars each and wraps them all. Each of her twenty-five students will receive one of the gifts during the year along with a note that says, "Just because you're so lovable!" This practice has become such a hit that her students have developed a tradition. When they spot one of the students with a present on their desk (which happens every ten days or so), they all shout in unison, "Just because you're so lovable!"

Twelve-year-old Sarah Vaugn gave her great-grandmother some gift certificates for her eightieth birthday. One of them read as follows: "This certifies that Grandma Kemper is entitled to one evening of storytelling, to be redeemed anytime, day or night, whenever she would enjoy some good, old-fashioned family storytelling." Five years later, when Sarah was seventeen, her great-grandmother had a stroke and spent an extended period of time laid up in bed. One evening, she managed to motion to Sarah to go into her wallet. Inside her wallet was a small, shriveled-up card with pink Magic Marker that read "Gift Certificate" in faded letters. It was the storytelling gift certificate! She had kept it all those years. Sarah stroked her great-grandmother's head and told her old family stories for the last time. Her great-grandmother went into a coma the next day. Sarah was touched by the fact that her great-grandmother had saved her gift certificate all these years, and she was even more grateful that she had taken the time to be thoughtful and reach out to her great-grandmother in such a small but meaningful way.

A mother of three children sends each of them a greeting card a few times a year in the mail. She includes a short poem or letter expressing her unique love for each child. "Sure, I could give it to them in person, but my kids usually get the mail each day, and most of the time there is no mail for them. This way, they can anticipate something special just for them."

Do something special and unexpected for your child today — whether she is five or sixty-five, whether he is close or far. Who knows? It could start a heartwarming new family trend for no reason at all!

> To keep a lamp burning, we have to keep putting oil in it.
> — Mother Teresa

70

Mission Esteem

**Create a Mission Esteem Statement and post
it in a high-traffic area to remind everyone
that self-esteem is on the rise in your home.**

*I celebrate myself,
and sing myself.*

— Walt Whitman

Corporations, businesses, and even schools are creating mission statements. The goal is to work together as a group to accomplish something greater than anyone could do alone. What an excellent idea for the most important organization of all — the family!

Here is a Mission Esteem Statement from a family of five.

The Mission Esteem Team

*We're a wonderful self-esteem team!
We offer a creative place for all to enjoy life,
And feel inspired by the dawning of each new day!
Since our own possibilities give us goose bumps,
We freely explore our own inner genius.*

Here is a Mission Esteem Statement that a third grade class wrote and posted in their entranceway.

Together We Grow

*Each one of us is unique and rare,
A gift to behold with tender loving care.
We take the time to notice and see*

Positive things about you and me.
We open our hearts to listen and share,
Our class is a family of friends who care.

Put your intentions into a statement and, voilà!, you will
have your Mission Esteem Statement.

Esteem Extras Chart

Read over the following chart of old beliefs and new beliefs, and help your child move from low esteem to full esteem while learning how to give and receive esteem extras.

From Low Esteem

1. Parents should do more extras with their children. It's hard to be a good parent with so much to do.

2. Most parents don't know how to do the extras. Many never got much attention, love, or nurturing themselves as children.

3. When children misbehave, they don't deserve any extra time or special attention. In fact, they should get less.

4. Most parents are not very creative or expressive. They don't know how to interact with their children.

5. The bottom line is that there just isn't time. Parents can hardly manage the essentials, much less any extras. They don't need any more pressure.

To Full Esteem

1. Parenting is an art and a skill that you are still learning. Any extras that you can do with your child are further steps toward progress rather than perfection!

2. Practice having patience and understanding for yourself. As you realize how lonely it was not to have much attention, you will find a way to give it to your child one step at a time.

3. Give your child special time consistently, not based on performance but because you want to share love and support.

4. By relaxing and showing vulnerability to your child, you become more real. Even when you are unsure, you can risk sharing your feelings or trying something new.

5. You can make time, even if a few of the essentials have to wait. You could probably use more playtime — why not make it with your child?

chapter
8

Esteem Holidays

Holidays are out-of-the-ordinary days created to commemorate a significant person, place, or event. Every culture the world over celebrates its own version of holidays, often accompanied by music, dance, celebration, or ritual.

Chapter 8 provides a wealth of ideas for creating self-made holidays that build self-esteem while offering a memorable experience for all involved. Imagine the look on a child's face when you announce, "We must keep our calendars clear next Saturday — it's Celebrating You Day!" Or consider the fun that you can have as a class or family by creating a Hometown Adventure Holiday. From laughing through a Backwards Day to dream-weaving a Treasure Mapping Holiday, this section will inspire you to set aside whole days out of the year for the purpose of pleasure, play, adventure, or learning.

The following poem, "Full Esteem Ahead," takes a new look at living a life of full esteem, not just on holidays but every day of the year.

Full Esteem Ahead!

by Diana Loomans

To feel the joy
And embrace the sorrow,
To live for today
And believe in tomorrow.

To laugh more laughter
And cry more tears,
To feel the feelings
And face the fears.

To have the strength to hold on
And the wisdom to let go,
To trust in the ebb
And move with the flow.

To have great vision
And be a dreamer by day,
To have the courage to be real
In each and every way.

To dare to rise
And to risk the fall,
To reach out to life
And connect with it all.

This is to have lived a life of full esteem.

One Hundred Strokes for You
by Diana Loomans

One evening, at the end of a long day, I took a few extra moments to sit beside Julia as she lay on her pillow. As we reminisced over the day's events, I began to stroke her hair slowly. She became tranquil and still, absorbing the attention as a plant draws in cool, refreshing water. With each gentle movement I made through her hair, I whispered an affirmation or blessing into her ear: "You are precious. You are a miracle. You are a wonderful friend. May you always be loved." Gathering thoughts from the garden of my mind, I offered a bouquet of loving intention to her as she lay hushed and motionless, with her eyes half closed. The more blessings I whispered, the more serene she became.

"Thank you for being alive. You are a blessing to your family and friends. You are a strong soul." I realized I was counting as I went along, with the intention of giving her one hundred strokes. Deep feelings of fondness and love welled within me as I watched my young teenage daughter curl up close to me and savor each stroke. My brushing strokes through her hair flowed the way an artist's brush graces a canvas with color. My whisperings became as a gentle breeze winding its sacred secrets through the sapling's dancing leaves.

This was a moment of quiet magnificence — one that perhaps only she and I and the heavens that moved between us would ever know of. But I knew that the repercussions of such an act would know no bounds. Years from now, she would stroke the hair of a daughter, niece, or grandson with her own litany of holy whisperings. In a moment of fear, she would recall that she was a strong soul and muster the strength to overcome her dark imaginings.

As I neared the last stroke, I experienced a rare moment of gratitude. I had seized a moment — ordinary in appearance — and turned it over to find its silver lining. What caused me to reach for Julia's hair and share a few treasured moments that night remained a mystery. But I knew I wanted to share more moments like this with my child before she grew up. On the one hundredth stroke, I said, "You will have many more moments like this in your life." She smiled sweetly without answering. She was fast asleep.

71

Holidays from around the World

Celebrate holidays from around the globe together for enrichment and enjoyment.

Children love holidays. What, then, could be more fascinating than joining in the celebrations of scores of holidays from around the world? Explore various holidays with your child and sharpen your cultural skills together. There are holidays every day in some part of the world. Since some celebrations fall on various dates depending on the country, you might want to pencil in selected international holidays on a family calendar, or celebrate them at your convenience. Here are a few to give you a boost on global festivities from east to west and north to south.

Each holiday around the globe is like a small light on a universal Christmas tree.

— Rebecca Everett

Global Holidays

1. **Id-Ul-Fítr:** In many Muslim countries, people fast from sunrise to sunset during the Muslim month of Ramadan. They spend their days praying in mosques (their places of worship), and they eat one large meal each night. As the fast draws to an end, they wait for the next full moon to break their fast. When the moon rises, they begin a three-day celebration known as Id-Ul-Fítr. They share a dish called Saiwiyan — thin noodles cooked with milk and coconut — and they play together for three days. On the last day of Id-Ul-Fítr, they visit relatives and family and share gifts and prayer.

2. **Tet Trung Thu:** This mid-autumn Vietnamese festival usually takes place around September 15 and is a holiday for the imagination. Children decorate soda cans and build colorful lanterns. They have a parade at night, swinging their lanterns to music and pretending to take a trip to the moon. Parents make moon cakes made of black beans and sugar, and they carve grapefruit slices into animal shapes.

3. **American Indian Day:** The purpose of American Indian Day is to honor the traditions of the many great Indian nations in the United States and to celebrate some Native American leaders, such as Cochise, Geronimo, and Chief Joseph. It is often celebrated on the second Saturday in May and includes storytelling from the great tribes as well as studying the customs of the various tribes and having a celebration feast in honor of the heritage Native Americans left for us.

4. **Diwali:** In India, Diwali is celebrated in late October and is actually a series of separate holidays all linked together. *Yama* is one of the holidays, in which brothers and sisters make promises of love and loyalty and share a special meal together. *Bali Worship Day* is the day that people tell stories about good winning over evil. Children make *dipas,* which are oil-burning lamps made out of clay saucers. One house may have up to one thousand oil lamps burning along balconies and sidewalks during the Diwali Festival Days.

5. **Shichi-Go-San:** On November 15, the Japanese celebrate the Seven-Five-Three Festival. It honors three-year-olds (who are no longer babies), five-year-olds (who are no longer toddlers), and seven-year-olds (who are growing up). They go to a Shinto shrine to express gratitude that their children have safely reached the age of three, five, or seven. They have a special party for their children and eat Chitoseame — a candy invented a thousand years ago that tastes like sugarcane and symbolizes long life.

The celebrations of the World are a reverent part of our human heritage.

— Joseph Campbell

6. **Tu B'Shvat:** A springtime holiday in Israel, it is celebrated by planting trees. Trees are an ancient and important symbol in Jewish culture, standing for all that is good, strong, and noble in life. On Tu B'Shvat, children parade down the streets with spades, hoes, and watering cans, traveling to an open field and planting trees. They decorate their homes with beautiful flowers and fresh green leaves. Everyone eats plenty of fruit — dates, raisins, figs, and pomegranates.

7. **Cinco de Mayo:** An important Mexican holiday, Cinco de Mayo is celebrated on May 5 and honors the love that the Mexican people have for their freedom and their country. Women wear skirts and flowered hats, and the men dress as soldiers who are proud of their country. There is much song and dance, and blindfolded children enjoy swinging sticks at the piñata — a clay pot filled with candy and covered with papier-mâché in the shape of an animal. When someone breaks the piñata, all the children scramble to pick up some of the candy.

8. **Songkran:** A three-day festival from April 13 to 15, Songkran is a joyous welcoming of spring and celebrates the Buddhist New Year. Children dress in costume in a parade and sprinkle scented water into the hands of their parents as a sign of respect. Family members wear their best clothes and sprinkle perfumed water on the statue of Buddha. They carry bowls of pet fish to a river and release the fish into the water, and they set birds free from cages into the blue heavens. Songkran celebrates freedom and the renewal of spring. Thai desserts include coconut and many tropical fruits.

If a child is to keep alive an inborn sense of wonder, he needs the company of at least one adult who can share it, and rediscover the joy and mystery of the world we live in.

— Rachel Carson

Begin to celebrate holidays from around the world together, and expand your fun to include interesting people and customs in faraway lands. This will give you an opportunity to bridge the global gap and try something new, too.

72

Learning Adventure Day

Share in the excitement of lifelong learning with your child. Visit museums, libraries, and bookstores; learn about different topics, or take a class together.

Author Leo Buscaglia used to go through a learning ritual each night at the supper table with his father. At the end of the meal, Leo's father would turn to each child and ask, "What did you learn today?" Leo claims that although he often had to scramble to the nearest dictionary or encyclopedia to scout for a word or fact before sitting down at the table, in the long run he felt enriched because of it.

One mother of three asks a "learning question" to her children each day, such as "What is the capital of Turkey?" Whoever comes up with the answer first gets a small reward.

Anyone who stops learning is old, whether at twenty or eighty. Anyone who keeps learning stays young.

— Henry Ford

The current generation of children is going to be absorbing more information than any previous generation. These children are growing up through the information age and the technology explosion. Their experience of learning is not limited to the classroom; instead, the whole world is becoming their classroom. Here are some ideas to help you to create learning holidays with your child.

Five Ways to Have a Learning Adventure Day

1. **Museum Adventure:** Spend a leisurely day at a nearby museum — taking in the interesting displays

and discussing feelings and reactions to what you are learning.

2. **Learning Something New:** Take a half-day computer class together, a ropes course, an astronomy class, or a sculpting workshop. A father and his two children took a one-month course together on video production that met for four consecutive Saturdays in a row. "We spent the mornings in class and the afternoons in the park practicing what we'd learned together," he said. "Now we have a goal — to win first prize on a local television show by producing the funniest home video!" Taking a class together is a great equalizer as well as an opportunity to bond.

3. **Bookstore Hopping:** Julia and I like to spend learning adventure days going bookstore hopping to new and used bookstores. We roam the aisles, read aloud together, look for unusual titles, or just wander around the store for fun. Sometimes we close our eyes and pick out a book at random. We usually end the adventure by buying a book and reading together at a local café.

4. **Library Visits:** Libraries are full of wonderful books, magazines, tapes, videos, classes, and learning opportunities. Become familiar with your local library and the enrichment programs offered. A family from Thailand who are still learning the English language take out fifteen books each bi-monthly. Even if they don't get a chance to read each book, they scan it and pick up some important cultural ideas. How many Americans are that committed to learning? If you haven't taken your child to a university campus library, treat yourselves to an informational smorgasbord. Most college libraries are loaded with resources, including children's literature.

5. **Learning Topics:** Choose a different learning topic

The illiterate of the year 2000 will not be the individual who cannot read and write, but the one who cannot learn, unlearn and relearn.

— Alvin Toffler

251

for each learning holiday, such as business, history, politics, religion, or technology. One father chooses a topic each month and records excerpts from different books onto tapes. When he's driving with his son, they listen to the tapes and have a lively discussion.

Life is a grand learning experiment, and we are the experimenters. So step into the learning lab of life with your child and share in the good chemistry of lifelong learning.

73

Backwards Day

**Choose a day to turn reality upside down.
Answer the phone with "Goodbye," get up and
put your pajamas on, have dinner for breakfast, walk
backwards, talk backwards, or reverse roles for the day.**

In the Native American tradition, certain tribe members were taught to become "contraries." Their job was to do things backwards, just to shake things up and keep tribe members on their toes. They walked, talked, danced, and rode their horses backwards, and they went about their everyday tasks doing everything from "finish to start."

Genius loves to turn reality upside down for the sheer pleasure of it.

— Diana Loomans

We have found that when we do something backwards, it stretches our thinking in ways unimaginable to the "right side up" perspective. Here are a few of our favorite backwards habits.

Twelve Ways to Have a Backwards Day

1. Read a short book from the last page to the first. Start with a children's book and progress to something more challenging.
2. Read a news article from last word to first, or from right to left (in many cases, the news became much more readable!).
3. Preview a video on rewind, or watch it backwards and guess what the plot is about.
4. Eat supper with dessert first and salad last. When the meal is over, set the table.

Age is one of those ideas which has outlived its uselessness.

— Professor Oops!

5. Write a letter to someone backwards with the signature at the top. For the more adventurous, write each word backwards.

6. Dress inside out, and see if anybody notices.

7. Make the bed backwards, and sleep at the foot of the bed.

8. Put up holiday decorations at the opposite time of the year.

9. Hang a picture upside down. Who knows — you might decide you like it better that way!

10. Walk backwards — first around the house, and then for a stroll in the neighborhood.

11. Take a view opposite from your own and hold that perspective all day in discussions and conversation (for example, the belief that all weeds should grow, and all flowers should be cut down).

12. Surprise someone on a birthday or special event by reciting a famous poem backwards.

Things don't turn up in this world until somebody turns them up.

— James Garfield

Try having a backwards day. It just may turn your life upside down in some very important ways.

74

Exploring Nature Day

Set aside a whole day to get out into nature, go exploring together, and share adventure, relaxation, and renewal.

Every child loves nature. The sounds, sights, and scents are stimulating, educational, and healing for all ages. A young man who was raised in South America near the Amazon River said, "I am still amazed by how much time American families spend indoors watching TV. If families could dig their hands in some soil, admire flowers, hug some trees, and watch some birds together, they would experience a new level of closeness." There are only three things needed to enjoy a wonderful adventure with your child in nature — the ability to look, listen, and enjoy! Here are some ideas to make your Exploring Nature Day memorable.

The clearest way into the universe is through a forest wilderness.

— John Muir

Seven Ways to Explore Nature Together

1. **Blindfolded Walk:** Form pairs and decide who will lead first and who will be blindfolded. The leader guides the partner along — being careful to watch for logs, branches, and so on. The leader can also guide the blindfolded partner to interesting objects, sounds, and smells. This exercise is a terrific way to heighten the senses.

2. **On the Ground:** The forest looks different when you see it from a brand new angle. Lie on the ground together and watch the animals, clouds,

swaying trees, and fluttering birds. Try lying motionless for a while, or cover each other's bodies with leaves, sticks, and pine needles, with only your faces exposed. This exercise offers an intimate sense of what it's like to be part of the forest.

3. **Tree Hunting:** Make a day of admiring trees of every size and shape. Sit and lean up against a tree while having lunch, hug a tree while imagining that you are koala bears, or study the tree ants as they cavort up and down the trees in dutiful mission. For the more adventurous, listen to the heartbeat of a tree. The best time to listen is in the early spring, when the trees send surges of sap up through their branches. Choose a tree with thin bark, such as a deciduous tree, and press a stethoscope firmly against the trunk. The sound and rhythm will show children that a tree truly is a living creature.

4. **Silent Pioneers:** Walk in total silence, taking in the beauty with all of your senses. Choose a leader and a follower, if you'd like, and take the time to stop, sit, climb a tree, or explore a more secluded area.

5. **Scavenger Hunting:** Create a list of things for your child to find on your outing, such as a leaf, a flat rock, a feather, something sharp, something square, something artificial, a seed, or a colorful object. The search for the objects on the list keeps the energy level high.

6. **Still Hunting:** Native Americans used to enjoy "still hunting." They would go to a familiar, comfortable place, sit down, and settle into a watchful mood. Their only desire was to observe and to learn. When you decide to "still hunt" with your child, let your quiet place find you. Be as unobtrusive as you can. Julia once curled up in a ball for a full hour near a swan pond imagining that she was a swan. She didn't budge an inch, and within half

When you appreciate the beauty and uniqueness of things, you receive energy.

— James Redfield

an hour, swans were sitting just a few feet from her, treating her as part of the scenery.

7. **Walking Under the Stars:** Share a stroll through a forest or your own neighborhood, gazing at the wonder of stars strewn across the sky. Find an inviting spot and lie on a blanket as you watch the nighttime show of lights.

Use your imagination as well as your senses on your nature adventure, and turn over a whole new leaf together!

75

Celebrating You Day

Devote an entire day from sunup until sundown pampering someone important with attention and small surprises, doing some of the things he or she loves to do.

A young boy of six was rolled out of bed at eight o'clock on a Saturday morning by his mother. "Wake up, Todd," she whispered. "It's Celebrating You Day today." He leaped out of bed with excitement, knowing it was his day to be pampered, surprised, and treated like a king. His two sisters had a special breakfast prepared for him in the kitchen, and they were scurrying around in preparation for some kind of adventure. As he ate his breakfast, his mom sat down at the table with him and read one of his favorite stories to him. He couldn't wait to see what the rest of the day would bring. Celebrating You Day has become a ritual in his household. Each year, three of the four family members plan a surprise day for the fourth person, who will be treated like royalty all day long. It was now a yearly ritual with his family, and everybody got a turn at some point during the year.

Everybody has to be somebody to somebody to be anybody.

— Malcolm S. Forbes

They spent the rest of the day together doing several of Todd's favorite things — playing Frisbee in the park, going to watch polo races, and playing a game of his choice together after having one of his favorite meals. Before bed, his mom and two sisters read him short poems they had written to him, expressing their love and appreciation for him. He fell asleep that night feeling important, special, and very much loved.

A Celebrating You Day is intended to let someone know just how special he or she is in your life here and now, and not at some point down the road "for a reason," such as a birthday, graduation, or holiday. Here are a few suggestions to help you create wonderful memories for someone you love.

Five Ways to Create an Unforgettable Day

1. **Treasure Hunts:** Everyone loves treasure hunts. Why not create a Celebrating You Treasure Hunt? A friend of mine once created an outdoor treasure hunt for me. Each cue card that I found had a verse from a poem that he had written to me, along with a clue for finding the next card. At the end of the hunt, I pieced an entire poem together, along with the final verse. It was one of the most wonderful things anyone has ever done for me. After that, I began to create treasure hunts for Julia at different stages in her life. It has become a great memory for both of us, and something that both of us will do again in the future.

2. **Wonderful Friend Day:** Plan a whole day with a special friend and shower him or her with adventure, small surprises, affirmations, and small testimonies of appreciation. Plan ahead, and ask your friend to block out a day from his or her calendar for a surprise.

3. **Ritual Day:** A Native American friend of ours took us on a Celebrating You Adventure Day to his favorite nature spot in the area. He read us prayers from some books, took us through an Indian Medicine Wheel, and taught us how to pick sage (a plant growing out in the wild that is often dried and burned as incense in Native American ceremonies). He took us to his "power spot" — a gorgeous area at the top of a bluff with a panoramic view — and ended the day by cooking

Always try to do something for the other fellow and you will be agreeably surprised how things come your way.

— Claude Bristol

us a wonderful Indian dinner. He does this periodically with friends to honor them and thank them for their friendship. It was a very adventurous and touching day for all of us.

4. **It's Your Choice Day:** A friend's way of creating a great Celebrating You Day for her kids is to say, "We've got the whole day — let's play your way!" The child for the day can then dictate what is done and when, for the entire day. "My kids enjoy their Celebrating You Day even more than their own birthday," she said with a grin. "When else will they have a chance to get their parents to do whatever it is they want to do, like playing catch for two hours in a row, or eating lunch in a treetop while playing Robinson Crusoe!"

5. **Happy, Happy, Happy Birthday All Week Long:** Make a significant other's birthday last a whole day, or even a whole week, rather than starting and ending with the birthday cake. One family celebrates a "birthday weekend" whenever someone in the family is one year older. For the entire weekend, the birthday baby is the star of the house and doesn't have to lift a finger. Each family member spends some special time with him or her, and small gifts are hidden around the house for the house celebrity to find.

He who does good to another does good also to himself.

— Seneca

There are many ways to spend a day celebrating someone you love. Do something unexpected, use your imagination, and act on that impulse that you've had for years. You'll be glad you did.

76

Animal Adventure Day

Take a day to celebrate animals together: Go to a pet store, the zoo, or the humane society, or read some books together on the wonders of the animal kingdom.

When Julia was two years old, she said, "I want to be an animal when I grow up — they have a lot more fun than grown-ups!" Although her remark generated much laughter at the time, there was a grain of truth in her comment. Animals are spontaneous, playful, fascinating, and full of life. Children of all ages love animals. Since animals bring so much enjoyment to life and teach so much, why not create a few Animal Adventure Days each season or in a year's time with your child? Here are a few ideas to help you learn more about animals with your child.

Watch a baby the first time he sees an animal — total delight, recognition, almost a look of I know you, we are the same.

— Polly Berrien Berends

Animal Ideas

1. **Animal Visits:** If you have a pet, such as a dog, take the dog along on a special one-day trip or hike, or take the dog on a visit to a school or a retirement home with your child. If you don't have a pet, consider borrowing one for a day and going on a long walk or to the park with your child. It's a nice way to have a trial run without all the responsibilities.

2. **Animal Adventures:** To experience a variety of animals, visit your local humane society, a large pet store, or, if you live near a large city, spend a day at the zoo together taking in all the sights and sounds.

Horseback riding can be a wonderful adventure for a day. If your child is very young, start with going to visit and pet horses at a nearby ranch.

3. **Animal Behavior Education:** To learn more about animals, watch specials on public television stations, take out educational videos, or go to the library and read some books together on animals.

4. **Animal Trivia:** A father-son team plays animal trivia games on their once-a-month Animal Adventure Day. Here are a few fun animal facts to help you get started in sharing unusual animal facts together.

Nine Fun Animal Facts

- The blue whale is the biggest animal in the world, weighing 150 tons and measuring 100 feet in length!
- The tallest animal in the world is the giraffe, at 20 feet in height.
- The smallest animals are protozoans — 5,000 in a group measure only $1/_2$ inch in diameter.
- The longest-lived animal in the world is the giant tortoise, who lives to be 200 years old.
- The slowest animal in the world is the three-toed sloth. It travels only 100 yards in an hour.
- The largest bird in the world is the ostrich. It's 8 feet tall and weighs 330 pounds.
- The longest snake in the world is a water boa. It lives in South America and is 36 feet long.
- The animal with the largest nose is the elephant, whose trunk is 6.5 feet long.
- The smartest animal in the world is the chimpanzee, who is capable of learning up to 1,000 words in sign language.

Share in the joy of the animal kingdom with your child, and celebrate the wonders of all creatures great and small.

77

Career Visits Holiday
by Julia Loomans

Take your child on a career visit to your place of work, or to a workplace that's of interest to your child, for fun and enrichment.

When I was in grade school, my dad was a medical student. We grew up studying together and quizzing each other on upcoming exams. When he was working on his cadaver, he would come to life as he described the skeletal bones, the size and shape of various organs, and the delicacy of the veins and arteries. "Take me along," I would beg. "I want to see what I look like inside!" One day, he took me along for the whole day. I sat in on all of his classes, ate lunch with the medical students, and, at the end of the day, spent some time in the dissecting room with my dad and his cadaver. It was an amazing experience that I will never forget. I was too young to be squeamish over the whole experience, and my memories of my day at the Medical College of Wisconsin are still vivid.

He who loves his craft is an artist of being.

— Krishnamurti

When my mom was teaching college courses, she used to bring me along once in a while and let me sit in the back of the room, coloring. She wanted me to know what she did with all those big adults, and I remember feeling excited to be a part of a college class at nine years old. A few years later, she was preparing a speech for a school convention, rehearsing a scene from *The Velveteen Rabbit*. "Can I do the scene with you?" I asked, since *The Velveteen Rabbit* was one of my favorite stories. I got the star role as the rabbit, and my mom played a character called the Skin Horse. It was my first time on a big stage in front of an audience, and I loved it! I realized that I never would have had the opportunity to go to my mom or dad's places of work if I hadn't asked.

Since then, I have gone on other career visits with some family friends. I've been to a kindergarten class, a hospital, a bookstore, and a day-care center for a day. Now that I'm in high school, I'd like to make some other career visits, just to experience what they're like. I'd like to spend a day on a Hollywood set and a day at a shelter for the homeless. I'd like to spend a night in the kitchen of my friend's large restaurant and sit in on a disc jockey's shift and watch her at work. There are so many things I want to experience before I grow up, just to get a sense of a job that I might not otherwise know about.

Take your child on career visits — to your place of work or to workplaces of interest to your child. One of my friends has never been to her dad's place of work. She doesn't really even understand what he does, even though he's a very talented engineer. Both of them have been missing an opportunity to get to know more about each other. I encouraged her to ask him if she could spend part of a day with him at his job to find out more about what he does forty hours a week. He was flattered when she asked and said yes. It's amazing what you can learn when you ask for what you want.

Just as there are no little people or unimportant lives, there is no insignificant work.

— Elena Bonner

78

Hometown Adventure Holiday

**Take a whole day to enjoy your hometown —
tour the streets, visit some landmarks, or get more
acquainted with your own neighborhood.**

You don't have to travel a great distance to have an adventure
with your child. Just find some activities to do together right
in your own hometown. Here are a few ideas to help you to
start getting to know your own neck of the woods better.

Four Ways to Have a Hometown Adventure

1. **Six-Hour Adventures:** We learned about this
    well-kept secret by watching a family of four who
    moved to a Midwestern city from France. Once a
    month, they would pack lunches and take off for
    a six-hour Hometown Adventure. They spent their
    mornings picking a section of town they weren't fa-
    miliar with and walking the streets together. They
    discovered cafés, art studios, novelty shops, small
    parks, unusual architecture, and businesses of every
    kind. "If you really want to become acquainted
    with your own city, travel by foot," they advised.

2. **Landmark Adventure:** In the afternoons, after hav-
    ing their lunch in a nice outdoor setting, they went
    to a landmark of their choice — city hall, the fire
    or police station, the central library or museum, or
    some historical building, such as the courthouse,

*There will always be a
frontier where there
is an open mind and
a willing hand.*

— Charles Kettering

university, theater, or some churches. "In just one year, after having twelve hometown adventure days, we probably know our city better than most of the locals," said the fifteen-year-old son.

3. **Neighborhood Projects:** Another way to become more familiar with your own hometown is to get to know your own neighborhood better. A family from Israel who moved to Northern California was amazed by the isolation they experienced when they moved into their San Francisco neighborhood. They had lived in a kibbutz, where they experienced a strong sense of community in every sense of the word. "When we moved here," said the father, "it was culture shock! People nodded and smiled with a brief hello coming and going, and then disappeared into their own dwelling, and we wouldn't see them again for days at a time. One night, my wife suggested that if the mountain wasn't going to come to Muhammad, then Muhammad must go to the mountain. It was at that point that we realized we had a gift to bring to our neighbors — the gift of community!" Over the next few months, the family organized a block party, a neighborhood yard sale, and an open house brunch. It was a big success. People became friends, and the connections snowballed. A small baby-sitting co-op began in the neighborhood, as well as a family neighborhood cleanup event that took place at the beginning of each season on a Saturday morning.

4. **Neighborhood Activities:** If you don't know your neighbors well, create a sense of community by reaching out to those who live near you. Set up an active neighborhood watch program, help organize a neighborhood social event, or host a family night, including seniors and non-parents. Start a

There's no hometown like my hometown.

— Shirley Wilder

parenting support group, join a neighborhood bartering group, or help establish a neighborhood association. Small families or single-parent families can weave an extended family by reaching out to others in a similar situation and by finding surrogates in the neighborhood.

Put aside a day to enjoy your neighborhood and hometown with your child and gain a greater sense of pride and caring for your own community.

79

Treasure Mapping Holiday

Create a visual collage that includes pictures, photographs, and positive phrases, mapping your way toward a treasured goal or dream.

The Chinese knew the impact that visual images can have on the mind when they created the proverb "A picture is worth a thousand words." A treasure map is a collage of magazine pictures, photographs, news headlines, positive phrases, or trigger words that stir the imagination and create a visual image of one's journey from vision to reality. Here are some ways others have put treasure mapping to creative use.

To treasure map is to map your way to your greatest treasures!

— Carlos Hegen

Five Ways to Use Treasure Mapping

1. **Yearly Goals:** A friend holds an Annual Treasure Mapping Holiday on January 1 of each year. Twenty or more people of all ages arrive with stacks of magazines, glue, a pair of scissors, poster board, and a list of goals and dreams for the following year. In the next few hours, clippings, phrases, images, laughter, and dreams are exchanged, and everyone shares a few tidbits from their treasure mapping masterpieces. Most are later placed in a good spot where they can be seen each day. During the year, stories trickle in on how the treasure map pictures are becoming a reality — one dream at a time.

2. **Dream Come True Adventure:** A sixth grade science class in California had a dream — to spend a whole week in Yosemite National Park. They created a large five foot by eight foot treasure map at the beginning of the year with photos of Yosemite and phrases posted all over, such as "A good time was had by all," and the headline "Brilliant science team brings awe to the world all over again!" By April of the same year, over three-quarters of the class was getting on the bus for a week in one of America's treasured parks — Yosemite!

3. **Vacation Goals:** A Persian family set aside a Treasure Mapping Day to create their vacation goals over the next five years. They included some national trips, such as Oregon, the Rockies, and the Grand Canyon, as well as a few international trips, such as Egypt, southern France, and Russia. They included family photographs, pictures of each place, and trigger words such as "A fabulous tour!" They now have a poster filled with fun vacations to look forward to.

4. **Healing Treasure Map:** After a forty-eight-year-old mother of three was in a serious car accident, her healing process included a three-month stay at a physical rehabilitation center. Her children made a treasure map for her that was filled with photos of women biking, gardening, walking, and dancing — the four things that she loved to do most. Phrases such as "Every day I feel better and better" were posted all over the large poster board. They posted it right across from her bed, and in exactly nine-and-a-half weeks, she was ready to go home, feeling determined and grateful to be alive.

5. **From Vision to Reality:** A high school boy who loved to bike had a dream. He wanted to bike across the country when he graduated from high

The big thing is to know what you want.

— Earl Nightingale

If you don't know
where you are going,
how can you get there?

— Basil Walsh

school and before he started college. He made a treasure map — posting pictures of the kind of equipment he wanted, along with beautiful nature scenes from all over the country. Six months later, he was on his way.

Begin collecting pictures, magazines, and fun phrases with your child, and set up a Treasure Mapping Holiday together. The results are sure to surprise you.

80

Be Here Now Holiday

Put aside a day, or a whole weekend, and plan to do absolutely nothing. Just be with your child in the here and now, and see what shows up.

A young man approached a master swordsmith and said, "How long would it take me to become an expert swordsmith like you if I start taking lessons three times a week now?" "Ten years," replied the teacher. "Well, what if I practice day and night, each day, for a whole year?" "In that case, it would take you twenty years!" was the master swordsmith's reply.

Teaching our children the art of relaxation and "doing nothing" is as valuable as teaching them to set goals, discipline themselves, or achieve success. Rest and repose recharge us so that we can go back to our day-to-day lives with added zest and vigor. Relaxation gives us a chance to sit back and look at our achievements, appreciate what we have in our lives, and listen to the "call of the wild" within us.

The way to do is to be.

— Lao-tzu

A Hawaiian family of four decided to spend a ten-day vacation in the Swiss Alps, to experience a whole different climate and to get in some skiing and snowmobiling. But instead, they found themselves trapped in their cabin due to the heavy snowstorms that arrived the same day they did. "We didn't have much to do, so we built fires, sang songs, and I told my children adventure stories, mostly fictional, to fill the time. We took naps together, talked a lot, played and wrestled, and tried to keep one another warm," the father told me. "At the end of ten days, we hadn't had a chance to leave the cabin at all, and skiing was out of the question. I apologized to my family and expressed my regret, when my youngest son of five piped in with, 'Dad, this was the greatest vacation ever! I never got to do nothing with everybody for this long before. Let's do it again next year!' I was amazed, but the whole family said they felt closer and that it hadn't been such an ill fortune after all. It caused me to rethink the idea of relaxation and taking a day off entirely."

Consider creating a Be Here Now Holiday for a day or even for a whole weekend with your child. Rather than making plans, plan to do absolutely nothing and see what shows up. If anyone asks you what time it is during your Be Here Now Holiday, just answer with, "Here and now." Do what comes naturally — play for as long as you like, take a rest midday without guilt if you feel like it, or act goofy. Young kids under five spend most of their time in the here and now — not worried about what happened yesterday, not concerned about tomorrow, but instead just taking it one step at a time, absorbing everything in their environment like a sponge — moment after moment. Researchers have concluded that children under five learn more than any other segment of the population. In fact, they learn so much more than most adults that it has been theorized that if children would continue to learn at the same pace as they grew up, they would all be actualized geniuses by the time they became adults. Maybe it's their genuine ability to stay in the moment that qualifies them as genius learners.

Planning a day to do absolutely nothing with your child may sound like an oxymoron, a ridiculous notion, or an impossible dream, but it's happening somewhere every day. If you need a little practice on how to go about the task of

Each second we live is a new and unique moment of the universe — a moment that never was before and will never be again.

— Pablo Casals

"no-task," if you've forgotten how to stop thinking about all there is to think about, or if you are longing to see a tree once again as though for the first time, enlist the help of your own child, or sentence yourself to a few hours of kindergarten playground duties — and dutifully watch all of the creative geniuses at play — busy at the task of doing absolutely nothing.

Esteem Holidays Chart

Read over the following chart of old beliefs and new beliefs, and help your child move from low esteem to full esteem while celebrating esteem holidays with you.

From Low Esteem	To Full Esteem
1. Holidays are demanding and stressful and take a lot of time.	1. Holidays are meant to be retreats from everyday life, a chance to renew relationships and relax.
2. Holidays never turn out well. The expectations are too high, and there is usually a crash that follows.	2. True holidays aren't so much about expectations but instead about fun and adventure.
3. It takes too much work to orchestrate any kind of holiday. When parents get a day off, they just want to collapse.	3. Create frequent mini-holidays to avoid a sense of burnout. Learn to see holidays as playful, rather than pressure filled.
4. Holidays can be expensive. Planning an outing or going on an adventure tends to mean spending money.	4. Fun holidays have more to do with expressing creativity than with spending money. Nature, games, laughter, and enjoying one another don't cost a thing, but will certainly "collect interest"!
5. Holidays aren't worth all the trouble.	5. You can enjoy holidays and look forward to them all — traditional, global, and self-created holidays. They can remind you to enjoy life.

chapter

9

Global Esteem

Global esteem is one of the most important qualities that adults can instill in their children today. The global child of tomorrow will be considered a citizen of the planet rather than a citizen of any particular
country or nation; he or she will manifest a deep love for the health and
well-being of the entire world.

Chapter 9 offers a number of ideas to help adults and children to
develop more global esteem each day. Practicing ecology at home,
school, and work and protecting the last great places on Earth will help
to increase planetary responsibility. Preparing for the future, becoming
aware of the wonders of creation, and celebrating cultural differences
will increase global awareness. Learning to find what's going right in the
world, being of service to others, and devoting five minutes a day
to world peace will help children and adults to become new world
thinkers who know how to focus on solutions rather than on problems.

The following poem, "You Are a Lovable Little Planet," reminds us
to love and appreciate the most amazing and diverse planet this side of
the Milky Way galaxy, our precious planet Earth.

You Are a Lovable Little Planet

by Diana Loomans

When my child was very young,
we loved to end our evening prayers
by hugging a round pillow of Earth,
and blessing our wondrous home planet.
One night, she whispered alone in the dark,
"Don't worry, it's not your fault.
It will be okay... you are so lovable!"
I peeked in her room and asked, "Who are you talking to?"
"I'm pretending to be God,
talking to my little planet," she said softly.
"Oh," I mustered, and silently closed the door.
At that moment, I saw the truth in my young child's words.
Earth was a lovable child of the Universe.
How many humans were taking the time to appreciate
this delicate blue marble spinning through space?
Soon after, I hung up a picture of Earth taken from space.
Whenever I gaze at it, I whisper in contrition,
"You are such a lovable little planet,"
and I think of astronaut James Irwin's words:
"The earth reminded us of a Christmas tree ornament,
hanging in the blackness of space.
Seeing this has to change a man,
has to make a man appreciate the creation of God,
and the love of God!"

Teachers of Peace
by Diana Loomans

I will never forget the morning of my eleventh year of life. It was my birthday, and my mom and I got up very early to go to the Audubon Center, one of our favorite natural wilderness preserves. The morning air was crisp and cool, and the sun was a rising blaze of color as we headed towards the woods. We had decided to usher in my new year in the forest while it was still early and quiet.

We hiked for quite a while up a long winding path amidst the crunching fall leaves, until we came to a clearing in the woods that seemed like the place to become still for a while. We sat down on a couple of large tree stumps and relaxed into the woods. As I absorbed the sights and sounds all around me, my mom suggested that I close my eyes and ask one of the birthday questions: What am I here to learn? I listened to the wind blowing through the tree branches and waited for an answer to come to me. The word *love* came to mind. I was here to learn more about how to love — this was my answer.

After a while, my mom suggested that I ask the second birthday question: What am I here to teach? I sat still for a long time listening to some blue jays singing in the oaks, until I began to feel very peaceful. I wished that everyone could have the gift of this peaceful feeling. I realized that I was here to teach people how to have more peace.

I slowly opened my eyes and, to my great surprise, there was a family of three deer standing within fifty feet of us. For a long time, all of us just watched one another with awe. I looked closely at the beauty of their dark eyes and marveled at their proud stance. I never realized what beautiful creatures they were before. I wondered if they were thinking the same thing about us!

My mom and I joined hands to silently share our delight that the deer had come to join us on my special morning. After what seemed like a long time, I began to hum a song quietly. My mom joined in, and we began to serenade the deer. They seemed entranced by our melody. The two grown deer perked up their ears, and the baby walked a few steps closer to us. We sang song after song for a good twenty minutes or more, as they stood motionless, taking it all in.

When we finally parted ways, I felt changed somehow. We had given the deer the joy of our song, and they had touched us with the beauty of their innocence. I wondered when we would see them again, and I realized that they had appeared at the moment that I had recognized myself as a bringer of peace. I didn't really understand what this meant, but I knew that I would find out over time. I saw that, like the deer, I needed to keep my innocence alive. I made a promise to myself that day to become more like the deer — to tread softly on the Earth, to notice the living creatures around me, to harm no one, and to stop to hear the songs along the way.

I went back home and had a birthday party that afternoon with all my friends. After the festivities were over, I described my day in my diary. "Dear Diary," I wrote. "Today was a super great birthday! I had a fun party and got a lot of neat presents. But the best gift of all wasn't even wrapped — it was meeting my deer friends in the woods, who taught me about what it means to be a teacher of peace."

81

Celebrating Cultural Differences

**Take cultural mini-tours of our global village
with your child by learning about the languages,
customs, and beliefs of people around the world.**

Welcome to the global village that we call home. Each hour, four thousand new human beings are born. If we could stand in a circle with hands joined, we would encircle the planet 153 times. If the world were a village of one thousand people, it would include:

We must acquaint ourselves with the best that has been known and said in all of the world.

— Matthew Arnold

- 584 Asians,
- 124 Africans,
- 95 Europeans,
- 84 Latin Americans,
- 55 Russians and other former Soviets,
- 52 North Americans,
- 6 Australians and New Zealanders.

In this village of one thousand, there would be:

- 329 Christians,
- 178 Muslims,
- 167 "Non-religious,"
- 132 Hindus,
- 60 Buddhists,
- 45 Atheists,
- 3 Jews,
- 86 all other religions.

And among these one thousand villagers:

- 360 are less than 15 years old.
- 60 are more than 65 years old.
- 200 have a radio.
- 50 have a car.
- 70 have a television set.
- 600 do not have clean drinking water near their dwelling place.
- 250 are undernourished.
- 80 are unemployed.

There are approximately five thousand languages spoken across the globe. We speak in different tongues, but all of us have a need to communicate with one another in our own way. Here are a few examples of languages from around the world. Why not incorporate words from other languages into your everyday conversations with your child?

Make our earthly ball a peopled garden.

— Goethe

Welcome

Willkommen (will-cah-mun) — German
Bienvenidos (byen-veh-nee-dos) — Spanish
Karibu (keh-ree-buh) — Swahili

I Love You

Je t'aime (jha-tum) — French
Ik houd van je (ik-hood-von-ya) — Dutch
Ich liebe dich (ik-leeb-diks) — German
Nini kupenda (nana-kuh-puhnda) — Swahili

Peace

Shalom (shah-lowm) — Hebrew
Paz (pahs) — Spanish
IIri'ni (ah-reen-nee) — Greek

Good-bye

Adios (ah-de-ohs) — Spanish
Adieu (ah-dyur) — French
Ciao (che-ow) — Italian

There are thousands of different gestures around the world to explore and enjoy with your child.

What sunshine is to flowers, smiles are to humanity. They are but trifles, to be sure; but, scattered along life's pathway, the good they do is inconceivable.

— Joseph Addison

Greetings

- *India:* Placing hands in a praying position about chest high, and making a slight bow.
- *Polynesia:* Embracing, followed by rubbing one another's backs in a circle.
- *Eskimos:* Rubbing noses together.
- *South America:* Shaking hands, and then giving each other a hearty clap on the back.

Farewells

- *Italy:* Turning one's hand toward oneself and making a gesture that looks like "Come here!" in America.
- *Africa:* Touching palms together and looking into each other's eyes for about ten seconds.
- *Japan:* Standing facing someone and bowing together.

There are thousands of interesting customs to explore with your child from around the world. For example, the Koreans, Chinese, and Japanese eat with chopsticks. In Thailand, it's a tradition to light up an entire room with candles to celebrate a birthday. Africans in Nigeria use a "talking drum" to send messages to others at a distance. In Malaysia, people live in houses that are elevated on stilts to accommodate the rain.

Read books together on customs and beliefs around the world, try out some of the new ideas and practices together with an open mind, and bring more of the global village into your own home.

82

What's Going Right in the World?

Instill a sense of hope by tuning into the good news that's happening on the local, national, and international scenes. Talk about it with your child and post a good news bulletin board for all to read.

When the Indigenous Peoples of the World held their first world conference in Brazil in June 1992, cultural and tribal leaders from all corners of the Earth gathered to create an international message of hope for the world.

You can spread a message of hope for the world in a small corner of your own dwelling place by posting a "What's Going Right in the World" bulletin board for all to read. Post any newspaper, magazine, or newsletter clippings that are uplifting or positive. Include local, national, and global events, and keep circulating good news. Here are a few excerpts from our good news bulletin board.

> *The White House has issued a strong executive order to increase federal purchasing of recycled paper. The action was a victory for over eighty environmental and consumer organizations, along with city and state governments who worked hard to reverse the industry trend.*

> *On the anniversary of the 1992 Los Angeles riots, a "gang summit" took place in Kansas City. Two hundred gang leaders from twenty cities spent four days together at the National Urban Peace and Justice Summit, discussing ways to extend a nationwide gang truce movement.*

When we look for the best in the world, we find it in ourselves.

— Irish proverb

A local philanthropist has recently allocated money to open a rooming house in Dallas, Texas for people with AIDS, feeding, nursing, and caring for them, without charging rent.

We recently included an added feature on our good news bulletin board — a good news to come area, listing good news headlines that we look forward to reading in the papers in the future. Here are just a few of them.

- International Olympics for Peace Gets Record-Breaking Attendance from 170 Countries.
- World Hunger — Now Just a Memory of the Past.
- United Nations Holds International Celebration for Monumental Progress toward World Peace.
- Special News Report: Recent International Study Finds That Every Child Born Now Is a Wanted Child.
- United States Military Funds Now Completely Obsolete: Funding Redirected to International Peace Negotiations.
- Rain Forests Thrive as Countries the World over Protect These Precious Areas.
- City Gangs Gather to Plant More Trees and Tend City Gardens.
- More People Found Dancing in the Streets without Reason in Large Metropolitan Cities in the United States.
- Universal Language Continues to Grow as Cultures Communicate Together across the Globe.
- Millions of Guns Donated to Museum's Ancient Weapons Floor.

We are what and where we are because we have first imagined it.

— Donald Curtis

A recent study indicated that up to 95 percent of all news reported in the media has a slant on the negative. Reverse this trend with your child by posting a good news bulletin board, and by staying up on positive trends and talking about them together. Consider sending postcards to media stations and newspapers, thanking them for the uplifting news they cover and encouraging them to include more news that instills hope for a better tomorrow.

83

Special Service Day

Reach out and touch a person, the community, the nation, or the world, and share in the joy of service with your child.

Half a century ago, drummers of Gabon, Africa, spread the news from village to village: "Oganga — the White Fetish-man has come among us." They were referring to Albert Schweitzer, a musician, physician, healer, builder, and peacemaker, who gave more than fifty years of his life in service to the African people. His hospital in Lambaréné was an island of peace, where people of different nationalities, races, and backgrounds lived in harmony with one another and with nature. He was a man of great stature who devoted his life to helping others. When he died, the drums of Gabon echoed again, with the drummers tolling the dirge "Papa Pour Nous is dead." His compassion, his plea for international peace, and his spirit of service set him apart from common humanity.

We exist to work and enjoy and to stir others to work and enjoyment.

— Goethe

Albert Schweitzer said, "The only ones around you who will be really happy are those who will have sought and found how to serve." If we want our children to learn to love, we must teach them how to serve family and friends, the community, and the world. Here are a few suggestions to help you to create a Special Service Day with your child.

Four Ways to Be of Service to Others

1. **Create a Reputation as a Family for Service and Help Others:** Become a block parent, put a

Neighborhood Watch sign in the window, and make your home a safe, friendly place where your child will want to bring friends. Reach out to help people in distress, and show your child that being of service to others is natural and rewarding.

2. **Be of Service in the Neighborhood:** A young man moved into a neighborhood that was rather removed and unfriendly. He decided to smile and be friendly to everyone he met and to help out in any small way that he could. He helped neighbors carry their groceries on occasion, talked with children, and petted dogs. Since he loved to cook, he would sometimes share part of his meal with one of his busy neighbors. "The whole neighborhood changed after Kyle moved here," said an elderly man who had lived there for over twenty-five years. "It's amazing what one friendly face can do!"

3. **Reach Out to Your Community:** A couple started a homeless project in San Diego that now involves over one hundred volunteer families, offering meals to the homeless seven nights a week. A mother and her two children began to take their pet rabbit to visit a local children's hospital once a month. She considers it one of the more important things she does with her children.

4. **Join Some National or Global Organizations That Support Causes You Believe In:** A father-son team joined the Sierra Club, and, as a result, they have planted trees together, cleaned up one of the large state park areas after a fire, and gone on several wilderness outreach weekends. A mother and her ten-year-old daughter joined a group called the Earth Foundation, which helps to empower Third World countries with food, health supplies, and other outreach programs. "This organization has changed our lives for the better," the mother said.

Sow much, reap much; sow little, reap little.

— Chinese proverb

"My husband died a year ago, and being involved in this group has revived my spirits and helped my daughter to move forward after her dad's death."

Reach out together and touch somebody's hand, and teach your child that it is in giving that we receive.

To love forever is to live forever.

— Henry Drummond

84

Ecology Each Day

Become stewards for the Earth by practicing home ecology, recycling, and environmental protection, and help save the Earth one day at a time.

The environment has now become a daily topic in the news around the world. The current predictions are often dire and frightening, warning us about the greenhouse effect, ozone depletion, hazardous waste, acid rain, and the overpopulation problem, to name just a few. Global warming, the burning and clearing of our rain forests, the poisoning of our air and water, cancer-causing chemicals in our food, and the extinction of living species are just a few of the major challenges that our children will contend with as they grow up. Although many families still minimize the problems that the Earth is facing right now, others take the doomsday approach and believe that it's too late to make a positive change for the better. Nothing could be farther from the truth. There are numerous things that we can teach our children to do each day to increase their sense of becoming "ecology detectors," as well as responsible, caring Earth citizens. Here are a few practical ideas to help you begin to do your part to help save the Earth one day at a time.

Never have nations of the world had so much to lose or so much to gain. Together we shall save our planet or together we shall perish in its flames.

— John F. Kennedy

1. **Home Ecology:** Our own home is the first place to teach our children to respect the precious resources of the Earth. Since we spend a great deal of time at home, it's important for us to instill a respect for

the Earth in the midst of our daily activities. Here are just a few ideas to help you to practice home ecology with your child each day.

- Use cloth napkins at the table, and use dish towels to dry glasses rather than paper.
- Ask local restaurants to wrap food to go on paper plates rather than Styrofoam, which is completely nonbiodegradable, takes up room in landfills, and is deadly to marine life.
- Use phosphate-free detergent, and avoid chlorine bleaches when possible.
- Buy energy-efficient refrigerators, or install an energy-saver switch on your current refrigerator. Keep the temperature set between 38° and 42°F in the freezer.
- Use microwaves and toaster ovens rather than the stove when possible, and put an electronic ignition system on your gas stove to conserve 40 percent of the energy. Choose electric ovens when possible.
- Shop at health food stores and food co-ops, and buy organic and fresh foods whenever possible.
- Use natural fibers for clothes and household linens instead of permanent press and no-iron materials.
- Avoid aerosol cans of all kinds.
- Flush the toilet less often, take short showers instead of baths, and turn off the water while brushing your teeth or washing your face. Check the toilet and all faucets regularly for leaks.
- Use a warm water wash and a cold rinse when you run the washing machine. Hang your clothes out to dry whenever possible.
- Run the dishwasher only when full, and select a short cycle with an air-dry option.
- Turn off all lights when not in a room, and use dimmer switches.

Man must cease attributing his problems to his environment, and learn again to exercise his will — his personal responsibility.

— Albert Schweitzer

Only the unity of all can bring the well-being of all.

— Robert Muller

- Open windows rather than using electric fans or air conditioning whenever possible, and weatherize and insulate your home to reduce heat loss during the cold months.
- Instead of toxic household cleaners, use baking soda, vinegar and soap, or mild detergent for cleaning.
- Control ants, roaches, silverfish, and termites with boric acid, bone meal, or silica aerogel. Control fleas with powdered borax.

2. **Recycling:** Children need to understand that there is no such thing as "throwing something away," since garbage remains with us long after it leaves our local garbage cans. According to the United Nations Environment Programme, each person in the United States generates nearly a ton of trash every year. Here are a few recycling basics to become familiar with together.

- Avoid all disposable items, such as disposable cameras, lighters, diapers, and razors.
- Avoid paper cups and plastic utensils, and store food in reusable containers rather than in aluminum foil or plastic wrap. Use biodegradable wax paper for sandwiches rather than plastic or foil.
- Become familiar with recycled symbols when buying household products, and support the businesses that make these products whenever possible.
- Buy items in bulk or large quantities whenever possible. An enormous number of trees can be saved each year by avoiding expensive packaged food items in small quantities, and you'll have less to throw away.
- Recycle all paper, glass, and especially aluminum. Make visits to the local recycling center if it doesn't pick up in your area.

- Refuse unneeded bags at the store. Use paper bags rather than plastic, and get into the habit of carrying food home in cloth bags. Reuse bags as many times as possible.
- Ask for recycled stationery at the store, and use the front and back sides of paper. Keep a box of scrap paper in the house for notes.
- Choose toys that last rather than breakable plastic toys that quickly end up in the garbage.
- Recycle clothes and toys that are no longer being used to a local community center.

3. **Environmental Protection:** A dramatic change in two key factors during our lifetimes has forever changed the way our children will relate to the Earth. First of all, there continues to be a startling surge in human population, with an expected 9 billion by the year 2032. Second, science and technology have accelerated dramatically, allowing for an enormous shift in our ability to affect the world around us adversely. Here are a few ideas to help you and your child to protect our precious and finite resources.

    Nature is an endless combination and repetition of a very few laws.

    — Ralph Waldo Emerson

    - Plant trees in your yard, parks, and neighborhood. Many of the world's forests are being destroyed for luxury items. An alarming one-third of all of the Earth's remaining forests will be destroyed in the next fifteen years. Every tree planted is a seed of hope for tomorrow's generation.
    - Support local and national groups that are committed to saving the rain forests. We are losing an alarming one-and-a-half acres of rain forest each second. Since rain forests are essential to the well-being of the planet, it is imperative that we do all that we can to protect these invaluable areas.
    - Help protect animals and wildlife by joining

boycotts, refusing to buy products that come from endangered animals, and supporting local and national wildlife refuges. Nearly 10 percent of all species on this planet are now endangered, and a species becomes extinct every twenty minutes somewhere on the Earth.

- Reduce CFCs (chlorofluorocarbons) in the air by avoiding the use of air conditioners and buying insulation that is CFC free. CFCs are gases that consist of chlorine, fluorine, and carbon. They are responsible for up to 20 percent of global warming, and they also destroy the Earth's ozone layer.

- Express your concern to television and radio networks as well as local newspapers and magazines regarding the environment, and ask them to increase programming and articles that educate the population about ecology and the Earth.

- Start a school or neighborhood ecology club, and share information, news clippings, and ideas on how to help save the Earth one step at a time.

Do not look back in anger, or forward in fear, but around in awareness.

— James Thurber

Teach your children what we have taught our children,
that the Earth is our mother
Whatever befalls the Earth befalls the children of the Earth....
One thing we know, which the white man may one day
discover — our God is the same God,
You may think now that you own him as you wish
to own your land, but you cannot.
He is the God of all people, and his compassion is equal for all.
This Earth is precious to God, and to harm the Earth
is to heap contempt on its creator.
So love it as we have loved it. Care for it as we have cared for it.
And with all of your strength, with all of your mind,
with all of your heart,
preserve it for your children, and love — as God loves us all.

— Chief Seattle (Suquamish people), 1854

85

Exploring the Wonders of the Earth

**Develop an awe for beauty and a deep
appreciation for the Earth through reflection
time and direct interaction with nature.**

A seven-year-old child was asked by her teacher what she
thought could be done in order to bring about peace on the
planet. She thought for a long time and finally said, "We
could notice all of the people and all of the creatures and tell
them how beautiful they are." An international peace nego-
tiator who addressed people from every culture at the Earth
Summit gave a similar answer to the same question. He said,
"If we could see and really appreciate the beauty in the diversity all around us, we would be filled with too much wonder and awe to be concerned with conflict. We must become
connoisseurs of beauty." The Navajo people have a prayer
that is recited in praise of the beauty that is teeming all
around us:

*Find tongues in trees,
books in the running
brooks, sermons in
stone and good in
everything.*

— William Shakespeare

> *I walk with beauty before me.*
> *I walk with beauty behind me.*
> *I walk with beauty above me.*
> *I walk with beauty below me.*
> *I walk with beauty all around me.*
> *Your world is so beautiful, Oh God.*

There is no end to the beauty in the world for the person
who is aware. Teaching children to develop the skill of awe
brings them more in touch with themselves and with the

Earth. Horticulturist Charles Lewis, who has been studying what he calls the people-plant connection for thirty years, said, "A great deal of stress exists because we are out of touch with natural forces. In our efforts to control nature, we have cut ourselves off from the source." There are two ways to become more attuned to the beauty around us with our children. The first is through reflection on nature, such as watching a sunset or listening to birds chirping, and the second is through direct interaction with nature, such as gardening or hiking. Here are a few ideas to help you to share reflective and active time exploring the wonders of the Earth together.

To see a World in a Grain of Sand,
And Heaven in a Wild Flower,
Hold Infinity in the palm of your hand,
And Eternity in an hour.

— William Blake

Ways to Explore the Earth

1. **Multisensory Wonder:** One grandmother takes her three grandchildren for frequent walks in the six-hundred-acre preserve near her home. One of their favorite ways to explore is to become more aware of using all their senses. Sometimes they walk for a full hour, magnifying their sense of sight and taking in all the colors, shapes, and patterns. Other days they focus on their sense of smell or touch. One of her young grandsons came up with a highly creative way to walk through the woods, which he calls "sense-swapping." "We see with our hands, touch with our eyes, hear with our nose, or smell with our ears," he said with a grin. "It's kind of like switching the radio to a station you've never heard before, with really interesting music." They also make use of a sixth sense that they call the silent sense. "When we walk in silence," said another of the grandchildren, "our senses become like a magnifying glass. We get smaller, and everything around us gets bigger!"

2. **The Wonder of Planting a Seed:** Anyone who gets his or her hands into some living soil knows that

the moment we become participants, rather than observers of nature, a much more intimate relationship occurs. A single father of two girls decided to plant some tomatoes in the backyard a few years ago, just for fun. With the help of his daughters, he has slowly progressed to include over fifteen different kinds of vegetables, and even a few small fruit trees. "Once we plant a seed, we become aware of caring for it through all its stages — growth, flowering, fruiting, and dying. Gardening has taught all three of us about the amazing cycles of renewal in nature — death, decay, fertilization, gestation, and rebirth."

A Russian family of five now living in the United States has adapted a wonderful tree-planting tradition from their native land. Each time someone is born or dies in their large extended family, they plant a tree on their land to commemorate a birth into this world, or the birth into a new life. As they watch the trees grow and flourish, they think of their loved ones.

3. **The Wonder of Nature's Community:** Most living things live and thrive in communities. Ecosystems are really nothing more than an elaborate dance among many living organisms. Biologist Lewis Thomas said, "The relationship between chloroplasts and mitochondria, which produce oxygen for all living things, is probably the most ancient and firmly established of all. There is nothing resembling predation on either side. Competition is not so much the law of the universe as is cooperation in community." A mother of a four-year-old frequently takes him on nature hikes to observe the ecosystems all around them. "We talk about how the trees help the air, and how the water helps the trees, how the insects help the Earth, and how the change of seasons keeps the whole cycle going," she

Interconnectivity is a habit of the universe.

— Rupert Sheldrake

said. "There are many profound secrets that nature has to teach," she said, "and I'm right in there learning with my son!"

A teacher of third graders makes it a point to teach her classroom about the wonder of community in the insect and animal kingdoms each year. "We go on a pilgrimage to a bee farm to observe the entire community working in cooperation with the queen bee. We also study the amazing cooperation that ants display in ant colonies over a period of several months, and then we try to mimic the same sort of cooperation in the classroom. It's amazing to watch my students begin to grasp the beauty of many living things working together for the good of the whole over time! I've learned that nature is one of the best teachers of cooperation, and my students are a living testimony of this!"

4. **The Wonder of Mindfulness:** Living each hour of the day in mindfulness may be the greatest way of all to attain the skill of awe. People who are mindful are present to their surroundings and more receptive to those around them. There are just two things needed to develop mindfulness — a conscious awareness of the breath and a willingness to stay in the moment. Practice saying this short verse with your child:

The love of wilderness is more than a hunger for what is always beyond reach. It is also an expression of loyalty to the earth, the only home we shall ever know, the only paradise we ever need — if we had the eyes to see.

— Edward Abbey

> *As I breathe in, I relax my whole body.*
> *As I breathe out, I feel my whole body smiling.*

Encourage your child to say this often during the day as a practice in mindful breathing. Since we eat of the bounty of the Earth three times a day, mindful eating is another way to practice mindfulness. Before eating, take a moment to breathe and look at the food before you. Doing something as simple as contemplating our food for a few moments fosters happiness and good digestion. Vietnamese Buddhist Thich Nhat Hanh recommends saying this verse before eating:

My plate, empty now,
will soon be filled
with precious food.
In this food,
I see clearly the presence
of the entire universe
supporting my existence.

This verse helps us to see that all aspects of existence are woven together in the web of life that sustains us.

The wonders of the universe abound all around us. Take the time to reflect and interact with nature, and you and your child will be on your way to becoming connoisseurs of beauty.

Lo! To behold the gifts that await in my own backyard.

— Anna Kelletia

86

Glimpses of the Future

**Prepare your child for the future by learning
about trends, predictions, hopes, and dream together.**

The world is moving so fast these days that the man who says it can't be done is generally interrupted by someone doing it!

— Harry Fosdick

The future isn't what it used to be, but there is one guarantee that never changes about the future — all of us will spend the rest of our lives there. Our children may have difficulty comprehending the lightning pace of current technology. Some scientists say that those of us living in urban areas have an equivalent of 120 slaves at our disposal through the many conveniences that modern-day life offers. There has been more change in the last twenty years in technology than the previous six hundred years. And in the next twenty years, the changes to come will surpass the changes that have taken place in the previous millennium. Another theory states that if all human knowledge could be stored in one hundred volumes by the year 2036, only three of those volumes have been written thus far. Scientists are comparing the advances of biotechnology to a second discovery of fire. And with Japan rising to become a major economic power, Japanese children are not experiencing a forty-year generation gap from their grandparents, but, instead, a four-hundred-year gap. Japanese young women no longer walk in clogs behind the men but work side by side with men in corporations.

All the technological advances have not come without a price, however. Environmental problems are at an all-time high. Our children will be making decisions that no other generation has had to consider. In the past one hundred years, the Earth has sustained more environmental damage than during the previous two million years. Environmental responsibility is now one of the biggest trends of this decade, along with worldwide business innovation, the changing global economy, the technology explosion, and a renaissance in cultural awareness. The following ideas are just a few suggestions to help your child prepare for the changes that the future is ushering in.

When it comes to the future, the key has been lost . . . but they left the door unlocked!

— Anonymous

Five Ways to Explore the Future

1. **Asking Future Questions Now:** Ask your child questions about the future, such as:

    - What scares you about the future?
    - What are you looking forward to about the future?
    - What would you like to learn more about in the future?
    - What do you feel is one of the most important things your generation can do in the future?
    - What would you like to contribute to the future?
    - What do you want to see changed in the future?
    - What is one of your biggest dreams for the future?

2. **Exploring Exciting Future Predictions:** Since children experience much fear about the future, read up on some of the exciting changes that we can expect to see in the next ten to twenty years. Here are a few examples from the World Future Society:

    - 2000–2010: Improved chemotherapy, artificial organs, electronic newspapers and magazines, wristwatch telephones, televisions, and computers, bionic legs, lightweight spacecraft, decision-making robots, fully automated farms, implantable health sensors, air super-freighters, earthquake forecasting.
    - 2010-2020: Reliable rainmaking, low orbit space tourism, plastic automobiles, permanent

moon station, electronic eyesight, diabetes cure, cancer cure, green energy, key understanding of human memory, humans on Mars, and artificial eyes.

Talk about the above possibilities to stimulate discussion about the future.

There is more to life than increasing its speed.

— Mahatma Gandhi

3. **Using Future Talk:** Learn some of the special words that will become everyday words in the future. Here is a list of some of the most common words used among futurists.

Advanced biotechnology	Electronic notepads
Advanced lasers	Endoscopic technology
Advanced robotics	Fiber optics
Advanced satellites	Global collaboration
Artificial intelligence	Genetic engineering
Biochemistry	Multimedia computers
Digital electronics	Multisensory mobiles
Digital interactive television	Nanotechnology
DNA technology	Superconductors

For I dipt into the future, far as human eye could see, Saw the Vision of the world, and all the wonder that would be.

— Alfred, Lord Tennyson

4. **Exploring Mental Blocks to a Positive Future:** Take some time to talk about the mental barriers that prevent productive thinking about the future. In 1899, the U.S. Patent Office was considering closing because they thought that perhaps all inventions of value had already been patented. They were victims of their own limited thinking. In 1958, the president of a major corporation said that he didn't see much value in the use of computers in the future. His name was Tom Watson of IBM. His mental blunder was basing the future on the past. Here are a few more examples of limited thinking regarding the future.

- We've already tried everything there is to try.
- Let's leave this problem to someone else.
- I'm not smart enough to figure out what to do!

- If it's not logical, leave it alone.
- We should stick to the rules no matter what.
- Some things will just never change.
- Some problems are only going to get worse.
- We can't possibly do that!
- It's too late!
- We made our mess, now we'll have to sit in it!

5. **Learning the New Rules for the Future:** According to technology forecaster and futurist expert Daniel Burrus, author of *Technotrends,* "In order to make technological change our friend, we must adopt a new set of rules to live by." Here are a few of them to acquaint your child with.

- Make rapid change your best friend.
- Don't fix the blame, fix the problem.
- Learn to creatively apply technology.
- Solve tomorrow's predictable problems today.
- Think ten years out and plan back to the present.
- Build change into the plan.

   As Dan says, "All of us will become either masters of change, or prisoners of it."

We're drowning in information and starved for knowledge.

— John Naisbitt

Before us is one of the most important decades in the history of civilization. Help your child to become a master of change by inviting the future into your thoughts with an open mind and a hopeful heart.

87

Creation Celebration

Explore the wonders of inner and outer space and the story of creation, and learn to appreciate the miracle of life together.

Our task is to explore, to celebrate, and delight in the depths of the universe.

— Brian Swimme

We live in an amazing universe that continues to unfold and expand. Science is beginning to look more and more like religion, and religion is beginning to wake up to the parallels between the spiritual world and the physical world. Our children are growing up in an age that no longer regards matter as solid, but instead recognizes that matter is composed of energy and information. The old space-time model of the universe has been replaced by a quantum field of flowing energy that is not separate from us, but in fact is a part of us. We now know that at any given moment in time, we are breathing in atoms that were once a part of the primordial fireball and the earliest stars.

Every breath that we inhale today might have been exhaled yesterday by someone in Africa, Australia, or somewhere near the equator, and the molecules of air that fill our lungs are the same molecules that were once breathed by King Tut, Jesus, Mozart, or Leonardo da Vinci. Perhaps this is what naturalist John Muir was referring to when he said, "Whenever we try to pick out anything by itself, we find it hitched to everything else in the universe." Here are a few suggestions to help you and your child learn more about the wonders of the universe.

Exploring Life's Wonders

1. **Exploring Inner Space:** Share in the wonder of creation by exploring the amazing universe that exists within our own bodies and minds. Read books together, watch television specials, visit the local museum's section on the human body and brain, and view videos and movies together that keep you updated on the many new discoveries that science is revealing to us. Here are a few amazing facts to consider.

   • Each of us is born with fifty trillion cells, which appear new but are actually made up of atoms that have been circulating in the universe for billions of years.

   • Every atom in our bodies was once fashioned in the blazing heat of temperatures a million times hotter than molten rock as the stars were formed. Quite literally, we are further expressions of the stars.

   • The body is renewable. The skeleton replaces itself every three months, the liver every six weeks, and the skin every month.

   • By the end of the year, over 95 percent of the atoms in your body will be exchanged for new ones.

   • We breathe in approximately fifteen quintillion molecules in a single breath of air.

   • Right now there are millions of chemical reactions taking place in your body, most of them happening at 1/10,000th of a second.

   • There are billions of atoms moving in and out of your brain each second, creating electrical waves that will never again create the same pattern.

   • The body is made up of 99.9999 percent empty space. It has been said that if you removed the space from fifteen billion human beings, their mass would fit inside a single aspirin.

   • DNA is not only the carrier of the secrets to

*As is the microcosm,
so is the macrocosm.
As is the atom,
so is the universe.*

— Deepak Chopra

life, but also of secrets that we are just beginning to understand, since scientists say that we understand as little as one percent of the total function of DNA.

- There are more than three trillion neurons in the brain (thinking cells). Although it weighs less than three pounds, the brain is considered to be the most complex matter in the universe. No computer of any size can even begin to perform the thousands of skills that our brain orchestrates effortlessly each moment.

- The human nervous system takes in only the most minute fraction, less than one part per billion, of the total energy vibrating in the environment at large.

2. **Outer Space:** We are just beginning to grasp how vast our universe really is. Einstein taught us that time is a construct of our minds and that traveling at the speed of light would allow us to see the past, the present, and the future as one continuum. Steven Hawking discovered that the universe continues to expand. It appears that entire galaxies simply show up and, conversely, disappear into the innocuous vacuum of a black hole. No science fiction story can compare with the story of the amazing universe, as science unfolds mystery after mystery. Explore the wonders of space with your child through books, special programs, videos, movies, and pop science magazines. Here are a few stunning facts about the wonders of outer space.

The scientific theory I like best is that the rings of Saturn are composed entirely of lost luggage.

— Mark Russell

- The known universe has been in existence for fifteen billion years.

- Scientists have discovered that the universe began as a silent fire that burned for almost a million years as hydrogen atoms gravitated together and fused to become what we call the first star.

- Each successive generation of stars created matter that had not existed before, until the whole spectrum of chemical elements and matter (the "stuff" that we are made of) spewed forth and scattered itself into the universe.

- There are at least 50 billion galaxies, each with at least 50 billion stars.

- The timing in the universe is so precise that had space unfurled one-trillionth of one percent more slowly, the entire universe would have collapsed back into quantum foam ages ago.

- The inflation theory suggests that there may be many other universes that we have yet to discover, and that the universe that we can measure may be just one of billions of universes, like a droplet of water in an ocean of universes.

- Giant stars live for approximately 100 million years, burning up their fuel and then exploding into a supernova.

- Supernovas are important to galactic ecology, since atoms of heavy elements are blasted into space, becoming future stars and planets.

- Even though light travels at 186,000 miles per second, the universe is so vast that it takes a few million years for the light from a star to reach our eyes. Therefore, when we look at a star, we are seeing it as it looked a few million years ago.

- Subatomic particles make up each atom, whirling electrons around a core of protons and neutrons that are so small they leave only minute trails of light.

- Earth is approximately $4^1/_2$ billion years old.

- Humans have been in existence for just a few

The new cosmic story can help us to overcome alienation so that awe and delight return.

— Matthew Fox

million years. In the scheme of the universe, we are a very recent development.

Explore the wonders of creation with your child, and celebrate the origins of all of life. We are all made up of elementary particles of the fireball, the supernovas, and all of the life forms that followed. We are a creative expression of the mysterious, ever-expanding, enchanting universe. What can compare with such a heritage?

88

The Last Great Places

Seek out some of the last great places on the planet that house endangered plant and animal species and help to preserve some of our greatest resources.

In the next several decades, organizations such as the Nature Conservancy and An Alliance for People and the Environment will protect millions of acres of important natural areas in the United States and Canada, many of which house endangered species as well. Since our planet is now in grave danger environmentally, teaching our children to protect and appreciate the last great places has never been more important. Children who have been taught a sense of reverence for the planet's diversity will be more apt to do all they can as adults to see that the environment is protected at all costs.

Study the last great places with your child via videos, books, or in person whenever possible. Join an environmental protection group, or attend special presentations and classes on some of these beautiful areas and how to protect them. Here is a listing of just a few of the last great places to appreciate.

It's not by accident that the pristine wilderness of our planet disappears as the understanding of our own inner wild nature fades.

— Clarissa Pinkola Estés

A Few of the Last Great Places

1. **The Horseshoe Lake Conservation Area:** This is part of the Cache River wetlands in Illinois, which is known for its rare trees and foliage, including the fat-bottomed cypress tree.

2. **Basque Country in Spain:** The Basque people still cling to the five-hundred-year-old farmhouses on beautiful land where nonmechanized chores are a matter of tradition. The rolling hills and pristine air make this part of Spain a paradise all its own.

3. **The Coral Reefs of the Florida Keys:** These are the world's most popular diving destination and host more than a million visitors each year. The biological diversity of these waterscapes has been compared to that of the tropical rain forests.

4. **Hawaii:** Hawaii offers a gold mine of natural diversity. It houses over one-fourth of the nation's endangered birds and tropical plants. The Hawaiian rain forests support many native species that cannot be found anywhere else.

5. **Lake Baikal in Siberia, Russia:** This is the world's deepest and purest freshwater lake, and also the largest. Lake Baikal contains more than 20 percent of the Earth's freshwater, with eight hundred animal species unique to the lake's environment. The lake is one of Russia's premier environmental causes.

6. **Aravaipa Creek:** This lovely creek rushes through a canyon in the Sonoran Desert of southeastern Arizona. The creek and canyon support seven rare fish species, desert bighorn sheep, desert tortoises, and many birds.

7. **The Galapagos Islands:** Located off Ecuador are the beautiful islands that Charles Darwin once explored. They are still home to a stunning variety of species, many that are now rare or endangered. Visitors can still approach many of the islands' creatures and get close enough to get a detailed look at their unique features. The islands become more popular each year, and the hiking trails and the variety of species make this area an inviting place to see.

Bambi walked under the great oak on the meadow. It sparkled with dew. It smelled of grass and flowers and moist earth, and whispered of a thousand living things.

— Felix Salten

8. **Big Darby Creek in Ohio:** This is the healthiest, most diverse aquatic system of its size in the Midwest. Of the forty species of mussels and eighty-six species of fish that breed there, several dozen are considered rare.

9. **The Amazon River:** This four-thousand-mile river flows through the largest rain forest in the world. More than two thousand different species of fish swim in these waters, and up to 40 percent of the area's plants have yet to be discovered.

10. **Panama:** Though it is smaller than the state of South Carolina, Panama has a wider diversity of birds than the United States and Canada combined. Several of these species are found only in this area.

11. **San Rafael Waterfall:** These beautiful cascades in Ecuador lie amidst one of the most biologically diverse areas in the entire hemisphere. People from all over the world have come to appreciate this lush area.

12. **Yucatan Coastal Reserve in Mexico:** The beaches offer nesting grounds for the globally endangered leatherback and hawksbill turtles, as well as the green sea turtle.

13. **Steens Mountain:** Located in the High Steens Wilderness area of southeastern Oregon, these mountains provide a high desert habitat to many endangered and rare plant species.

Walk quietly in any direction and taste the freedom of the mountain air. Nature's peace will flow into you as sunshine flows.

— John Muir

There are thousands of great places on the planet that house precious and limited plant and animal species. Commit yourself to seek out, study, and support a few of these areas with your child, and help to preserve our greatest resources and to make the world a better place.

89

Five Minutes a Day
for World Peace

**Devote five minutes a day thinking,
talking, imagining, praying, or reading about
world peace with your child.**

*There is no way to
peace. Peace is
the way.*

— A. J. Muste

In one twenty-four-hour period, there are 1,440 minutes and 86,400 seconds. By developing the habit of devoting just five minutes a day to world peace with your child, you are contributing 300 seconds to the pursuit of world peace each day. That leaves 1,435 minutes, or 86,100 seconds for other things. It's a small contribution that can make a big difference over time, and it will teach your child that every contribution to world peace is valuable, in thought, word, or deed. Edmund Burke said, "No one could make a greater mistake than he who did nothing because he could only do a little."

*If we have no peace,
it is because we have
forgotten that we
belong to each other.*

— Mother Teresa

Devoting five minutes a day to world peace is a little bit like steering the trim tab on a large sailing ship. The trim tab is a small rudder that is placed within the main rudder. It takes only a small amount of energy to turn the trim tab, but when it turns, the main rudder turns, and the entire ship changes its course of direction. Imagine what it will be like when a large part of the population devotes at least five minutes a day to world peace. The thought is staggering. Here are some ways that you can focus on world peace during your five minutes of time each day.

Ten Ways to Bring More Peace into Your Life

1. Describe a peaceful world in detail together often. Here are some comments children have made about a world without war or violence.

   People would all wait in circles visiting, instead of waiting in lines with a serious look on their faces!
   — Twelve-year-old boy

   Every child would be treated as precious, and adults everywhere would be nice to them when they made mistakes. — Eight-year-old girl

   The varieties of races would be treated like varieties of flowers —the greater the variety, the more beautiful the bouquet becomes! — Fourteen-year-old boy

2. Write the word peace on something each day. Write or stamp peace phrases such as "Picture World Peace!" or "Whirled Peas Forever!"

3. Read together about famous leaders who were advocates of nonviolence, such as Martin Luther King, Jr., or Mahatma Gandhi. Talk about ways that you can exercise nonviolence in your thinking each day.

4. Talk about ways to disagree with others without being against them. Learn to be for your own beliefs, rather than against the beliefs of others. Remember that what you are *for* strengthens you, while what you are *against* weakens you.

5. Create an affirmation together to say each day after prayers, or at the beginning of meals, such as "Let there be peace on Earth, and let it begin with me."

6. Come up with a picture of world peace together, such as visualizing a golden thread of light that links all people in the world together from one heart to another. Hold the picture in your mind each day.

7. Clear resentments and grudges whenever possible by writing letters, talking it out in person, calling someone, or talking to a friend. Develop the skill

Never in this world can hatred be stilled by hatred; it will be stilled only by non-hatred — this is the law eternal.

— The Buddha

of empathy — the ability to walk a mile in the other person's moccasins.

8. Honor yourself for your own uniqueness. Talk about how the differences in others are often disguised gifts that help you to become more tolerant and open-minded.

9. Face one another and take turns answering the question, "How can I create peace in my world today?" Give each person three minutes, and ask the question over and over again. You will be surprised at how many valuable answers can be generated in a short period of time.

10. Know that each act of kindness and each thought that we hold regarding world peace create a ripple effect that will move like a wave over the ocean of humanity. Remember that world peace happens one mind at a time. If you spread peace today through a kind thought, word, or deed to 2 people, then 3 people will have it. If each one spreads it to 2 more people, and those 6 pass it along to 2 people each, before long it will reach 12; then 24; 48; and all the way to 384; 1,536; 3,072, and on and on and on!

I say a prayer for a compassionate world each and every day.

— The Dalai Lama

Teaching children to devote five minutes a day to world peace will help them to develop the skill of hope. And in the future, it will be those who have hope who will encourage others to make a positive difference in the world.

The World Peace Prayer

Lead me from death into life,
from falsehood to truth;
lead me from despair to hope,
from fear to trust;
lead me from hate to love,
from war to peace.
Let peace fill our heart, our world, our universe.
— Fellowship of Reconciliation

90

New World Thinking

Explore the differences between old world thinking and new world thinking with your child and learn to see crisis as opportunity, rather than danger.

We are living in one of the most exhilarating and challenging decades in all of history. Our children are growing up through a time of unrest, upheaval, and monumental change. This shift is a profound one that implies a revolution in our way of thinking about ourselves and the world. Our old way of thinking is rapidly being replaced by a new way of thinking that turns many of our ingrained conceptions about life and human beings upside down.

Significant problems cannot be solved at the same level of thinking that created them.

— Albert Einstein

The Chinese believe that every crisis carries within it both danger and opportunity. Study the chart on page 316 with your child, and discuss the differences between old world thinking and new world thinking. Explore the notion that this period of history is a rare opportunity to learn and to be of service in the world.

The new world thinker realizes that every human being has much larger capacities than we were able to imagine in the past and knows that we are capable of solving the problems that we have created. There is a burning desire to pass on the torch of hope and belief in a peaceful world. The new world thinker knows that every individual is capable of changing the world for the better. As Margaret Mead once said, "Don't think that a small group of awakened individuals cannot change the world. Indeed, it is the only thing that ever has."

Encourage your child to look for new world thinking in everyday life, by listening to the beliefs expressed in classes, daily conversations, the news media, and books.

From Old World Thinking to New World Thinking

Fifteen Symptoms of Old World Thinking	Fifteen Signs of New World Thinking
1. Sees change as threatening.	1. Sees change as opportunity.
2. Thinks in a logical, linear way.	2. Thinks both logically and creatively.
3. Refers to the future from the past.	3. Refers to the future with new vision and high ideals.
4. Believes that more is better.	4. Believes that acting from integrity is better.
5. Needs to measure and evaluate everything.	5. Enjoys explanations, but also trusts in the mystery of life.
6. Measures growth in terms of money and power.	6. Measures growth in terms of win-win for everyone.
7. Instills fear to maintain power.	7. Instills love to empower others.
8. Believes that whoever has the control has the power.	8. Believes in the power of connection.
9. Tries to fix symptoms, rather than going to the root of a problem.	9. Goes to the root of the problem when symptoms appear.
10. Creates distance from others.	10. Bridges gaps and brings people together.
11. Wants to achieve without regard for the good of the whole.	11. Knows that all achievement rests on the good of the whole.
12. Believes in "us and them."	12. Believes in "we."
13. Intolerant of differences.	13. Encourages and appreciates differences.
14. Takes up sides and believes in allies and enemies.	14. Knows that each side needs to be acknowledged. Believes in humanity.
15. Feels hopeless and powerless to make a difference in the world.	15. Feels empowered with a sense of hope, believing that each person can make a difference in the world.

Global Esteem Chart

Read over the following chart of old beliefs and new beliefs, and help your child move from low esteem to full esteem while contributing to global esteem.

From Low Esteem

1. The world is on a downslide, and it's only going to get worse!

2. There's nothing one person can do about all the problems in the world.

3. There will always be conflict and war. That's just the way people are. Look at history — it never changes!

4. The environment is doomed for disaster. It's too late. We have to deal with the fact that the damage has already been done.

5. There will always be rich people and poor people. That's just the way it is.

6. Differences must be tolerated in the world, but at least we are civilized and educated and have many of the advantages.

To Full Esteem

1. It's not too late to turn the tide of events. As long as there is life, there is hope.

2. Each person can make a difference in the world. Better to light one candle than to be in the dark.

3. Someday, war will become obsolete. The future does not equal the past.

4. We must face the deep regrets that result from our misuse of power. But change is still possible, and all effort to save the environment is positive effort.

5. In the future, global unity will include a more equal distribution of power. It's a big order; but if we can dream it, we can do it.

6. Differences are to be celebrated! There are advantages as well as disadvantages to each culture. Every culture on Earth has lessons to teach and gifts to share.

chapter
10

Spiritual Esteem

The spiritual life of children begins each day as they open their eyes and greet the world with a "holy curiosity" that often brings us to our knees. Children are born with an enormous amount of spiritual esteem — a sense of being connected to the whole. Our task as adults is to be willing to learn from their spontaneity and to help them keep their joy intact as they grow through the marvels and mysteries of life.

Chapter 10 offers ideas to help children explore religions from around the world and approach a variety of cultural beliefs with an open mind. Reading from the great books of timeless wisdom, finding teachers and guides, and learning to meditate will enhance children's sense of inner spirituality. Developing an attitude of gratitude, performing angel deeds, creating a peaceful place, and participating in rituals and rites of passage will reinforce the idea that spirituality is love in action. Ideas to help children cope with trauma, loss, and death are included, along with ways to help children grow and learn through the grieving process.

The following poem, "For the Caretakers of the Children," offers a few words of wisdom to parents.

For the Caretakers of the Children

by Diana Loomans

To the Caretakers of the Children,
Who do the most honorable and challenging work
on the face of the Earth,

May you live with compassion,
And teach with great love.

May you love the children as they are,
And inspire them to be even more.

May you see the world through their eyes,
And remain rooted in your own ground.

May you guide the children with direction,
And allow them to find their own way.

May you teach them self-discipline
And treat them with great respect.

May you show the children your humanness,
And be a model of strength.

May you be present for the children,
And give them freedom to explore.

And may you blossom in your own garden,
As you nurture the seedlings to full bloom.

Nicholas Webster
by Julia Loomans

It was Easter Sunday morning, and I was eager to pay a visit to my pet rat, Nicholas Webster, as I had done every morning for the past three years. As I got close to his cage, I sensed something was strangely different. I had a habit of calling out his name in a quiet voice from across the room and watching Nicholas peek out from beneath the basket in his cage. But that day, there was no response to my call, and the basket remained still and motionless. I stopped in my tracks and paused before I had the courage to look directly into his cage. Somehow, I already knew that he was gone. I felt a wave of sorrow as I reached into his cage and found a cold, lifeless body, instead of receiving the warm, spirited greeting I had come to expect from my beloved little pet. I picked Nicholas up in a daze of emotion, still half in disbelief as tears spilled down my face.

For the next several hours, time seemed surreal. I held Nicholas for a long time, trying to comprehend that he was really gone. It was strange. I had had lots of pets before Nicholas, but never had I bonded with any other animal the way I had with him. He was intelligent and affectionate, and we shared a nonverbal language all our own. He spent countless hours perched on my shoulder as I did my homework, painted, cooked, or talked on the phone. I'd dressed him like a doll on more than one occasion, and all my friends knew him by name. Throughout all the changes that I'd been through in the last few years, Nicholas had always cheered me up and brought a lift to my spirits. It seemed almost silly that something as insignificant to the rest of the world as a rat could have such an impact on me. And yet somehow that made him even more special. I cried and cried that day, and I knew that I would miss him for a long time. I wanted him to know what he had meant to me, so I sat down and wrote out my feelings in my journal. Then, as I looked back over what I had written, I was inspired to express my feelings in a poem that would become part of his burial ritual.

I read the poem aloud the next day with my mom as I buried Nicholas. I put him in a special box, along with some of his favorite things — a chewed-up wool sock, some dried food, some cotton bedding, and a strand of my hair, and I enclosed the following poem to him.

Farewell My Friend

Shine on, my friend.
I'm honored to have had you as my pet.
We have shared many lessons together.
I love you, I love you, I love you forever!
Thank you for the gift of your presence.
Thank you for all the times you made me laugh.
I'm sorry for the times that I grew impatient with you.
Thank you for being so patient with me.
You are so beautiful!
Being with you the last few years has been so real.
Did you know that when I held you my heart would glow?
Did you know how warm you made me feel?
You are so very precious.
You are no longer with me,
And yet a part of you remains within me.
A piece of your life lives on in me.
And where is the rest?
I smile inside beneath my tears.
I know where you are,
And it is good.
And now, although I cannot hold you,
My heart will glow just knowing that somewhere
You'll be shining on.
Even now in your new world,
You will live on in my heart.
We are closer now that we have shared this time.
I let you go, Nicholas Webster,
Knowing that we are one in spirit.

Although it helped to do the burial ritual, I was left with many questions. I wondered about my death, and the death of those I loved. I realized how little we really know about the mysteries of life. We go about our day-to-day lives as though each day will be like the last. And yet, in the blink of an eye, everything can be changed forever. I realized how precious life was — all of life, from the smallest of creatures to the largest of mammals, and I had a sense that it was all part of one big sacred picture. Although my beloved little pet was gone, and I knew that I'd miss him for a long time, he had left a gift behind for me. It was a new appreciation of life — and many happy memories.

91

Religions around the World

Whether you are religious or not, explore some of the major world religions with your child for cultural enrichment and global awareness.

Four-year-old Alan was listening intently to a special news report with his mother. As two religious leaders carried on in heated debate, he turned to his mother and said, "Why can't they be friends?" "Because they have different beliefs about God," she answered. "Well, are they fighting with God?" he asked in bewilderment. "No, I think they are fighting about God," she said. Alan became increasingly disturbed and finally said, "Well, don't they realize that God is everybody's friend?"

Many wars over the centuries have occurred in the name of God, using the infamous claim that "God is on our side." The Renaissance child of the new millennium knows that, as Alan said, "God is everybody's friend," and develops a deep respect for all religious beliefs regardless of personal preferences. To help your child develop a sense of religious tolerance and global understanding, consider the following ideas.

Six Ways to Learn about World Religions

1. **Read about the Major Religions:** Become familiar with the major religions of the world, along with a basic understanding of the rituals, beliefs, and history of each one. The main religions include

Christianity, Islam, Hinduism, Buddhism, Confucianism, Shintoism, Taoism, Judaism, and Sikhism.

2. **Discuss Various Beliefs about God:** Discuss the various names for God, along with the various beliefs that accompany the names. People of the Christian religion understand God as a Trinity, with Father, Son, and Holy Spirit as one. People of the Jewish faith understand God as the teacher of Moses. The Muslims understand God as the teacher of Mohammed. People of the Buddhist religion understand God as the teacher of Buddha. In India, there are many gods, including Brahmin — the god of the dance — and the great goddess Devi. In Africa, there are many gods, including Yoruba, the storm god. In Asia, there are people who worship the sun as a god, and in China, there are many goddesses, including the goddess of the moon. Talk about the varieties of beliefs about God, and explore your own understanding of God together.

3. **Read Some of the Great Religious Texts:** Most religions have a holy book in which someone wrote down what their leaders taught about God. Reading excerpts from various holy books is culturally enriching and offers many different perspectives on God for your child to learn from. People of the Muslim religion read a holy book called the Koran, Buddhists read the sutras, Christians read the Bible, Hindus read the Vedas, and the people of the Jewish religion read the Torah. We keep several of the great books from various religions in our library, reading from different texts on different days.

4. **Worship Together:** People worship in churches, synagogues, mosques, temples, or meditation centers. For a real flavor of a particular religion, attend a service or ceremony, remaining open-minded and taking in the sights, sounds, and songs with your child. A Buddhist family of four makes it a

To be at all is to be religious more or less.

— Samuel Butler

One truly conscious being can awaken millions.

— Mahatma Gandhi

point to attend a few services from different religions each year. Their favorite from last year was a small inner city Baptist church where they claim they "rocked out with the Lord, and sang in the aisles while stomping our feet and clapping our hands." It was a definite alternative to their quiet walking meditations and readings from the sutras.

5. **Learn Some Cross-Cultural Prayers:** Every religion on Earth believes in the power of prayer. A great teacher once said, "A day hemmed in by prayer is not likely to unravel." Collect various prayers from different religions and cultures — American Indian, Jewish, Sufi, Christian, Hindu, Buddhist, and so forth. Read them at the end of your meals, at bedtime, or any time you share in spiritual practice together. Keep a prayer box near the dining room table where you can reach in and pick a prayer for the day.

6. **Seek the Similarities:** Talk about differences in spiritual practice with your child, but even more important, talk about the similarities among various religions. Most religions acknowledge a divine power and promote "doing unto others as you would have them do unto you." Help your child to recognize the unity that underlies the diversity, and discuss the importance that valuing differences will bring to world harmony. In India, there is a proverb that says, "One string alone holds up little, but many strings weaved together become rope, and rope can hold up an elephant." If the string of religions in the world today can unite together for the common good, they will become a rope of hope that can hold up the world.

Seek and ye shall find. Knock and it shall be opened unto you.

— Matthew 7:7

92

The Gratitude Attitude

Develop an "attitude of gratitude" with your child, and learn to appreciate the gift of life more.

There is an old English proverb that says, "Absence makes the heart grow fonder, but gratitude makes the heart spilleth over." Gratitude reminds us that there is much to be thankful for, even amidst struggle and strife. Several countries celebrate the gift of gratitude as a holiday, such as Thanksgiving in the United States. In the United States, September 26 has been declared World Gratitude Day. Although it doesn't receive the attention that Easter or Christmas does, it is easily as important.

Why not declare every day Gratitude Day. Here is a three-step exercise to go through together to help develop a "gratitude attitude."

Three Steps to Developing an Attitude of Gratitude

1. **Appreciating the Unnoticed Gifts:** We think of all the gifts we are grateful for that often go unnoticed — another sunrise, the Earth, our health, the gift of choice, freedom, change, and life itself — and give thanks.

2. **Appreciating Gifts from Others:** We think of all the gifts that others bring into our lives, such as companionship, love, compassion, playfulness, acceptance, challenge, new ideas, encouragement,

and surprise. We think of people in our lives we would like to thank, and we take a few minutes to fill our hearts with goodwill for each person who comes to mind. If we are harboring anger or resentment toward anyone, we look forward to the gift that will be ours when we can give and receive empathy and understanding together.

Gratitude is not only the greatest virtue, but the parent of all others.

— Cicero

3. **Finding Hidden Gifts:** We look at the gifts in our lives that come disguised as limitations, pain, loss, problems, setbacks, disappointments, or failures. Although it may be painful, we get in touch with the ways that we are softened, molded, pruned, or redirected by challenges. We begin to see that sadness brings with it the gift of cleansing the soul, that the fire of rage can bring forth the torch that lights the darkness, and that fear brings the opportunity to stand on the threshold of courage. We become aware of ourselves as "peaceful warriors," to use author Dan Millman's term, and we learn to use every life lesson as grist for the mill. We go over these three steps at bedtime, so that each day can end on a note of gratitude.

Gratitude in action is another powerful way to take what we know and let it show. Sending short thank-you notes for small kindnesses, or acknowledging others out loud for the gifts that they bring will increase our sense of well-being and help others to feel appreciated. A teacher with a strong interest in peacemaking has a "gratitude attitude hour" one Friday a month with her fourth grade class. They take the first fifteen minutes to brainstorm a list of all the things they are grateful for — both large and small. The next forty-five minutes are spent writing short gratitude notes to a known friend or relative, a leader in the country, and an international leader or organization that is making a difference in the world. "I believe that writing these three simple gratitude letters each week will plant seeds that will later produce great leaders," she said. "After all, every great leader knows that peacemaking starts with an attitude of gratitude."

True gratitude is expressed in deeds, rather than words.

— Maria Carleton

93

Angel Deeds

Sow good seeds in the world together by reaching out to help others. Give from the heart to family, friends, neighbors, the community, and those you admire, and experience the joy of committing random acts of kindness.

When Julia was getting the mail one day, she decided to place a tiny jasmine blossom in our neighbor's mailbox. A big smile came across her face and she said, "I'm going to do this every day for a whole week. They will wonder who in the world keeps leaving small flowers in their mailbox!" For the next week, she left tiny flowers in our neighbor's mailbox each day before they returned from work. She probably had at least as much fun doing this "angel deed" each day as they did receiving it. After her daily jaunts to the mailbox, she would delight in pondering their possible reactions. "I wonder what they'll think when they see the flowers again today, Mom," she would say beaming.

A fourteen-year-old boy recently decided to start committing "random acts of kindness" at home whenever possible. "I started out by sneaking into my sister's bedroom and making her bed while she was in the shower. Then later that day, I took the garbage out for my older brother, and put some flowers from the garden on my mother's dresser. It felt so good to do something unexpected, and when they wondered who was behind these senseless acts, I never let out a peep!" He claimed that it started a household trend in his

The more one gives, the more one has.

— Chinese proverb

family, with all six family members beginning to perform un-expected acts of thoughtfulness for one another. "The best one of all was last week, when someone changed my hamster cage for me. Now that was a real act of kindness!"

We have recently begun to leave surprise notes for strangers underneath their windshield wipers. Recently, we put a twenty-dollar bill in an envelope underneath the wind-shield wiper of an unknown car and wrote on the envelope, "To Lovable You." We enclosed a note that said:

> *"Hello. I am a connoisseur of fine human beings. Con-gratulations for being a unique and lovable person! Since your presence on Earth enriches us all, please take this twenty-dollar bill, and be good to yourself in some way today. I ask for just one thing in return, and that is that you gift someone else in your world with a surprise act of kindness, preferably someone you don't know. Thanks for being you! Please go out and celebrate yourself!"*

It would be hard to describe how much fun it was to sneak through a parking lot with Julia and find just the right car that was screaming out, "The driver of this car needs some acknowledgment!" It probably made the driver's day and kept that person wondering for quite a while.

I don't believe in angels; I know them.

— Terry Lynn Taylor

Humor educator Joel Goodman believes that people need to cultivate more "inverse paranoia" — the belief that the world is out to do them good. Angel deeds are gifts to others that offer a sense of renewed hope and gratitude. We have derived immense satisfaction from performing angel deeds together, especially when we do them anonymously! Here are some suggestions that will help you to spread your angel wings with your child.

Fourteen Ways to Soar into Service Together

1. Send a surprise gift, card, or flowers to someone special to say, "I appreciate you."

2. Put a positive message under someone's windshield wipers whom you don't know.

3. Make it a point for one whole day to smile at everyone you meet.

4. Lift someone's load at home or work by doing one of his or her jobs when least expected.

5. When out in public together, give sincere compliments to every person that you meet.

6. Throw an appreciation party in someone's honor for no special reason.

7. Deliver a home-cooked meal for someone who is overworked, sick, or in crisis.

8. Donate some uplifting books to a library, school, or organization that would appreciate it.

9. Send a thank-you card to someone who is making a difference in the world in some way.

10. Decorate someone's room or office with balloons and party trimmings and tell them it's Celebrating You Day!

11. Bring blankets, clothes, or food to a homeless shelter or halfway house.

12. Buy a small animal, such as a turtle, fish, or bird for a lonely friend who needs cheering up and is open to caring for a pet.

13. Take a friend for a surprise day out in nature, taking him or her to a few of your favorite spots.

14. Craft something for a friend (a sculpture, picture, collage of photographs) to show how much you care.

Kind words can be short and easy to speak, but their echoes are truly endless.

— Mother Teresa

Try doing an angel deed with your child, and you'll discover that angel deeds bring heavenly gifts for all.

94

Rituals and Rites of Passage
by Julia Loomans

Create rituals and rites of passage with your child to honor and celebrate significant events on your journey through life.

In northern Spain, people practice a ritual to protect newborn babies from harm. Some babies are placed on a mattress in the street. A man leaps over them, and when he lands safely, it is believed that the babies have been blessed and are now prepared for a safe passage through childhood. In Tibet, parents teach their children to use prayer flags, by writing a prayer on the fabric of a flag and hanging it out in the breeze. This simple ritual is their way of making their desires known to the higher realms. Rituals have been a part of every culture since the beginning of time. Through prayer, blessing, ceremony, or celebration, people have always had a need to express themselves and their experiences of life.

The following examples describe a few of the significant rituals and rites of passage that I have gone through over the years.

> *Ritual has its genesis in the soul and our need to express deep emotions and intuitions in story, symbol, and action.*
>
> — Frederic Brussat

Significant Rituals and Rites of Passage

1. **The Blessing Ritual:** The first ritual I remember when I was little was a blessing ritual. I would go on long walks along the lake with my mom or dad, and collect colorful pebbles and rocks of unusual shapes. The stones represented people in my life and I would place them in shapes on the floor and

bless each one of them at night before I went to sleep. Often I would leave them in unique shapes for several days before changing the pattern, thinking of my friends and family as I looked at them.

2. **The New Home Ritual:** When I was a toddler, I remember a moving ritual my family went through when we moved into a new house. We took a few minutes to stand in the middle of each empty room before we unpacked, lit a candle, and imagined all the good times we'd share with family and friends in the future. It was a fun way to get acquainted with our new surroundings and to hold a picture of happiness in our minds.

3. **The New Year's Ritual:** Another one of my favorite rituals happened each year on New Year's Eve. Usually we would have some friends over and pass out six cards to each person. On the first three cards, we would write down three farewells — things that we did not want to take with us into the new year. On the second set of three cards, we wrote three welcomes — things that we most wanted during the following year. When we were done writing, we threw all the farewell cards into a bowl and read them aloud. After reading them out loud, we'd throw them into the fire one by one and watch them burn. We kept our welcome cards to post in a place where we'd see them every day.

4. **The Childhood Rite of Passage:** When I was four, I went through a rite of passage into childhood at my school. All the children in my class sat in a circle, and my parents came to school and read a poem they had written about my first four years of life. As they read each verse, I walked a full circle around my classmates to represent one full year around the sun. As they ended the poem, all of us celebrated with food, dance, and song.

Rituals and rites of passage are to humans what water is to fish.

— Joseph Campbell

5. **The Teenhood Rite of Passage:** When I was twelve, my mom had a ceremony for me to honor the passage from my childhood into my teens. This one was a surprise to me. Twelve of the most significant adults in my life were there, including parents, grandparents, and a few family friends. Each person brought a symbol of something that reminded him or her of me. Everyone sat in a circle and took turns one by one giving me the symbol and describing its meaning, along with kind words of admiration and a few tidbits of wisdom. Along with that, they gave me their blessings for my future. The ceremony was followed by food, laughter, and play. It was a night that I will never forget.

6. **The Coming of Age Rite of Passage:** Recently, my mom took me through a rite of passage that she called the Coming of Age Ceremony. She said that now that I was sixteen, it was time to begin to let go of any "Deity Daddy or Almighty Mommy" illusions I might still be carrying with me. Although she still wanted my respect, she knew that it was time for me to begin to let go and walk on my own path. We wrote something called the "Unconscious Pledge of Allegiance," which was a funny poem about all the ways that children become "addicted" to their parents' approval, living out the habits of their parents (including those that they would rather leave behind), and trying to please their parents, rather than following the beat of their own drum. I wrote a poem called "My Own Pledge of Allegiance," which was about learning to trust myself more and to realize that my parents were guides, not gods, with feelings, needs, dreams, and fears, just like me. We went to a mountaintop and I read the "Unconscious Pledge of Allegiance" aloud. After that, I burned it and threw the ashes over the mountain. Next, I read

Being loved and lovable, valued and valuable as we are, regardless of what we do, is the beginning of the most fundamental kind of self-esteem.

— Gloria Steinem

"My Own Pledge of Allegiance," and we burned some sage (a plant found in the wild that is often dried and burned at Native American ceremonies) to honor my learning to trust my instincts. Although I knew that this simple ceremony was just the first step, it felt good to know that I could become my own person and still have my parents' love and support, too.

If you only had one prayer, "Thank you" would suffice.

— Meister Eckhart

Here are a few simple guidelines for creating your own rituals and rites of passage with your child.

Five Steps to Creating Your Own Rituals

1. Use your intuition and creativity to come up with your own unique ideas together.
2. Keep the ceremony short and simple, from ten minutes to an hour.
3. Make sure that everyone who attends the event gets involved in it in some way.
4. Include music, dance, and the power of the spoken or written word in your ceremony.
5. See that the ritual benefits everyone and harms no one.

Rituals and rites of passage are wonderful ways to celebrate change in a personal and meaningful way. They have been an important part of my childhood and are some of the nicest things my parents have ever done for me.

95

Peaceful Place

**Set aside a small room or a corner of a room, and
create a sanctuary area or peaceful place.
Decorate the area, and use it for reflection or meditation.**

*My people will abide
in peaceful habitation,
in secure dwellings,
and in quiet resting
places.*

— Isaiah 32:18

When Julia went on a trip to India with her dad, she was fascinated by the "puja areas." In the Hindu culture, the puja area is a sacred spot in the house for meditation. Families decorate the area with bright fabric, flower petals, and incense. They spend quiet time in prayer together there.

Many religions encourage families to create a quiet corner in their dwelling place for reflection and prayer. Christians often create a shrine area, placing statues of Jesus and the saints and posting prayers to read aloud. Traditional Muslims often create a quiet place in an area of the house for chanting the name of Allah, which they do five times each day. Most Buddhists meditate each day, and many families have a small room set aside for meditation.

Here are a few ideas for creating a peaceful place of your own.

Five Ways to Create a Peaceful Place

1. Find a small, low table and decorate it with flowers, candle holders, candles, and a few of your favorite objects.
2. Decorate the area with fabrics, paintings, or photographs.

3. Keep the lighting soft or light candles.
4. Play quiet, peaceful music, or play small instruments, such as bells, chimes, gongs, or a Tibetan singing bowl.
5. Scents can help to create a relaxed atmosphere. Burn incense or spray oils or plant essence to soothe the soul.

He who talks does not know. He who knows does not talk.

— Chinese proverb

Having a peaceful place in your house will give you and your child a chance to unwind and listen to the stillness.

96

Helping Children Cope with Trauma, Loss, and Death

Help children cope with the losses in life and teach them how to grow and learn through the grieving process.

We have been loved from before the beginning.

— Julian of Norwich

When Julia was two years old, she developed a case of croup, and within an eight hour period, her temperature rose to 103 degrees. It was just four days before Christmas, and all of us were anticipating a happy holiday week. Instead, Julia was in the hospital by midnight with a severe case of pneumonia. In fact, doctors told us that her lungs were almost completely filled when she arrived, and that had we waited even an hour longer, she probably would have died. She was immediately put in an oxygen tent, and for the next few days the only contact her dad and I had with her was holding her hand through a small opening in the tent. It was a frightening time for all of us, but also a bonding time that helped us realize how precious life really was.

Within twenty-four hours after Julia was admitted to the hospital, we contacted a number of friends, asking for their prayers and support. We asked each person to hold the same picture in their minds at the stroke of each hour, which was an image of hundreds of angels surrounding Julia in her hospital room, watching over her and singing to her, as she became well once again. Although our friends were from all walks of life, each person agreed to hold the image in mind, along with his or her own personal prayers for her safety and healing. We believed that twenty-one people focusing on Julia's recovery at the beginning of each hour would surely add some powerful support.

Although the doctors told us that her stay would be up to a few weeks, Julia's speedy recovery amazed everyone. Within four days, she was home with us and opening presents. It was Christmas Day. That night, when we tucked her in bed, we said a special prayer of thanks. We went over a long list of friends, family, and even some of the hospital staff who had gone out of their way to be kind to her. "And don't forget the angels," she said. "The ones who were singing to me on the ceiling when I was sick," she added matter-of-factly. I gave her a long hug and tucked her in bed. It was only after I went downstairs that I realized that Julia hadn't known about the circle of friends we'd called or about our images of the angels. She had been too sick to speak at all, much less hear us talking amidst the noise of the oxygen tent. Our only mode of communication with her had been through touch. I lay awake that night filled with a sense of wonder over the whole experience. Had she picked up on our thoughts, or did she really see angels, I wondered. I realized that it didn't really matter. The only thing that mattered was the healing power of love and the joy all of us felt that she was still in our midst.

Several weeks later, Julia began to ask numerous questions about death. With her own close brush with death, she had a new sense of the value and frailty of life. "If I had died at the hospital, Mom, would you be sad?" she asked inquisitively. "Yes, for a while," I answered her honestly. "Would I still be able to see you if I wasn't here anymore?" she wondered. "I don't know," was all that I could answer. Over the next several weeks, I found myself answering "I don't know" all too often to Julia's questions about death. Out of frustration, one day she blurted out, "Well, if you don't know, then who is going to teach me how to die, Mom?" That was a very good question. Who does teach others how to die in this country anyway? Most of us are busy trying to figure out how to live! But isn't death an integral part of life — the other side of the coin?

In some countries, such as India, many of the spiritual teachers believe that teaching others how to die is as

Any disaster you can survive is an improvement in your character, your stature, and your life. What a privilege!

— Joseph Campbell

important as teaching them how to live. In Hermann Hesse's classic novel *Siddhartha,* there is a scene concerning a man preparing for his own "conscious death." A ferryman named Vasudeva, who had lived a long, productive life, sensed that the end of his life was near. Serenity shone from his face as he looked deep into the eyes of his companion, Siddhartha, and said, "I have waited for this hour, my friend. Now that it has arrived, let me go. I have been Vasudeva the ferryman for a long time. Now, it is over. Farewell hut, farewell river, farewell Siddhartha. I am going into the woods; I am going into the unity of all things," he said with radiance in his eyes. He went deep into the woods and sat under a tree, fully awake, sitting quietly, until his spirit slipped from his body into the next realm.

Most children in our culture will learn to fear and deny their own death rather than prepare for it as Vasudeva did. Children are not taught to court the dark side of life or to embrace feelings of emptiness or sadness. When loss or trauma does occur, shock and denial often follow. Many children watch the adults in their world numb themselves to the reality of pain and loss with busyness, addiction, or by simply shutting down their feelings. Woody Allen summed up the all-American attitude on death when he said, "I have no fear of my own death; I just have no intention of being there when it happens!"

To me, every hour of the light and dark is a miracle.

— Walt Whitman

Dr. Elisabeth Kübler-Ross, a pioneer in the field of death and dying, encourages families to talk about trauma, loss, and death before they occur, so that when they do happen, children will have some understanding to lean on. Children need to learn about the various stages that they will most likely go through when they experience trauma, loss, or death. Here are the five stages of coping with loss that Kübler-Ross suggests that most human beings will go through.

The Five Stages of Coping with Death or Loss

1. **Denial and Isolation:** A sense of shock and disbelief about the loss.

2. **Anger:** A feeling of rage over having to face the loss.
3. **Bargaining:** A deep desire to gain control over the loss by attempting to bargain (e.g., I'll never fight with my sister again if my mom lives).
4. **Depression and Sadness:** A feeling of deep sorrow or remorse over the loss.
5. **Acceptance:** A willingness to come to grips with the loss and accept it.

It's important for children to understand that going through these stages is a natural part of coping with loss. Children often want to know how long it will take to move through the above stages. The best answer to give a child is that it will take as long as it takes. Grieving has a time clock all its own and does not occur in a straight line but rather on a zigzag path that gradually leads to a place of surrender and acceptance. The five stages don't necessarily occur in the above sequence, but most children will experience each of the five stages to some extent in their grieving process. When children do go through a trauma or loss, it will be useful for them to know that whatever they are feeling is a part of the process of learning to let go. Here are seven of the most common ways that children experience loss.

The lowest ebb is the turn of the tide.

— H. W. Longfellow

Seven Ways That Children Experience Trauma or Loss

1. **Failure:** Failing at something significant, such as an important event or tournament, a class, or grade in school, or being fired from a job.
2. **Loss:** Losing a valuable possession, ending a friendship or love relationship, moving to a new area and leaving the old area behind, or the loss of a valuable opportunity.
3. **Illness:** Losing one's health, either temporarily or permanently, or watching a significant other lose his or her health or well-being.

4. **Divorce:** Losing one's family system and one or both parents in the household due to a marriage ending.

5. **Violence:** Being violated physically, mentally, or emotionally; coping with the violence that a significant other has experienced; or dealing with the violence that societies past and present have endured.

6. **Death:** Coping with the knowledge that one's own death is near or coming to grips with the death of family, friends, pets, people in the community, or the world. Violent deaths are included, such as war, murder, and suicide.

7. **Catastrophe:** Facing the unexpected, such as floods, famine, fires, earthquakes, riots, tornadoes, accidents, and all other natural and unnatural disasters.

When children experience any one of these traumas, they will need ongoing support, empathy, and guidance to move through the five stages of loss. When any of the above traumas do occur, children need to be informed in a loving and direct manner. A friend of ours came home one day after school when she was seven years old and found her mother in bed, despondent and surrounded by comforting friends with somber expressions. She was told that her father had a heart attack and was in the hospital, when in fact he had committed suicide and was dead. After twenty-four hours of hushed voices and tearful faces, she made the announcement herself and said, "Daddy is dead, isn't he!" The silence and their grief-stricken faces had been more than she could bear. "I had to figure out that my dad was dead for myself at seven years old because no one had the courage to tell me," she said regretfully fifty years later. She remained haunted over the years by her father's death, with a nagging sense that there was something that she hadn't been told about her father's "heart attack." Many years later, she read the coroner's report and finally received the full truth about her father's death. It

There are two big forces at work, external and internal. We have very little control over external forces such as tornadoes, earthquakes, floods, disasters, illness and pain. What really matters is the internal force. How do I respond to those disasters? Over that I have complete control.

— Leo Buscaglia

was only after she had all of the facts that she could finish grieving and let go of her father. Here are a few simple ideas to keep in mind when helping children face trauma or loss.

Ten Ways to Help Children Cope with Trauma, Loss, or Death

1. **Be Honest:** Tell children the truth. Find a comfortable or familiar place to talk and share the facts quietly and honestly, in a soothing voice tone. A seven-year-old boy whose four-year-old sister died in a car accident said, "My mom took me to my favorite chair and held me close. She told me that my sister wouldn't be coming back home from the hospital because she died. I cried and asked lots of questions. She cried, too. I was really scared, but it helped that she answered all my questions."

    This is a miracle that happens every time to those who really love: The more they give, the more they possess.

    — Rainer Maria Rilke

2. **Give Empathy:** Give children plenty of empathy and support for as long as it is needed, whether there are any visible signs of emotion or not. Offer a listening ear, a kind deed, a warm smile, and a reassuring hug often. When thirteen-year-old Jake found out that his father was moving out, he didn't cry for a month. He had a very understanding aunt who gave him attention and empathy. One day, he began to cry, and, as he put it, "I let the lid off the pressure cooker and cried all day at her house. After that, it was easier to cry about it when I needed to."

3. **Encourage All Feelings:** Assure children that there is no right way to feel, there is just their way. Let children know that it's okay to feel sad, mad, confused, scared, or lonely. A fourteen-year-old girl whose dog died after eleven years said, "At first, I couldn't feel anything. Then I would swing from mad to sad. My dad told me that whatever I was feeling was perfectly okay. That helped a lot."

4. **Talk about It:** Let any regrets, fears, questions, or

"should haves" flow, knowing that feeling the feelings and asking the questions are all part of the healing process. Encourage children to talk about it as much as they need to. In the Jewish faith, some families spend a week of time sitting on a special bench, which is called "sitting shivah." All of the deceased one's friends come to sit on the bench with the family to share thoughts and feelings about the loved one, which often brings comfort and relief to the family members.

In the middle of difficulty lies opportunity.

— Albert Einstein

5. **Find Peer Support:** If the trauma or loss is significant, help children to find other children to talk to who have gone through a similar experience. Being heard and understood by one's peers is one of the most powerful ways to heal. A fifteen-year-old girl who experienced a violent gang beating attended a support group with other teens who had been physically abused. She said, "As we helped each other, we helped ourselves."

6. **Help Children to Reach Out:** Encourage children to ask family and friends for attention, support, comfort, or a shoulder to cry on. Let them know that asking for help is a sign of strength, not weakness. When a twelve-year-old boy went through an earthquake with his family, he said, "We all learned what it means to say the words 'I need help.' And we found that there are many people who really do want to help."

7. **Use the Arts:** Help children to express feelings that are difficult to talk about through drawing, painting, pottery, poetry, journaling, music, or movement. When six-year-old Lisa witnessed a violent murder in her neighborhood, she was quiet and withdrawn for several weeks. One afternoon, her parents got out some paints and paper, and she painted a picture of the entire scene. When she was done, she screamed and cried for a long time. Drawing the picture helped her to let out the

frozen sounds that were lodged in her throat from watching the gruesome scene.

8. **Use Ritual:** Creating a personal ritual can help someone who is grieving to move through the loss. A woman whose husband died had a Native American teacher and a group of women gather in the woods to help her through the agony of the early stages of her grief. They gathered in a circle and put their hands on her heart and back, encouraging her to "cry it all out." When she was through, they had her lie on the ground and say good-bye to her husband for the last time. They ended by singing together and sharing their feelings. She said it was so powerful and healing that she went home and repeated the ritual with her grown children.

9. **Reassure Children that There Is Life after Loss:** Although it will take as long as it takes, it's important for children to know that relief will come. C. S. Lewis was happily married to a poet for four brief years when she died of cancer. Shortly after her death he wrote, "Her absence is like the sky, spread over everything," and talked of his need to know that someday the pain would cease.

10. **Trust in the Cycles of Life:** As time passes, help children to look for "gifts from the abyss," and assure them that they will smile again, live again, and love again. Help them to realize that we are only seeing one small part of the picture. An eleven-year-old girl said, "For a while, it was so hard to live without my mom, but now I can see more of the big picture, and I know that I am going to be okay."

In the midst of winter, I finally learned that there was in me an invincible spring.

— Albert Camus

Teaching children to understand more about coping with trauma, loss, and death will give them tools that will help them to survive the loss of a pet, a job, a significant other, or any other losses that may come into their lives as disguised teachers.

97

Meditation

Teach your child to get still, breathe with awareness, and listen to the wisdom within through the art of meditation.

A gospel singer once defined the difference between prayer and meditation by saying, "When I pray, I talk to God, but when I meditate, God talks to me." Meditation is the purest form of listening. Meditation helps children continue with all of life and experience the worlds within, as well as the worlds without.

Meditation helps children realize that one of the greatest teachers they will ever have is sitting inside their own hearts. Although techniques can be useful, the only true requirement for meditation is a willingness to get still, breathe slowly, and listen. Whether a family is religious, eclectic, agnostic, or atheistic, teaching children to meditate is an invaluable tool to help them learn to tap into the realm of infinite possibilities. The psychologist William James said, "Our ordinary waking consciousness is but one form of consciousness. All around us lie infinite worlds, separated only by the thinnest veils." Setting the stage is an important part of daily meditation. Here are a few suggestions for children who are beginning to learn how to become quiet and still.

Be still and know that I am God.

— Psalm 46:10

Preparation for Meditation

1. **Timing:** Put aside twenty minutes at a quiet time of day, such as morning or evening. (For the very

young, start with five minutes and work up to twenty minutes. Older children may want to meditate longer.)

2. **Quiet Place:** Create a special area of the house in a corner of a room that is just for meditating. Sit in the same spot each day if possible.

3. **Sitting:** Sit in an upright position, with legs crossed and spine straight, in a comfortable posture, on a soft rug, mat, or a firm pillow.

4. **Breathing:** Spend a few minutes completely focused on the breath, just breathing in and out very slowly, until the breath begins to flow in a rhythm of its own.

5. **Music and Singing:** Play relaxing music or sounds from nature in the background, or spend the first five minutes singing a spiritual verse over and over again to help the body and mind become still and quiet.

The longest journey is the journey inward of him who has chosen his destiny, who has started upon his quest for the source of being.

— Dag Hammarskjöld

Meditation is simple, but it's not easy. Although techniques aren't necessary, they can be useful, especially in the beginning. Here are a few ideas to consider.

Techniques for Meditation

1. **Following the Breath:** Most of us begin to forget how to breathe by the time we are ten years old. Simply learning to follow the breath in and out lies at the root of all meditation. Breathing in a slow and conscious manner does more to alleviate stress and tension than almost anything else.

2. **Focusing:** Have your child, with eyes open, focus all attention on an object, such as a candle or a flower, and breathe in a slow, relaxed manner.

3. **Visual Imagery:** Help your child create a peaceful scene from nature to focus on, such as a warm shining sun, a soft fluffy cloud, or a colorful rainbow.

Lead your child on a short guided journey if you'd like, to heighten the imagination while quieting the body.

4. **Singing or Chanting Meditation:** Sing an inspirational verse in repetition out loud together while you sit, or have your child silently repeat a phrase over and over, such as "I sit in the seat of great stillness." Or perhaps recite a spiritual verse silently and repeatedly in your native tongue or in another language. Christians sometimes repeat a verse from the Bible over and over again, such as "Know the truth, and the truth will set you free," and Hindus often repeat a Sanskrit line, such as "Om mani padme hum."

We dance round in a ring and suppose, but the Secret sits in the middle and knows.

— Robert Frost

5. **Walking Meditation:** For those who have a difficult time keeping still, walking meditations are a useful way to still the mind. Buddhists have used mindful walking as a meditation for several centuries. Find a small area (twenty to thirty feet or so) and simply walk back and forth with a sense of heightened awareness. Feel each movement as you walk, and become aware of your feet as they come in contact with the Earth. Walking meditations can be done outside as well as inside.

6. **Naming the Thought:** Shamans of the ancient cultures used to have a habit of naming each thought as it came up while meditating, taking notice of the thought, and simply acknowledging it, such as "This is a joyful thought," or "This is a sad thought." Buddhist teacher Jack Kornfield suggests that one consider the insistent thoughts that come up again and again as "tunes on the hit parade list." If your child continues to have the thought "I wonder how I did on the math exam," for example, an inner response might be, "Thoughts of worry about the math exam — ah, this is number three on the hit parade list this week!"

7. **Welcoming the Guest:** William Moreau, a Christian minister from the Caribbean, suggests that one learn to welcome all thoughts in meditation as guests. "All of our thoughts have something to teach us. Often they must be heard and honored before they will vanish." If your child has a persistent thought or fear in meditation, encourage him or her to say, "Oh, it's you again — nice to see you! What would you like to tell me today?" After receiving an answer, continue to meditate.

Although meditation is its own reward, there are a number of special benefits for children. Here are a few.

Benefits of Meditation

1. **Deeper Relaxation:** Meditation slows down the heart rate, alleviates stress, and calms the nervous system. Recent research suggests that twenty minutes of meditation are equal to a full cycle of sleep (one and one half hours) and improve overall health and longevity.

2. **Enhanced Creativity:** Meditation helps children to tap into deeper levels of mind, allowing them to have more creative resources to draw from and more innovative ideas for problem solving.

3. **Deeper Concentration:** Children who know how to deeply relax have a greater attention span and more capacity to remain alert and calm while learning.

4. **Expanded Sensitivity and Intuition:** Meditation is one of the best ways to develop children's intuition and to help them to become more attuned to all walks of life.

5. **Greater Self-Esteem:** Children who meditate learn how to tap into more of their inner resources and trust themselves. A child with a rich inner life is a

The most beautiful and most profound emotion we can experience is the sensation of the mystical.

— Albert Einstein

confident child who takes more risks and reaches out to others more.

Meditation teaches children to live one moment at a time, one day at a time. It helps them to experience more of the present, and more of themselves. A nine-year-old boy who meditates with his father several mornings a week said, "Meditation helps me to go inside and ask myself, 'How am I doing in here?'" Perhaps the benefits of meditation are best summed up in this statement made by a ten-year-old boy: "I've finally figured it out. No matter where I go, there I am. Since there's no getting away from me, I might as well take the time to get to know me!"

98

Books of Timeless Wisdom

**Read the works of the great poets, philosophers,
and spiritual leaders from various traditions
and share in the gift of timeless wisdom together.**

Wouldn't it be nice if all of us were born with an instruction manual entitled *How to Grow Up to Be a Healthy and Happy Human Being?* As a speaker, I have often asked groups of adults to brainstorm a fictitious table of contents for the manual that we never received at birth. The chapter headings they come up with never center on fame, power, fortune, good grades, or mastery of knowledge, but rather on mastery of values. Having faith, taking care of one's health, learning to love, having healthy relationships, coping with change, crisis, or loss, and developing one's talents are always near the top of the list.

> *You are a principal
> work, a fragment of
> God himself. Why then
> are you ignorant of
> your high birth?*
>
> — Epictetus

It's curious that the "big stuff," such as birth, death, love, and life, doesn't receive much attention at school. Education still tends to focus on the "small stuff," like mastering subject material, passing tests, following rules, and academics. Although these things are important, they don't provide a foundation of spiritual values that each child needs to lead a fulfilling life. The findings of archaeology show us that the needs of the spirit are ancient; humans carved their spiritual longing in images and painted on cave walls long before the invention of the alphabet. Centuries later, we are still beckoned by a compelling force that urges us to look within. In times of inspiration, it is the light that illuminates our way. In times of sorrow, it is the armature that we all rely on. This thread of timeless wisdom weaves through the events of our lives with precision and care.

Many of the great thinkers over the ages have attempted to capture the essence of this wisdom through art, music, poetry, essays, stories, or a philosophy of life. They have left behind a legacy of their journeys through the gift of their works, many of which transcend personal beliefs or religious preference. Here are a few ideas to help you to deepen your appreciation for the works of timeless wisdom that have been passed along through the ages.

Six Ways to Share in the Gift of Timeless Wisdom

1. **The Rise and Shine Reading:** A family of three from India makes it a habit to start each day with a short reading from a spiritual text. They often read together from the Khandogya-Upanishad, the Bhagavad Gita, the poetic works of Rainer Maria Rilke, or from a daily meditation book. Said the father, "I want my children to wake up each day with a sense of joy and gratitude in their hearts that they can carry with them as they go about their busy day. I can think of no better way to accomplish this than to show kindness to them as they awaken and to read each morning from the great works as they eat their breakfast."

2. **Five Minutes of Wisdom a Day:** Adapt the traditional family custom of reading five minutes of timeless wisdom at the end of each meal. A Christian family of four rotates between reading the Bible one day and reading from a classic work the next day for variety. Some of their favorite readings are from the works of the beloved C. S. Lewis, Thomas Merton, Robert Frost, and the writings of

There are single thoughts that contain the essence of a whole volume, single sentences that have the beauties of a large work.

— Joseph Joubert

Thomas à Kempis. For weeks after hearing Robert Frost's poem "The Road Not Taken," the three-year-old proudly recited the last three lines aloud to anyone who would listen:

> *Two roads diverged in a wood, and I —*
> *I took the one less traveled by,*
> *And that has made all the difference.*

3. **Quotation of the Day:** A busy family of seven chooses a simple line from a poem or reads a quotation each day at the end of their meal, taking a few minutes to discuss the meaning of the words. Some of their favorites are from the works of Walt Whitman, Dag Hammarskjöld, Buddha, Emily Dickinson, e. e. cummings, the Psalms from the Bible, the Talmud, and Anne Morrow Lindbergh. They take turns providing quotations from various texts, or they read from books of compiled poems and quotes.

This above all: to thine own self be true.

— William Shakespeare

4. **Fireside Readings:** Choose an evening each week to curl up together near a fire (or, if you don't have a fireplace, a blanket or a mug of hot tea will do) and read aloud together for an hour or two. I started this tradition with Julia a few years ago, and it has become a cherished time to explore the great works and share ideas together. We have read from the I Ching, the Viking Book of Runes, *The Life and Teachings of the Masters of the Far East,* the poetry of Kahlil Gibran, the Tao Te Ching, and the Bible, as well as from works by Ralph Waldo Emerson, Paramahansa Yogananda, William Blake, Rabrindranath Tagore, and William Shakespeare. We keep a list of future readings that we'd like to share together, so that we have more wisdom to look forward to in the future.

5. **Wisdom on Tape:** A man with five grown children and twelve grandchildren began to record excerpts

from many of the great works on tape according to categories, such as love, challenge, creativity, faith, and persistence when his own children were growing up. He now has several hundred cassette tapes in his library that are available on over two hundred different subjects. Each tape begins with some readings and is followed by his own personal commentary, including examples from his own life. "The tapes are great," his fourteen-year-old grandson said. "They are interesting and often funny. I feel like I know more about life and a lot more about Grandpa because he took the time to make these tapes for us."

6. **The Family Book of Wisdom:** Gather your favorite prayers, poems, great ideas, and quotations and create your own family book of collected wisdom. We have a book that we have titled Golden Threads. It is a handwritten compilation of many of our most beloved works, to be read again and again, to our children's children's children. It includes some of the brilliant ideas that our family and friends have expressed, as well as some of the timeless classics. Here are a few samples from the book.

> *I am a spiritual being having a human experience, not a human being having a spiritual experience.*
>
> — Wayne Dyer

> *When it is dark enough, you can see the stars.*
>
> — Ralph Waldo Emerson

> *The general message of the Universe is, when in doubt, expand!*
>
> — Matthew Fox

> *The quality of the moment depends not on what we get from it, but on what we bring to it.*
>
> — Dan Millman

For peace of mind, resign as general manager of the universe.

— Larry Eisenberg

We have been loved from before the beginning.
— Julian of Norwich

The journey of the spirit is rarely a straight line between two points. The road of life our children are traveling will include some detours, uphill climbs, circular paths, and, at times, a willingness to travel without a map. Books of timeless wisdom remind us that life is a journey, not a destination, and that every ending brings a new beginning.

Oh wisdom of the ages, lead us and be our guide!

— Celtic prayer

99

Spiritual Retreat

Go on spiritual retreats with your child periodically, and share in the gift of reflection and renewal.

Several years ago, I was visiting a European family who lived in New York City. The father of the house, I was told, was away on a spiritual retreat in the wilderness by himself — something that his children spoke of with respect. I found out that there were three different kinds of spiritual retreats in their household. Each of the six family members did at least one solo retreat per year for a weekend to get some time alone to think and reflect. They also held a family retreat, which usually lasted three days, to renew family ties and breathe new life into their spiritual values. The third retreat was a private retreat for the parents, which usually lasted three to five days, to renew their marriage commitment and to spend some time in spiritual reflection together.

I was fascinated by the idea, and I began to converse with the family about retreats and vacations interchangeably. "A retreat isn't the same thing as a vacation," the ten-year-old informed me. "On a vacation, you go on an adventure in the world. On a retreat, you go on an adventure inside of yourself." When the father returned, I asked him about the family retreats. He informed me that six years ago, when he was just forty-two, he had had a serious heart attack that he believes was related to stress and overwork. During the same time period, he came across Socrates' well-known quotation: "The unexamined life is not worth living." This idea hit him right between the eyes, and he decided to make some major changes in his life. He stepped down a notch in his high-level executive job so that he would have more time to spend each day with his family, whom he now admits he "hardly knew." He decided to take at least three vacations a year with the family and three spiritual retreats each year — one alone, one with his wife, and one with the whole family. Within two years, he was experiencing a level of wellness that he never knew was possible when he was, as he put it, "chasing my own tail in the rat race of life."

I asked him how he spent the time on their spiritual retreats. "Usually," he said, "the time is divided up in three ways — silence, long walks in nature, and meditation. We don't talk a whole lot and we make an agreement before we go that we won't discuss any problems or issues or dwell on current affairs. This is a time to go inward, to listen, and to reflect on how far we've come since our last retreat." Over time, this family has discovered a wealth of retreat centers in the wilderness, all within a few hundred miles of their home. Most of these places offer a simple dwelling place at a reasonable price, making them accessible for solo as well as group retreats.

Here are a few ideas to help make spiritual retreat time more meaningful for you and your child.

we are so both
and oneful
night cannot be so
sky
sky cannot be so
sunful
i am through you
so i

— e. e. cummings

Five Ways to Make Your Retreat More Meaningful

1. **Eat Light to Feel Right:** Eat healthy foods and drink a lot of water on your retreat. Make it a period of rest and repose for the body by providing the best sources of nutrition available. Many families eat only raw food during their retreat time.

2. **Commune with Nature:** Spend a large part of each day communing with all of the life forces surrounding you when on a spiritual retreat. A great spiritual teacher once said, "If a person would spend but one

uninterrupted hour communing wholeheartedly with nature, all of my teachings would be unnecessary!"

3. **Find a Special Spot:** When going out into the wilderness, look for a sanctuary area that speaks to you. Imagine that you are putting up your "power spot antennae," and let the right place find you.

4. **Listen from the Soul:** Many people go on a spiritual retreat with lofty expectations of "clearing this," or "healing that." The best way to begin a spiritual retreat is to have just one goal in mind — listening from within. We're bound to meet up with our "ten thousand thoughts" along the way, and we will surely encounter what Buddha calls "the drunken monkey" — that part of the mind that races here and there in a drunken stupor. With humor and persistence, we can learn to listen to it all — our questions, fears, needs, hopes, and dreams, as well as the messages that nature whispers to us.

One should lie empty, open, choiceless as a beach — waiting for a gift from the sea.

— Anne Morrow Lindbergh

5. **Open Up to Receive Gifts:** There is a fable about a man who prayed in earnest that God would bestow unto him all manner of good things. The angels stormed the heavens and opened the floodgates so that he would have every one of his wishes rushed to him. On the delivery date, the man's heart was filled with doubt, and he decided that he was not worthy of these great gifts after all. The angels were greatly disappointed and could no longer deliver his gifts, because the man's *doubt canceled the order.* The opposite of doubt is trust. Practice trusting that you will receive exactly what you need on your spiritual retreat. Gifts may arise in the brushing of the leaves, messages may whisper in the sound in the wind, and insights may be heard in the calling of the birds. Remember the Zen phrase "Expect nothing, but receive everything."

Take some retreat time periodically with your child, to visit the secret garden within and learn of its sacred teachings.

100

Teachers and Guides

Learn and study together with teachers, mentors, and guides for self-awareness, inspiration, and growth.

There is a Zen parable about a student and teacher sitting together to share some tea. As the student expressed his desire to learn and grow, his teacher began to pour some tea into the student's cup. When the tea reached the brim of the cup, the teacher continued pouring the tea, which spilled over the cup and onto the floor. "If you want to take in new knowledge," the teacher said calmly, "you must first be willing to empty your cup."

The really great make you feel that you, too, can become great.

— Mark Twain

A very powerful and strong samurai once went to visit a small humble monk. "Monk," he said, "teach me about heaven and hell!" The monk looked up at the powerful warrior and said, "Teach you about heaven and hell! I couldn't teach you about anything! You're dirty, you smell, and your blade is rusty! You're a disgrace and an embarrassment to the samurai class. Get out of my sight. I can't stand you."

The samurai was furious. He shook, got red in the face, and was speechless with rage. He pulled out his sword and raised it above him, preparing to slay the monk.

"This is hell," said the monk softly.

The samurai was overwhelmed by the courage and compassion that the little monk had displayed. He had risked his own life to offer him this teaching. He humbly put down his sword, filled with gratitude, and felt very peaceful.

"And that's heaven," the monk quietly said.

Like the samurai and the Zen student, there are times when it is important to have a relationship with a teacher or spiritual guide who can help us grow past current limitations and find new understanding. In America, we place a strong value on self-sufficiency. And yet, the willingness to learn from a wise, compassionate teacher can be the greatest step of all toward true self-sufficiency. A good teacher models virtue and strength, touches our hearts, and reminds us of what is possible.

My life is my message.

— Mahatma Gandhi

A few years ago, I recognized a need within me to work closely with a teacher who could offer some counsel and guidance. Although I had guidance through written works and spiritual groups, I knew that I needed one-on-one contact with someone who could help me to move through some blind spots and encourage me to continue on in my life with courage.

There is an old saying that goes: "When the student is ready, the teacher appears." As my desire became very strong, I met a teacher who served the role of "life coach" and helped me to see many of the fears that were stopping me from acting on what I knew in my heart to be true. A few more teachers have appeared over time, and I now appreciate the value of mentorship more and more. We recently returned from a spiritual retreat with a wonderful teacher we have been studying with, and we are currently learning from a "compassion coach," who helps us to relate as parent and teen with more empathy. The gifts we have received from the teachers and mentors who have appeared on our path over the last few years have been enriching and rewarding. Below is a summary of the qualities we have found most beneficial. As you will see, they include several of the key qualities needed to become a great parent as well.

"Are you a god?"
they asked. "No!"
"An angel?" "No."
"A saint?" "No."
"Then what are you?"
Buddha answered,
"I am awake!"

— Huston Smith

Ten Qualities of a Great Teacher

1. Models what is taught with integrity and wisdom.
2. Offers compassion and encouragement, rather than control or judgment.

3.   Respects you as an equal, and enjoys learning from you.

4.   Believes in your ability to succeed, and holds the vision with you.

5.   Has a good sense of humor.

6.   Encourages you to trust yourself and follow your heart.

7.   Helps you find your own answers rather than giving you the answers.

8.   Inspires you to do what you most want to do.

9.   Has patience and understanding with all phases of your growth.

10. Gives you complete freedom to leave when it's time.

There are as many different teachers as there are individuals. It's not so much who the teacher is, but the quality of what the teacher has to offer. A father-son team has a martial arts teacher who is teaching them the ancient Chinese discipline of meditative movement, tai chi chuan. They are learning skills that involve physical discipline, mental clarity, and spiritual principles. They see him twice a week, and they both feel that their teacher has changed their lives dramatically for the better. "We used to argue and bicker a lot," the father said, "but now we're so busy practicing our art form together that we don't have much interest in conflict. Besides, our teacher has taught us the value of nonresistance, and we're applying it to our relationship more and more."

A Christian family of five has a wonderful mentor from their church. "He's just like one of the family and has inspired all of us to get closer and to be more honest," said the mother. They receive counseling from him as a family every other week, and they have him over for dinner once a month or so. Since both parents came from families where there was a lot of struggle and conflict, they have been especially appreciative of their teacher's simple, compassionate listening skills and suggestions.

A wise teacher would rather underplay his power than preen his feathers; screen you from his power than burn you by it; walk gently by your side rather than crush you from an upraised throne; and enlist your approval with wisdom rather than imposing opinion by force of will.

— Pir Vilayat Khan

A woman from India studied under a wise teacher for many years before she had a family of her own. Her teacher had modeled a great deal of faith and trust, and when she was dying, her students were crying and weeping outside the door. When she heard this, she said, "Why are they crying? Have they forgotten where I am going?" Several years later, when the woman's own seven-year-old son was dying in the hospital, she took great solace in remembering her teacher's words. "It made it bearable to let him go," she said, "because I could sense the presence of my teacher, and I knew that, like her, my son wasn't really going away," she said.

The kingdom of Heaven is within you.

— Jesus

The Greek philosopher Plato studied under Socrates for a number of years, learning from his wisdom and insight. One day, as they walked along the shoreline together, Plato expressed a deep yearning for truth and asked Socrates what he must do to become more aware. Socrates led him deep into the water, and when Plato was standing up to his neck in waves that were splashing against his face, Socrates grabbed the top of Plato's head and dunked him under the water. Although befuddled, Plato dutifully held his breath, trusting that his beloved teacher had good reason to be doing such an unconventional thing. A full minute passed, and Plato began to get very uncomfortable. His lungs became strained and his muscles taut as Socrates continued to hold his head firmly underwater. After another full minute had passed, Plato began to squirm violently, no longer concerned with his teacher's intentions. He wanted one thing and only one thing — to get his head above water! He kicked and splashed and yanked and shoved until Socrates finally freed him.

As he came up from the depths, panting and gasping for air, Socrates said, "When you want truth as much as you wanted this breath, you shall have it!" Like Plato, you and your child will discover that when you desire to learn as much as Plato wanted a breath of air, your teacher or guide will surely appear on your path.

Spiritual Esteem Chart

Read over the following chart of old beliefs and new beliefs, and help your child move from low esteem to full esteem while developing spiritual esteem.

From Low Esteem

1. Children are resistant and selfish by nature. They must be trained to become spiritual.

2. The spiritual beliefs we teach our children are the best of all. Everyone should believe as we do. There is only one true way — our way.

3. Children should follow their family's spiritual beliefs without question, to show respect.

4. Children will inevitably fall short of their spiritual values because they are inherently weak.

5. Children should be taught to feel guilty when they don't act in accord with their spiritual values.

6. With so many different religions in the world, we will never have spiritual unity.

To Full Esteem

1. Children have great capacity to love when they are raised with love. They are naturally spiritual.

2. Our spiritual beliefs work for us, just as others have beliefs that work for them. There are many paths leading to truth.

3. Children ask questions to learn and grow. Asking questions is a dynamic part of the spiritual journey and fosters self-awareness.

4. Children will make mistakes because they are learning. With compassion and guidance, they will learn to strengthen their commitment to their values.

5. Children need acceptance and understanding when they aren't in harmony with their values. It is self-understanding that raises awareness, not guilt.

6. Underneath the many religions is a similar heart's desire for spiritual unity. The more we recognize this and honor religious differences, the sooner we will have world harmony.

resource
guide

Recommended Reading

Books on Self-Esteem

Barksdale Foundation. *Building Self-Esteem.* Idyllwild, Calif.: Barksdale Foundation, P.O. Box 187, Idyllwild, CA 92349, 1974.

Borba, Michele. *Esteem Builders K-8.* Rolling Hills Estates, Calif.: Jalmar Press, 1989.

Branden, Nathaniel. *Experience High Self-Esteem.* New York: Simon & Schuster, 1988.

————. *How to Raise Your Self-Esteem.* New York: Bantam Books, 1987.

Canfield, Jack, and Hansen, Mark. *Chicken Soup for the Soul: 101 Stories to Open the Heart and Rekindle the Spirit.* Deerfield Beach, Fla.: Health Communications, 1993.

Canfield, Jack, and Wells, Harold C. *100 Ways to Enhance Self-Concept in the Classroom: A Handbook for Teachers and Parents.* Englewood Cliffs, N.J.: Prentice Hall, 1976.

Clarke, Jean Illsley. *Self-Esteem: A Family Affair.* Minneapolis: Winston Press, 1978.

Espeland, Pamela, and Wallner, Rosemary. *Making the Most of Today.* Minneapolis: Free Spirit Press, 1991.

Kaufman, Gershen, and Raphael, Lev. *Stick Up for Yourself! Every Kid's Guide to Personal Power and Positive Self-Esteem.* Minneapolis: Free Spirit Press, 1990.

Krawertz, Michael. *Passport to Self-Esteem.* New York: Henry Holt, 1990.

Loomans, Diana. *The Lovables in the Kingdom of Self-Esteem.* Tiburon, Calif.: H J Kramer, 1991.

————. *Today I Am Lovable: 365 Activities for Kids.* Tiburon, Calif.: H J Kramer, 1996.

Loomans, Diana, Kolberg, Karen and Loomans, Julia. *Positively Mother Goose*. Tiburon, Calif.: H J Kramer, 1991.

Marston, Stephanie. *The Magic of Encouragement*. New York: Pocket Books, 1992.

Mather, Anne, and Weldom, Louise. *The Cat at the Door: Affirmation Stories for Children*. Minneapolis: Hazelden, 1991.

Palmer, Pat, and Froehner, Melissa. *Teen Esteem*. San Luis Obispo, Calif.: Impact Publishers, 1989.

Parsley, Bonnie. *The Choice Is Yours: A Teenager's Guide to Self-Discovery, Relationships, Values, and Spiritual Growth*. New York: Simon & Schuster, 1992.

Rosenberg, Ellen. *Growing Up Feeling Good*. New York: Puffin Books, 1987.

Satir, Virginia. *Self-Esteem*. Milbrae, Calif.: Celestial Arts, 1975.

Williams, Mary. *My Precious Child: Affirmations for the Child Within*. Deerfield Beach, Fla.: Health Communications, 1991.

Books on Parenting

Baldwin, Rahima. *You Are Your Child's First Teacher*. Berkeley, Calif.: Celestial Arts, 1989.

Bennett, Steve, and Bennett, Ruth. *365 TV-Free Activities You Can Do with Your Child*. Holbrook, Mass.: Bob Adams, 1991.

Berends, Polly Berrien. *Whole Child, Whole Parent*. New York: Harpers Magazine Press, 1975.

Childre, Doc Lew. *Heart Smarts: Teenage Guide for the Puzzle of Life*. Boulder Creek, Calif.: Planetary Publications, 1991.

Clarke, Jean, and Dawson, Connie. *Parenting Ourselves, Parenting Our Children*. Minneapolis: Hazelden, 1989.

Cutright, Melitta. *Growing Up Confident — Making Your Child's Early Years Learning Years*. New York: Doubleday, 1992.

Dacey, John, and Packer, Alex. *The Nurturing Parent*. New York: Fireside Books, 1992.

Durfee, Cliff. *Feel Alive with Love, Have a Heart Talk (The Heart Talk Book)*. San Diego: Live, Love, Laugh, P.O. Box 9432, San Diego, CA 92167, 1979.

Eyre, Linda, and Eyre, Richard. *Teaching Children Joy*. Salt Lake City, Utah: Shadow Mountain, 1984.

Fram, Joel, Boswell, Carol, and Maas, Margaret. *I Heard It Through the Play-Ground: 616 Best Tips from Parents.* New York: HarperCollins, 1993.

Greene, Lawrence. *1001 Ways to Improve Your Child's Schoolwork.* New York: Dell, 1991.

Hart, Dr. Louise. *The Winning Family: Increasing Self-Esteem in Your Children and Yourself.* New York: Dodd, Mead, 1987.

Jenkins, Peggy. *The Joyful Child.* Tucson, Ariz.: Harbinger House, 1989.

Johnson, Spencer, M.D. *The One-Minute Mother: The Quickest Way for You to Help Your Children Learn to Like Themselves and Want to Behave Themselves.* New York: Morrow, 1983.

Louv, Richard. *101 Things You Can Do for Our Children's Future.* New York: Anchor Books, 1994.

Mann, Richard. *The Wonderful Father.* Chicago: Turnbull & Willoughby, 1985.

McMahon, Tom. *It Works for Us! Proven Child Care Tips from Experienced Parents across the Country.* New York: Pocket Books, 1993.

Miller, Alice. *The Drama of the Gifted Child.* New York: Basic Books, 1980.

———. *For Your Own Good.* New York: Farrar, Straus and Giroux, 1984.

———. *Thou Shalt Not Be Aware.* New York: New American Library, 1986.

———. *The Untouched Key.* New York: Anchor Press, 1991.

Nelson, Jane. *Positive Discipline.* New York: Ballantine Books, 1981.

Newell, Peter. *Children Are People Too.* London: Bedford Square Press, 1989.

Perry, Susan. *Playing Smart: A Parents' Guide to Enriching, Offbeat Activities for Ages 4–14.* Minneapolis: Free Spirit Press, 1990.

Rich, Dorothy. *MegaSkills: How Families Can Help Children Succeed in School and Beyond.* Boston: Houghton Mifflin, 1988.

Stem, Ellen Sue. *I'm a Mom: Meditations for New Mothers.* New York: Dell, 1993.

Taffel, Ron, and Blau, Melinda. *Parenting by Heart.* Reading, Mass.: Addison-Wesley, 1993.

Vissell, Barry, and Vissell, Joyce. *Models of Love: The Parent-Child Journey.* Aptos, Calif.: Ramira Publishing, 1986.

Weston, Denise, and Weston, Mark. *Playful Parenting.* New York: Putnam Books, 1993.

Miscellaneous Books

Armstrong, Thomas. *In Their Own Way: Discovering and Encouraging Your Child's Personal Learning Style.* Los Angeles: Tarcher Books, 1987.

Bagley, Michael T., and Hess, Karin. *Two Hundred Ways of Using Imagery in the Classroom.* New York: Trillium Press, 1984.

Barrett, Susan L. *It's All in Your Head: A Guide to Understanding Your Brain and Boosting Your Brain Power.* Minneapolis: Free Spirit Press, 1985.

Berends, Polly Berrien. *How to Teach Your Children about God while Finding Out for Yourself.* New York: Collin Books, 1991.

Berkus, Rusty. *Life Is a Gift.* Encino, Calif.: Red Rose Press, 1982.

————. *To Heal Again: Towards Serenity and the Resolution of Grief.* Encino, Calif.: Red Rose Press, 1984.

Cassidy, John. *Juggling for the Complete Klutz.* Palo Alto, Calif.: Klutz Press, 1990.

Coles, Robert. *The Spiritual Life of Children.* New York: Houghton Mifflin, 1990.

Cornell, Joseph Bharat. *Sharing Nature with Children.* Nevada City, Calif.: Ananda Publications, 1979.

Davy, Gudrun, and Voors, Bons. *Lifeways: Working with Family Questions.* Gloucestershire, England: Hawthorn Press, 1983.

Deranja, Michael Nitai. *The Art of Joyful Education.* Nevada City, Calif.: Ananda Publications, 1980.

Dickson, Paul. *Family Words: The Dictionary for People Who Don't Know a Frone from a Brinkle.* Reading, Mass.: Addison-Wesley, 1988.

Durfee, Cliff. *More Teachable Moments.* San Diego: Live, Love, Laugh, 1983.

Elwell, Patricia A. *Creative Problem Solving for Teens.* New York: DOK Publishers, 1990.

Fisher, Richard. *Brain Games.* New York: Schocken Books, 1982.

Goelitz, Jeffrey. *The Ultimate Kid. Levels of Learning That Make a Difference.* Boulder Creek, Calif.: Planetary Publications, 1986.

Gross, Ronald. *Peak Learning.* Los Angeles: Jeremy Tarcher, 1991.

Herzog, Stephanie. *Joy in the Classroom.* Boulder Creek, Calif.: University of the Trees Press, 1982.

Hirsch, E. D., Jr. *A First Dictionary of Cultural Literacy: What Our Children Need to Know.* Boston: Houghton Mifflin, 1989.

Javna, John, and The Earthworks Group. *50 Simple Things Kids Can Do to Save the Earth.* Berkeley, Calif.: Andrews McMeel, 1990.

Jenkins, Peggy. *A Child of God: Activities for Teaching Spiritual Values to Children of All Ages.* Englewood Cliffs, N.J.: Prentice Hall, 1984.

Katz, Adrienna. *Naturewatch: Exploring Nature with Your Children.* Reading, Mass.: Addison-Wesley, 1986.

Kincher, Jonni. *Dreams Can Help.* Minneapolis: Free Spirit Press, 1990.

———. *Psychology for Kids: Forty Tests That Help You Learn about Yourself.* Minneapolis: Free Spirit Press, 1990.

Krementz, Jill. *How Does It Feel When a Parent Dies?* New York: Alfred Knopf, 1981.

Lewis, Barbara. *The Kids' Guide to Social Action.* Minneapolis: Free Spirit Press, 1991.

Loomans, Diana, and Kolberg, Karen. *The Laughing Classroom: Everyone's Guide to Teaching with Humor and Play.* Tiburon, Calif.: H J Kramer, 1993.

Martin, Bette. *The Children's Material.* Tucson, Ariz.: Miracle Experiences and You Publishing, P.O. Box 64146, Tucson, AZ 85740-1146, 1978.

McCutcheon, Randall. *Get Off My Brain.* Minneapolis: Free Spirit Press, 1990.

Milord, Susan. *Hands around the World: 365 Creative Ways to Build Cultural Awareness and Global Respect.* Charlotte, Vt.: Williamson Publishing, 1992.

Orlick, Terry. *The Cooperative Sports and Games Books.* New York: Pantheon Books, 1978.

Parlett, David. *Over One Hundred of the World's Best Word Games.* New York: Pantheon Books, 1981.

Rifkin, Jeremy. *The Green Lifestyle Handbook: 1001 Ways You Can Heal the Earth.* New York: Henry Holt, 1990.

Rofes, Eric. *The Kids Book about Death and Dying by and for Kids.* Boston: Little, Brown, 1985.

Rozman, Deborah, Ph.D. *Meditating with Children.* Boulder Creek, Calif.: University of the Trees Press, 1983.

Saunders, Antoinette, Ph.D., and Remsberg, Bonnie. *The Stress-Proof Child: A Loving Parents' Guide.* New York: Holt, Rinehart and Winston, 1984.

Simon, Sarina. *101 Amusing Ways to Develop Your Child's Thinking Skills and Creativity.* Los Angeles: RGA Publications, 1989.

Sobel, Jeff. *Everybody Wins: 393 Noncompetitive Games for Young Children.* New York: Walker, 1983.

Tanner, Joey. *Futuristics.* Scottsdale, Ariz.: Zephyr Press, 1981.

Viner, Michael, and Hilton, Pat. *365 Ways for You and Your Children to Save the Earth One Day at a Time.* New York: Warner Books, 1991.

Walker, Barbara. *Laughing Together: Giggles and Grins from around the World.* Minneapolis: Free Spirit Press, 1992.

Watson, Susan. *Sugar Free Toddlers.* Charlotte, Vt.: Williamson Publishing, 1991.

Weinstein, Matt, and Goodman, Joel. *Playfair: Everybody's Guide to Noncompetitive Play.* San Luis Obispo, Calif.: Impact Publishers, 1980.

Other Resources

This section highlights listings of a few national groups that may be of interest to your family or organization.

Adult Children of Alcoholics World Service Organization, Inc.
P.O. Box 3216
Torrance, CA 90510
www.adultchildren.org
Offers help to adults raised in addictive or dysfunctional environments, with cost-free support groups meeting in cities across the country.

National Audubon Society
700 Broadway
New York, NY 10003
www.audubon.org
Provides information on organizing youth groups in environmental education.

Center for Nonviolent Communication
2428 Foothill Boulevard, Suite E
La Crescenta, CA 91214
www.cnvc.org
With centers in twenty-two countries, this group offers seminars and education materials based on the work of Dr. Marshall Rosenberg, international peace activist, for all ages.

Children's Rainforest
1064 Kingston Avenue
London, Ontario, N6H 4C6
Canada
http://childrenrainforest.tripod.com
Provides information on children's projects to save the rain forest in
Costa Rica.

Difference Makers International
449 Santa Fe Drive, Suite 252
Encinitas, CA 92024
www.blueribbons.com
A group that focuses on raising self-esteem in children and adults of all
ages. Offers seminars and products of acknowledgment.

Earthstewards Network
P.O. Box 10697
Bainbridge Island, WA 98110
www.earthstewards.org
Offers international peace ventures, classes, and materials on peacemak-
ing and environmental protection.

Earthwatch International
3 Clock Tower Place, Suite 100
Box 75
Maynard, MA 01754
www.earthwatch.org
Recruits volunteers for field research expeditions (archaeology to zool-
ogy). Ages sixteen and older. Operates in thirty-six countries and the U.S.

Human Values Foundation
Lower Wallbridge Farmhouse, Dowlish Wake, Ilminster, Somerset
TA19 0NZ, UK
www.ehv.org.uk
An organization dedicated to teaching children to develop positive val-
ues. Direct inquiries to: June Auton, president.

Educators for Social Responsibility
23 Garden Street
Cambridge, MA 02138
www.esrnational.org

Information about how to involve your teachers in creating new ways of education for active and responsible participation in the world.

Friends of the Earth
1025 Vermont Avenue, NW, Suite 300
Washington, DC 20005
www.foe.org

Offers newsletters, information, and volunteer programs to help preserve the Earth.

The Giraffe Project
P.O. Box 759
Langley, WA 98260
www.giraffe.org

Recognizes the courage of individuals of all ages who "stick their necks out" for others. Also offers training in community action.

Global Family
11689 Lowhills Road
Nevada City, CA 95959
www.globalfamily.net

Offers seminars and educational materials, and support groups to foster peacemaking, cooperation, and nonviolent communicating.

Global Learning
P.O. Box 389
Santa Monica, CA 90406
www.DianaLoomans.com

Offers national seminars for teachers and parents on The Laughing Classroom, 100 Ways to Teach Values and Build Self-Esteem, and a number of other topics for children and adults based on the work of author Diana Loomans.

Partner Service Center
Habitat for Humanity International
121 Habitat Street
Americus, GA 31709
www.habitat.org
Deals with problems of the homeless and people with disabilities.

International Pen Friends
P.O. Box 340
Dublin 12, Ireland
www.iol.ie/ipf
Headquartered in Dublin, Ireland, this group can connect you with 250,000 pen pals of all ages in 153 countries. Visit their website or send a self-addressed, stamped envelope (SASE) for information.

Joyful You – Joyful Child
P.O. Box 3808
Sedona, AZ 86340
www.joy4u.org
Offers classes, a newsletter, cassettes, and videos on raising a healthy and joyful child.

KAP (Kids Against Pollution)
at the Children's Museum
311 Main Street, 3rd Floor
Utica, NY 13501
www.kidsagainstpollution.org
This is a kids' networking group against pollution. Send $6.00 to join the network.

Kids for Saving the Earth Guidebook
P.O. Box 421118
Minneapolis, MN 55442
www.kidsforsavingearth.org
Tells how to join this kids' organization or start your own KSE neighborhood club; gives environmental information and activities. To order free copy, write to the above address.

Model U.N. (United Nations)
U.N. Association of the U.S.A.
801 Second Avenue
New York, NY 10017

Opportunities for young people to participate in model United Nations and youth programs.

Mothers and Others for a Livable Planet
40 West 20th Street
New York, NY 10011

Focuses on environmental issues of particular relevance to children's health. Cofounded by Meryl Streep. Provides a quarterly newsletter.

National Storytelling Network
101 Courthouse Square
Jonesborough, TN 37659
www.storynet.org

Offers a national conference, newsletter, and books on storytelling.

Sierra Club National Headquarters
85 Second Street, 2nd Floor
San Francisco, CA 94105
www.sierraclub.org

Environmental information for all ages, plus inner city outings and wilderness adventures.

The Quantum Success Coaching Institute
P.O. Box 389
Santa Monica, CA 90406
(310) 712-7040
www.quantumsuccesscoaching.com

This innovative institute, founded by author Diana Loomans, offers cutting-edge coaching programs for children, teens, adults, and businesses. The institute also offers a certified training program for those interested in becoming a success coach/seminar presenter for schools or businesses.

Technotrends
Burrus Research Associates, Inc.
557 Cottonwood Avenue, Suite 106
Hartland, WI 53029-0047
www.burrus.com

Offers videos, books, multimedia, and learning systems regarding technology and the future for business and education.

World Happiness and Cooperation
P.O. Box 1153
Anacortes, WA 98221

Offers Dr. Robert Muller's copyright-free material on peace education. Dr. Muller is chancellor of the University of Peace, Costa Rica.

Youth for Environmental Sanity (YES!) Action Camps
420 Bronco Road
Soquel, CA 95073
www.yesworld.org

Organizes talks, workshops, and camps for students about environmental issues.

About the Authors

Diana Loomans is the founder of the Quantum Success Coaching Institute and president of Global Learning in Los Angeles. As a speaker and success coach, she has worked with hundreds of schools, businesses, and individuals and developed numerous coaching programs, including her renowned Quantum Success 90-Day Life-Mastery program, and her training program entitled Quantum Success Coaching.

She is an international speaker, best-selling author, poet, and journalist, with several million books, poems, and short stories in print. Her books include *The Laughing Classroom* and her renowned children's titles, *The Lovables, Today I Am Lovable,* and *Positively Mother Goose.* She has appeared on hundreds of radio and television shows nationally as a spokeswoman and author. Her inspirational poetry is found on gift items, posters, tea boxes, and in numerous books, including the Chicken Soup for the Soul series.

She has delivered over 1,500 speeches and created more than twenty workshops, including Soul Intelligence, Quantum Success 90 Day Life-Mastery Program, Maximizing Human Potential, Full Esteem Ahead, The Laughing Classroom, The Enlightened Entrepreneur, Radical Pattern Shifting, The Identity Wheel, Write Your Book Now, The Enlightened Leader, Quantum Success Coaching Training, and Defining Your Destiny.

As a pioneer in the field of human potential and a previous college instructor with three universities, Diana has cultivated a reputation as a dynamic and rare presenter — leaving her audiences inspired and highly motivated. She combines hands-on skills with cutting-edge ideas — delivering her message in an "entertaining" style that is memorable and transforming.

She can be reached at dmloomans@aol.com. Her websites are www.dianaloomans.com and www.quantumsuccesscoaching.com.

Julia Loomans Faye, now a young adult, wrote the excerpts for this book at fifteen and sixteen. She has also coauthored the popular children's book *Positively Mother Goose* with her mother, Diana. Her short stories and poetry appear in numerous books and publications, including the Chicken Soup for the Soul series and the Hot Chocolate for the Soul series. She is currently an artist, writer, and actor in Hollywood.

She can be reached at juliafaye9@aol.com.

If you enjoyed reading this book, you'll love the workshop!

100 Ways to Build Self-Esteem and Teach Values

From coast to coast, Diana Loomans's dynamic program has met with rave reviews. It offers solid content, entertaining delivery, and practical hands-on value. As the founder of Full Esteem Ahead Workshops, Diana offers the program as a keynote speech, workshop, or forty-hour graduate level course for corporations, schools, conventions, and community groups. Loomans is a college teacher, national speaker, and director of Global Learning and The Quantum Success Coaching Institute in Los Angeles. She has degrees in community education and adult education from the University of Wisconsin.

Other topics by Diana Loomans include The Laughing Classroom, Creating a Positive Future, The Enlightened Leader, and The Power of Laughter and Play in the Workplace.

For more information contact:
dmloomans@aol.com or dianaloomans.com

Global Learning, P.O. Box 389, Santa Monica, CA 90406
Phone: (310) 712-7040

Other Books by Diana Loomans

The Laughing Classroom: Everyone's Guide to Teaching with Humor and Play by Diana Loomans and Karen Kolberg.

The Lovables in the Kingdom of Self-Esteem by Diana Loomans, illustrated by Kim Howard; The Lovables board book format.

Positively Mother Goose by Diane Loomans, Karen Kolberg, and Julia Loomans, illustrated by Ronda A. Hendrichsen.

Today I Am Lovable: 365 Activities for Kids by Diana Loomans.

If you are unable to find these books in your favorite bookstore, please call (800) 972-6657.

CHILDREN'S BOOKS FROM H J KRAMER / STARSEED PRESS

SECRET OF THE PEACEFUL WARRIOR
by Dan Millman
Illustrated by T. Taylor Bruce
The heartwarming tale of one boy's journey to courage and friendship. Recipient of the Benjamin Franklin Award.

QUEST FOR THE CRYSTAL CASTLE
by Dan Millman
Illustrated by T. Taylor Bruce
The inspiring story of a child's search for confidence, kindness, and the power to overcome life's obstacles.

WHERE DOES GOD LIVE?
by Holly Bea
Illustrated by Kim Howard
Beautifully illustrated by best-selling artist Kim Howard, *Where Does God Live?* is a fun way to introduce children to the concept of a loving deity.

MY SPIRITUAL ALPHABET BOOK
by Holly Bea
Illustrated by Kim Howard
Four youngsters lead the way in a lively, colorful romp through the letters of the alphabet. Lighthearted rhyming verse and joyful illustrations combine to teach children the alphabet and introduce them to the world of spirit.

BLESS YOUR HEART
by Holly Bea
illustrated by Kim Howard
In this newest collaboration by popular children's book author Holly Bea and illustrator Kim Howard, children are reminded to appreciate every little thing in life from the early morning light to hugs to the freckle on a knee as a gift.

If you are unable to find these books in your favorite bookstore, please call 800-972-6657, ext. 52, send an e-mail request to escort@nwlib.com, or visit www.nwlib.com. For a free book catalog, please send your name and address to H J Kramer, c/o New World Library, 14 Pamaron Way, Novato, CA 94949, or fax request to 415-884-2199.

H J Kramer and New World Library are dedicated to
publishing books and audios
that inspire and challenge us to improve the quality
of our lives and our world.

Our books and tapes are available
in bookstores everywhere.
For a catalog of our complete library
of fine books and cassettes, contact:

H J Kramer/New World Library
14 Pamaron Way
Novato, CA 94949

Phone: (415) 884-2100
Fax: (415) 884-2199
Or call toll free (800) 972-6657
Catalog requests: Ext. 50
Ordering: Ext. 52

E-mail: escort@nwlib.com
Website: newworldlibrary.com